Romania and the Quest for European Identity

Exploring the largely positive representations of Romanian Germans predominating in post-1989 Romanian society, this book shows that the underlying reasons for German prestige are strongly connected with Romania's endeavors to become European.

The election, in 2014, of Klaus Iohannis as Romania's president was hailed as evidence that the country chose a 'European' future: that Iohannis belonged to Romania's tiny German minority was also considered to have played a part in his success. Cercel argues that representations of Germans in Romania, descendants of twelfth-century and eighteenth-century colonists, become actually a symbolic resource for asserting but also questioning Romania's European identity. Such representations link Romania's much-desired European belonging with German presence, while German absence is interpreted as a sign of veering away from Europe. Investigating this case of discursive "self-colonization" and this apparent symbolic embrace of the German Other in Romania, the book offers a critical study of the discourses associated with Romania's postcommunist "Europeanization" to contribute a better understanding of contemporary West-East relationships in the European context.

This fresh and insightful approach will interest postgraduates and scholars interested in Central, Eastern and Southeastern Europe and in German minorities outside Germany. It should also appeal to scholars of memory studies and those interested in the study of otherness in general.

Cristian Cercel is postdoctoral researcher at the Institute for Social Movements within Ruhr University Bochum. He holds degrees from the University of Bucharest (BA), Central European University (MA) and Durham University (PhD). Before his current appointment, he held research positions and fellowships at New Europe College (Bucharest), Swansea University and the Centre for Advanced Study (Sofia). He has published in refereed academic journals such as *Nationalities Papers*; *East European Politics and Societies and Cultures*; *Nationalism and Ethnic Politics*; and *History and Memory*.

Southeast European Studies
Series Editor: Florian Bieber

The Balkans are a region of Europe widely associated over the past decades with violence and war. Beyond this violence, the region has experienced rapid change in recent times though, including democratization, economic and social transformation. New scholarship is emerging which seeks to move away from the focus on violence alone to an understanding of the region in a broader context drawing on new empirical research.

The Southeast European Studies Series seeks to provide a forum for this new scholarship. Publishing cutting-edge, original research and contributing to a more profound understanding of Southeastern Europe while focusing on contemporary perspectives the series aims to explain the past and seeks to examine how it shapes the present. Focusing on original empirical research and innovative theoretical perspectives on the region the series includes original monographs and edited collections. It is interdisciplinary in scope, publishing high-level research in political science, history, anthropology, sociology, law and economics and accessible to readers interested in Southeast Europe and beyond.

Changing Youth Values at the European Periphery
Beyond Ethnic Identity
Edited by Tamara P. Trošt and Danilo Mandić

Security Community Practices in the Western Balkans
Edited by Sonja Stojanovic and Filip Edjus

Social Movements in the Balkans
Rebellion and Protest from Maribor to Taksim
Edited by Florian Bieber and Dario Brentin

Romania and the Quest for European Identity
Philo-Germanism without Germans
Cristian Cercel

For more information about this series, please visit: www.routledge.com/Southeast-European-Studies/book-series/ASHSER1390

Romania and the Quest for European Identity

Philo-Germanism without Germans

Cristian Cercel

LONDON AND NEW YORK

First published 2019
by Routledge
2 Park Square, Milton Park, Abingdon, Oxon OX14 4RN

and by Routledge
605 Third Avenue, New York, NY 10017

First issued in paperback 2021

Routledge is an imprint of the Taylor & Francis Group, an informa business

© 2019 Cristian Cercel

The right of Cristian Cercel to be identified as author of this work has been asserted by him in accordance with sections 77 and 78 of the Copyright, Designs and Patents Act 1988.

All rights reserved. No part of this book may be reprinted or reproduced or utilised in any form or by any electronic, mechanical, or other means, now known or hereafter invented, including photocopying and recording, or in any information storage or retrieval system, without permission in writing from the publishers.

Trademark notice: Product or corporate names may be trademarks or registered trademarks, and are used only for identification and explanation without intent to infringe.

Publisher's Note
The publisher has gone to great lengths to ensure the quality of this reprint but points out that some imperfections in the original copies may be apparent.

British Library Cataloguing-in-Publication Data
A catalogue record for this book is available from the British Library

Library of Congress Cataloging-in-Publication Data
Names: Cercel, Cristian, author.
Title: Romania and the quest for European identity : Philo-Germanism without Germans / Cristian Cercel.
Other titles: Philo-Germanism without Germans
Description: Abingdon, Oxon ; New York, NY : Routledge, 2019. |
Series: Southeast European studies | Includes bibliographical references and index.
Identifiers: LCCN 2018054223 | ISBN 9781472465054 (hbk) |
ISBN 9781315606873 (ebk)
Subjects: LCSH: Germans—Romania—History. | Romania—Ethnic identity. | National characteristics, Romanian. | Germans—Public opinion, Romanian. | Romania—Public opinion.
Classification: LCC DR214.G4 C47 2019 | DDC 305.8009498—dc23
LC record available at https://lccn.loc.gov/2018054223

Typeset in Times New Roman
by Apex CoVantage, LLC

ISBN 13: 978-1-03-224131-9 (pbk)
ISBN 13: 978-1-4724-6505-4 (hbk)

DOI: 10.4324/9781315606873

Contents

Acknowledgments vi

1 "Only another German can jolt us out of our eternal boycotting of history" 1

2 Between the West and the East in Europe 7

3 Germans in Romania: A brief historical background 18

4 The Self and the Other 36

5 "A valuable and unmistakable contribution to the life of Romanian society" 70

6 "They who have no Germans, should buy some" 102

7 "The rich villages around Sibiu and Brașov have been invaded by the Gypsy migration" 135

8 Conclusions 163

Bibliography 173
Index 197

Acknowledgments

This book is a revised version of my doctoral thesis, defended in June 2012, at the University of Durham. My primary supervisor, Dr. Ruth Wittlinger, deserves my deepest gratitude for her ongoing intellectual, academic and personal support during my doctoral studies and after their completion. Without her, writing the dissertation would have surely taken much longer. I am also thankful to my second supervisor, Dr. Stephen Welch, for his intellectual assistance. The external readers of the dissertation, Dr. Claire Sutherland and Prof. Karl Cordell, have offered valuable comments as well. The financial support granted by the University of Durham through the Durham Doctoral Fellowship Scheme provided me with the lack of financial constraints needed in order to undertake the research for the dissertation.

In part or as a whole, various drafts of the manuscript – first of the doctoral thesis, then of the book – have been read by several people, whose feedback was more than welcome and useful. I therefore have to thank Annemarie Weber, Gruia Bădescu, James Koranyi, John Gledhill, Alex Drace-Francis, Natalia Bănulescu-Bogdan, Monica Stroe and Cosmin Cercel for finding the time to read chapter drafts and for offering me their suggestions. I have highly appreciated their input. I am thankful to Hannelore Baier for her indications of primary and secondary sources. Jenny Watson deserves my special gratitude for the effort she put into reading big chunks of the final manuscript on short notice and helping me improve it wherever possible.

Between 2009, when I started my doctoral studies in Durham, and 2018, when I finally managed to submit the manuscript of the book to the publishing house, many people provided emotional support in different ways. Some of them definitely have to be named here. In Durham, Lucy Abbott, Daniele Atzori, Marc Owen Jones, Mari Kolehmainen, Fouad Gehad Marei, Matthias Mösch and Dima Smayra helped me integrate and cope with the sometimes lonesome experience of conducting academic research.

For quite a while, Raluca Răpan put a lot of effort into being close to me. Throughout the years, Gruia Bădescu has offered me not only valuable intellectual feedback whenever necessary, but also a loyal and stable friendship that has withstood the test of time. Anca Militaru has constantly and carefully listened to me, even when I didn't actually have anything to say. Flatmate for a while, and,

Acknowledgments vii

more importantly than that, a close friend since 2006, Tudor Roşu hosted me in Budapest more times that I can remember, always seemingly enjoying it. Smaranda Şchiopu can jolt one out of sullenness and is incredibly kind. After years of silence, Ruxandra Ana has all of a sudden reappeared into the picture, with a flair all her own. Adam Altăr is a beacon of stability. Elena Trifan's readiness to encourage me deserves my full appreciation. Andrei Mihail's camaraderie is something I very much cherish. Thank you all!

Netanel Anor, Alex Cistelecan, Ettore Costa, Dimitrios Gkintidis, Christian Hagemann, Ágnes Kiss, Klaus Richter, Oana Sandu Ştefănescu, Marc Schroeder, Doina and Ionică Simion, Marius Stan, István Székely, Tibor Toró, Bálint Varga, Tom and Hossai Willis also have to be thanked for support, hospitality, and friendship.

At some point in the spring of 2015, Roxana Dobrin (Spi) unexpectedly entered my life. Playful and witty, she has come to mean a lot to me emotionally, in rather unconventional ways. She has also made me realize that a great deal of reciprocity is necessary in interpersonal relationships, no matter how unconventional they are.

In Bochum, where I moved in 2016 to work on a project at the Institute for Social Movements, I found a great group of peers. The director of the Institute, Prof. Stefan Berger, ought to be thanked for his cordiality and intellectual comradeship. Alrun Berger and Julia Sittmann are the best colleagues one could wish to share an office, take lunch breaks and discuss serious and less serious stuff with. Outside the workplace, hanging out with Lucía Martínez is something that I very much relish.

I am grateful to the editor of the Southeast European Studies series, Florian Bieber, for accepting this book to be published in the series, to Rob Sorsby and Claire Maloney from Routledge for their patience, and to Gordon Hammy Matchado for the efforts he put into proofreading the manuscript.

Writing this book would not have been possible without the help of my parents, Nicoleta and Vasile Cercel. They deserve my gratitude not only for their unwavering support during these years but also for their constant confidence in me and for pushing me to learn German when I was a child who was far from finding this language in any way attractive. I am thankful to my brother, Vlad Cercel, for being of help whenever necessary. The Nedea family also have to be thanked, for their openness and warmth. My grandparents are sorely missed.

Of course, the failures and shortcomings of this book are my responsibility alone.

1 "Only another German can jolt us out of our eternal boycotting of history"

In June 2000, the Transylvanian town of Sibiu (called Hermannstadt in German and Nagyszeben in Hungarian) was rocked by a shock election victory. Klaus Iohannis, a newcomer to local politics, an outsider when it came to the Romanian political establishment and an ethnic German, was elected mayor of his majority Romanian hometown.[1] Iohannis was standing for the Democratic Forum of Germans in Romania, an organization nominally representing the country's tiny German minority. His victory was surprising because in Sibiu itself, only roughly 2,500 of the around 170,000 inhabitants were ethnic Germans (Iohannis, 2010, 18). The town could, however, refer to a German past, having been founded in the late Middle Ages by Saxon (German) settlers and having traditionally been one of the main centers of Saxon (German) life in Transylvania (Roth, 2007). As Timothy Garton Ash (1999, 284) puts it, Sibiu, which used to be "a German town in Hungary", has in the twentieth century become "a Romanian town in Romania". A large-scale migration of the German minority from Romania to the Federal Republic of Germany took place during the Cold War and in the early 1990s. Against this background, the election of Iohannis in the summer of 2000 – as well as his subsequent electoral successes (Iohannis was reelected as mayor of Sibiu in 2004, 2008 and 2012 before being elected president of Romania in 2014) – looked like a political expression of a Romanian nostalgia for the German past and for the former German presence in Sibiu. According to an article published in the *New York Times* in 2009, "the fact that Mr. Iohannis comes from the country's tiny German minority, which would be a major liability in other countries in Eastern Europe, puts him at a distinct advantage here in Romania".[2]

Within a few months of first being first elected mayor of Sibiu, in September 2000, Iohannis was interviewed in the popular weekly magazine *Formula As*. The interviewer, Ion Longin Popescu, obviously fascinated by Iohannis and his success, echoed some of the opinions that were already circulating about the significance of the latter's German ethnicity:

> people saw the 'German' in you. They hoped you would bring more cleanliness and order, more seriousness. . . . They even hoped you would bring back their former compatriots. Because, it is known, Romanians have never

regarded gladly the departure of the Saxons. According to such a scenario, you could successfully run in four years for the country's presidency.[3]

Iohannis answered in negative with respect to the possibility of a candidature for Romania's presidency. Subsequently, he was thrice (in 2004, 2008 and 2012) reelected mayor of Sibiu, each time with an overwhelming majority of the votes.

In October 2009, high-profile Romanian author Mircea Cărtărescu, whose penchant for political commentary was at the time nurtured by a weekly op-ed in the daily newspaper *Evenimentul zilei*, published a piece on the presidential elections due to take place by the end of the same year. Like many other Romanians, he appeared not to know whom to vote for. Cărtărescu expressed dissatisfaction with what the existing candidates for Romania's highest political office had to offer. Yet there was someone who, in his view, was undoubtedly worthy of becoming the president of Romania, even if he was not running for office at the time. This someone was the mayor of the Transylvanian town of Sibiu, the president of the Democratic Forum of Germans in Romania, Klaus Iohannis.

How was Cărtărescu arguing on behalf of Klaus Iohannis, a man who was not even among the candidates for the presidency? In his own words: "I want Klaus Iohannis, the one who transformed Sibiu into a town worthy of Tyrol or Bavaria. I honestly believe that, after King Carol, only another German can jolt us out of our eternal boycotting of history".[4]

Iohannis did not run for office in the elections of 2009, yet he did play an important role in them. The Social Democrat candidate, Mircea Geoană, ran on a de facto electoral ticket with the German mayor of Sibiu in that he promised to appoint Iohannis as his prime minister if he won. Nevertheless, in what was one of Romania's most contentious and closely contested recent ballots, Geoană narrowly lost to incumbent Traian Băsescu, who went on to run the country for another five years.

When, in 2014, Iohannis, who had in the meantime joined the ranks of the National Liberal Party, did finally run for president, he was elected. During the electoral campaign, political scientist and Liberal Party member Radu Carp made a passionate plea in favor of a vote for Iohannis on the blog platform hosted by the daily newspaper *Adevărul*. The title of the blog post was "Why must Klaus Iohannis be elected?" One of the main arguments that Carp resorted to was simply the fact that Iohannis is German:

> The fact that this community still exists is a miracle. . . . Romanians developed an attraction to the ethnic Germans next to whom they lived, an attraction based upon positive experience. . . . Klaus Iohannis is, currently, the most representative product of this community from a political point of view. . . . I have been waiting for fourteen years to write such an article. Back then I had already realized that Iohannis was the aspiration of many towards normality. . . . If Romanians want to give a sign to the ethnic Germans who have stayed by their side for more than 800 years, who in 1918 chose Transylvania's unification with Romania, showing loyalty, but who went through

the calvary of deportations and humiliations, a sign that they are trying to repair the errors of the past, they have the chance to do this by electing Klaus Iohannis as president of Romania. . . . Klaus Iohannis is not 'the lesser evil', he is simply the good.[5]

Iohannis, the preferred candidate of Longin Popescu (a journalist), Cărtărescu (a writer), Carp (a politician and academic) and of the more than 6,000,000 Romanians who voted for him in the second round of the 2014 presidential elections, is a member of the once thriving German minority in Romania. As the previous statements indicate, this in itself seems to be considered a positive quality by some of his fans: rather than just being a Romanian German representative, he has been on the one hand regarded by such supporters as representing Germanness in Romania per se, while on the other hand Germanness has been regarded as representing him.

According to the results of the census conducted in 2011, there are only 36,042 ethnic Germans in Romania, an incredibly small figure compared to the approximately 745,421 ethnic Germans who were registered during the census conducted in 1930 (Institutul Naţional de Statistică, 2011; Manuilă, 1938, XXIV). Although boasting a historical presence in the western and central regions of today's Romania ever since the twelfth century, Germans from Romania emigrated *en masse* in the second half of the twentieth century to their imagined homeland, the Federal Republic of Germany, which has positioned itself as a kin state and intervened on their behalf throughout the twentieth and the twenty-first centuries. Iohannis is one of those few ethnic Germans who remained in Romania.

Academic literature does indicate that Iohannis's membership in the Transylvanian Saxon community played a decisive role in his electoral success among both the inhabitants of Sibiu and the country at large (Dragoman, 2005; Dragoman & Zamfira, 2008; Stroe, 2011a; Dragoman, 2013; Cercel, 2015). In various places in Transylvania and Banat, the two main regions in Romania where there has traditionally been a significant concentration of ethnic Germans, a phenomenon of cultural branding has been taking place over the past two decades, a shift in regional self-perception and self-promotion at the local level in which much emphasis is being placed on the German past (Batt, 2002; Botea, 2008; Câmpeanu, 2008, 2012; Koranyi, 2011; Stroe, 2011b, 2017). One researcher speaks of the existence of a "privileged Romanian-German relationship" in Banat, for example (Gavreliuc, 2003). Anthropological and oral history fieldwork has also documented relevant incidences in which special prestige is attached to the German population as well as the existence of a "German identity model" in the eyes of the non-German inhabitants of various localities (Chelcea & Lăţea, 2000, 63–86; Mihăilescu, Coman & Pozsony, 2002; Budeancă, 2016). Various surveys on interethnic relations in Romania conducted since 1989 also suggest that "hetero-images" of the Germans have been predominantly (and consistently) positive (Liiceanu, 2005, 61).

The aforementioned article by Mircea Cărtărescu, as well as the interventions by Longin Popescu and Carp, is a prime example of the philo-Germanism referred

4   *"Only another German"*

to in the subtitle of this book. The experienced author built his argument using two different comparisons. First, he praised the development of Sibiu under the administration of Klaus Iohannis, describing it as a town "worthy of Tyrol or Bavaria", thus indicating that his main points of reference and his benchmarks for judging success are abroad, in "Tyrol" and "Bavaria". This comparison illustrates a typical peripheral view whose points of reference are in imagined or real "centers". By calling Sibiu a town "worthy of Tyrol or Bavaria", Cărtărescu alluded to the transformation that had taken place in the city between 2000 and 2009 and interpreted it as a process of symbolic Germanization under the leadership of a German mayor. If, at the end of the 1990s, Ash had remarked that Sibiu had finally become "a Romanian town in Romania" (as opposed to a German town in Hungary), then by the end of the 2000s, Cărtărescu was almost regarding Sibiu as a German town in Romania.

Second, the Romanian writer explicitly acknowledged his view of German ethnicity as a quality in itself, juxtaposing it with what he saw as a deeply embedded Romanian flaw: "only another German can jolt us out of our eternal boycotting of history". Furthermore, by referring specifically to Carol I of Romania – the Prussian prince who became Romania's leader in 1866 at the age of twenty-five and ruled the country until 1914 – he evoked a broad set of historical representations in which the monarch, a member of the Sigmaringen branch of the Hohenzollern family, is perceived as the one who transformed 'backward' Romania into a truly modern, European country.

Cărtărescu's argument is based on two sets of interconnected images and ideas with a distinct lineage in Romanian (and wider European) cultural history and politics. On the one hand, he reinforces the representation of the paternalist German/Western European Other as a modernizer and provider of cultural and civilizational models worthy of emulation for the rather underdeveloped autochthonous population. On the other hand, he perpetuates the representation of the Romanian people as "boycotting history", lying in a deep slumber and hence missing out on progress, development and prosperity. Such views can also be found in various forms and guises if one looks beyond German-Romanian entanglements because they inform and regulate a great deal of West-East relationships in Europe, both on the discursive and on the more concrete material and political levels. They are, in effect, fundamental to "the colonizer's model of the world", according to which "Europe eternally advances, progresses, modernizes", whereas "the rest of the world advances more sluggishly, or stagnates" (Blaut, 1993, 1).

The contours of Romanian philo-Germanism without Germans are informed by the entangled subject matters that constitute the primary material of the present book: tensions and frictions within Romanian identity constructions, discursive colonization and self-colonization and representations of Germanness and of Europeanness. As will become apparent, a plethora of other examples can be brought to the fore in this context, demonstrating the prestige associated with German ethnicity and with "our Germans" in post-1989 Romania, also drawing on older traditions. This prestige is closely linked to specific tensions within discourses on Romanian identity. Positive views of Germanness and of German ethnicity are most often accompanied by self-disparaging views of Romanianness and of who "we Romanians" are. This book places this Romanian philo-Germanism without Germans under the spotlight, exploring this discursive endowing of the Other with positive characteristics. It investigates the connections between the especially positive representations of German otherness in Romania after 1989 and the never fully fulfilled yearning to "belong to Europe" that informs Romanian identity constructions. It examines the ways in which German prestige is depicted in Romanian discourses about the country's German minority, and it unravels and explains what such depictions most often represent and stand for.

The central argument of this book is that post-1989 Romanian philo-Germanism without Germans is strongly connected with Romanian aspirations toward Europeanization, which in turn inform identity discourses, as expressed in a variety of fields and by a variety of actors, but also politics and policies on a more general level. By applying concepts such as Orientalism, self-Orientalization and intimate colonization, the book reveals the connections between representations of Germanness in Romania, Romanian identity and memory discourses, and visions of Europe, of the West and of the Occident. By analyzing the positive representations of Romanian Germans in contemporary Romanian society, I am able to draw broader conclusions regarding the Romanian wish to assert a European identity as well as its underlying mechanisms. The valorization of Germanness in the Romanian context discloses a great deal about the country and the visions and positions – which are more often than not troubling rather than reassuring – that emerge when one scratches the surface of this apparent embrace of otherness. Indeed, as the book will show, in some cases, no such scratching is required, because the surface is in effect very transparent.

The expression "philo-Germanism without Germans" is both a pastiche and a borrowing. It is a pastiche to the extent that it parallels the better-known "anti-Semitism without Jews", first used by Paul Lendvai (1971) to describe the situation in several Eastern European countries in the late 1960s and early 1970s. Subsequently, the expression was also employed in order to describe the anti-Semitic phenomena and discourses present in Romania in the immediate aftermath of the fall of state socialism (Shafir, 1991). The similarities between "philo-Germanism without Germans" and "anti-Semitism without Jews" stem from the fact that they both refer to a set of representations about a specific ethnic group in a setting in which the said group is largely absent, following nonetheless a long history of presence. The expression is also a borrowing because it was used in a different form by Monica Stroe (2011a), who referred to a phenomenon she called "philo-Saxonism without Saxons" in connection to the electoral success of Klaus Iohannis and subsequent efforts to rebrand Sibiu as "Saxon" despite the tiny number of ethnic Germans (Transylvanian Saxons) still residing there. Finally, the expression "Germanicity without Germans" has been employed in order to describe the underlying tenets of social and cultural processes currently promoted in a top-down manner in villages formerly inhabited in significant numbers by a Transylvanian Saxon population (Hughes, 2011). My use of the expression "philo-Germanism without Germans" does, however, differ somewhat from the above mentioned "philo-Saxonism without Saxons" and "Germanicity without Germans". Although both Stroe and Hughes looked at local mobilizations of the prestige of "Germanness"/"Saxonness", they did this at the local level and on a rather small scale, according to the foci of their respective investigations. In contrast, my own approach will be to examine the phenomenon of philo-Germanism in post-1989 Romania at the broadest level while also integrating this examination of the phenomenon into a more comprehensive explanatory analytical framework, which is so relevant to other contexts as well.

Notes

1 I use the spelling "Iohannis" instead of "Johannis," because the former is the one in use in official documents, although its origin has to do with an administrative error. See Turnul Sfatului TV, "Iohannis sau Johannis," www.youtube.com/watch?v=V-5wawrDRIE (accessed 6 September 2017). For the sake of simplicity and consistency, I write "Iohannis" even when the original texts used the spelling "Johannis".
2 Nicholas Kulish, "Grim Romanians Brighten Over a German Connection," *New York Times*, 5 December 2009, www.nytimes.com/2009/12/06/world/europe/06romania.html?scp=1&sq=grim%20romanians&st=cse (accessed 12 June 2018). For similar approaches in the German-language press, see Thomas Roser, "Ein paar Deutsche sind Rumäniens größte Hoffnung," *Die Welt*, 3 December 2009, www.welt.de/politik/article5413600/Ein-paar-Deutsche-sind-Rumaeniens-grosse-Hoffnung.html (accessed 12 June 2018). See also Felix Hügel, "Allianz für einen Deutschen," *Die Zeit*, 5 December 2009, www.zeit.de/politik/ausland/2009-12/rumaenien-wahl?page=1 (accessed 12 June 2018).
3 Klaus Iohannis, "Vrem să facem din Sibiu ceea ce-a fost cândva. Un oraș european, un avanpost al integrării în Uniunea Europeană," interview by Ion Longin Popescu, *Formula As* 431, 18 September 2000. (All translations from Romanian and German into English were made by the author of this book.)
4 Mircea Cărtărescu, "Cine-o să iasă?" *Evenimentul zilei*, 9 October 2009, www.evz.ro/detalii/stiri/senatul-evz-cine-o-sa-iasa-870920.html (accessed 12 September 2017).
5 Radu Carp, "De ce trebuie votat Klaus Iohannis," *Blogurile Adevărul*, 8 November 2014, http://adevarul.ro/news/politica/de-trebuie-votat-klaus-iohannis-1_545dd0390d133766a8a6bb1b/index.html (accessed 8 July 2018).

2 Between the West and the East in Europe

2.1. The East and the West in Europe

Larry Wolff (1994), in his classic study investigating the discursive imagination of "Eastern Europe", set out to demonstrate that the concept was essentially concocted during the Enlightenment and that it continues to play the role of the Other to "civilized Western Europe". In doing so, Wolff explicitly acknowledges his intellectual indebtedness to Edward Said's *Orientalism* ([1978] 2003). He suggested that "Eastern Europe" and "the Orient" are two cultural inventions/constructions that share the same maker, namely the reasoning power of the Western European Enlightenment. According to Wolff, philosophers and other intellectuals of the Enlightenment, the likes of Voltaire or Rousseau among them, constructed "the idea of Eastern Europe", ascribing to it characteristics such as ambiguity, backwardness and underdevelopment. The construction of Eastern Europe was directly linked to the self-definition of Western Europe, the latter synecdochically purporting to be identified with "Europe" as a whole.

Wolff's work has been the target of several well-founded criticisms. In rebuking his line of thought as well as the theoretical tenets on which he based his elaborations, some scholars remarked that in reality the authors that Wolff referred to did not even use the term "Eastern Europe" (Confino, 1994; Adamovsky, 2005, 594). In a similar vein, his argumentation has been described as a way of "projecting Cold War divisions back into the eighteenth century" (Franzinetti, 2008, 364). Indeed, there is significant evidence suggesting that the cultural imagination of Eastern Europe by means of a so-called Euro-Orientalism did not take place during the Enlightenment but rather later, in the nineteenth century, when an East-West division replaced the traditional one, which had been drawn along a North-South axis (Adamovsky, 2005, 2006; Lemberg, 1985). Moreover, Wolff's use of a Saidian conceptual framework in order to refer to a process of cultural construction putatively taking place during the eighteenth century has also been attacked on the basis that Said himself placed the invention and the subsequent reproduction of the discourse of Orientalism in the nineteenth and twentieth centuries. Thus, speaking of "Euro-Orientalism *before* Orientalism" would be a fallacy (Adamovsky, 2005, 592–593). Finally, the "failure to specify adequately the social agents" that played a role in the process of invention of Eastern Europe as well as the presentation of an apparent immutable and eternal character of "Western Europe" and "Western European interests" represent significant deficiencies in Wolff's argumentative thread (Dupcsik, 1999, 7). In other words, Wolff's scholarly confrontation with the emergence of an essentialized image of Eastern Europe projects discursive processes and phenomena of the nineteenth and twentieth centuries back onto the Enlightenment and, paradoxically, relies on an implicit essentialization of Western Europe. Given that the conceptualization of the so-called East and the so-called West (and, by extension, of "Eastern Europe" and "Western Europe") "as two homogenous zones" is a discursive reification that impedes an investigation of the complexity of the relationships taking place within and between social, cultural and political structures, it follows that such essentialist conceptualizations should be analyzed and deconstructed rather than reproduced in scholarship (Maxwell, 2011, 1).

Nevertheless, recognizing these weaknesses in Wolff's approach should not lead us to throw the baby out with the bathwater. References to "Western" and "Eastern" Europe *do* set in motion a complex discursive apparatus that needs to be accounted for analytically.[1] Details regarding the emergence of this apparatus and the historicization of the unequal relationship between Western and Eastern Europe are undoubtedly open to debate, yet Wolff was right in pinpointing the existence of such a relationship. This relationship has informed and continues to inform a wide range of political, cultural and social discourses (although the contours of this relationship are neither static nor immanent). Thus, despite the obvious incongruences in his argumentation, Wolff's general thesis regarding the discursive construction of Eastern Europe against the background of the growing economic, military and political dominance of the West has not lost its relevance (Bideleux, 2015, 9, 11–12).

However, when it comes to looking at the concrete details of this process of discursive construction, it is more useful to leave Wolff aside. The phenomenon Ezequiel Adamovsky termed Euro-Orientalism (yet situating its birth in the second half of the nineteenth century, in contrast to Wolff) – that is, the "discursive formation by means of which the West symbolically organizes and regulates its relationship with the area of the world called Eastern Europe" – has been configured around a series of cultural, moral and sociohistorical binary oppositions, such as "civilization" versus "barbarity" or "modernity" versus "traditionalism". In his elaborations, Adamovsky (2005, 608) also emphasized that "discursive formations are not made of words, concepts, or representations alone; they are structured by means of social practices and institutions, through which they gain consistency and strongly condition the way we perceive the world". Despite the nominal reliance on a Foucauldian and Saidian conceptual framework, this almost all-encompassing and all-permeating character of discursive formations and apparatuses lacks from Wolff's account.

Against this backdrop, Adamovsky's critical engagement with the meanings of the Euro-Orientalist discursive formation has also shed some light on its links with "liberal-bourgeois ideology", demonstrating that Euro-Orientalism is a constitutive aspect of a specific class ideology (Adamovsky, 2005, 609, 613–628).

This is a particularly important addition since class is a key, albeit often silenced, underlying feature of the way in which what Pamela Ballinger (2017, 62) calls "easternisms" have been shaped after the fall of state socialism in Europe: "analytical frameworks on easternism powerfully illuminate the mappings of new hierarchies of class, not just ethnicity and race, within European societies and across them (particularly within the context of European integration)". At the same time, such frameworks can also function (or perhaps ought to function) as a device allowing us to understand the place of Eastern Europe "in the broader context of global modernity and development, which are comparative categories par excellence" and which suggest that other "incarnations of modernity" are inferior (Bodnár, 2014, 257).[2]

"Eastern Europe" is not the only discursive construction underpinned by hierarchizing frameworks and power relationships. In a book first published in 1997, which almost instantly acquired the status of a scholarly classic, Maria Todorova ([1997] 2009) discussed the process of "imagining the Balkans", the liminal territory being not fully East, and definitely not fully West, neither Occidental nor Oriental, but somewhere in between, although rather closer to the East than to the West. Her argument drew on Wolff, yet Todorova also parted ways with him in several significant respects. In contrast to Wolff, whose focus was solely on the eighteenth century as the period in which he believed to have discovered the emergence of the concept of Eastern Europe, Todorova brought to the fore a critical overview of the uses of the term "Balkans" and of the related Balkanist discourses from the sixteenth century up to the end of the twentieth century. In doing so, she exposed the various shifts in the perception of the Balkans by outside observers, thus emphasizing the significance of historical context and the fluid and processual character of self- and hetero-identifications. When analyzing the concrete expressions of such discourses, their contingency ought to be emphasized. In her discussion, Todorova also underlined the almost self-evidently unequal character of the relationship between the "West" and the "Balkans", which is bound to lead to an interpretive dominance of the former over the latter.

Another central aspect of Todorova's argument is the concept of "liminality", the state of being paradoxically situated both inside and outside Europe, like an "inside other" with an unclear status. She contended that this "liminality" is the most important characteristic of "Balkanism", a discourse related to, yet structurally different from, the Saidian "Orientalist" one (Fleming, 2000; Todorova, [1997] 2009, 194). This issue had also been implicitly touched on by Wolff. For him, one of the key features of representations of Eastern Europe was its being placed both inside and outside the European continent: "Eastern Europe's ambiguous location, within Europe but not fully European" (read: Eastern Europe's constructed geographical proximity) enabled it to arise as "the curious space between civilization and barbarism" (Wolff, 1994, 9, 23). Todorova's "liminality", just like Wolff's "demi-Orientalism", refers to this alleged feature of Eastern Europe, namely its symbolic location somewhere between Europe proper and the Orient, which entails to a certain extent the possibility to appropriate the (putative) acquisitions of Western civilization. Yet this appropriation is most often constructed as taking place only in part; that is, only some Eastern Europeans, allegedly more European than eastern, have been and continue to be imagined in various contexts as actually capable to fully (or largely) get rid of their easternness and to embrace Europeanness. This also underlines the fact that the discursive imagination of cultural constructs such as Eastern Europe or the Balkans is interconnected with various processes of social, cultural and political hierarchization.

A consequence of the liminality and hierarchization embedded in discourses about Eastern Europe and the Balkans is the phenomenon referred to as "nesting Orientalisms". Milica Bakić-Hayden (1995), in her analysis of the radicalization of identity discourses in former Yugoslavia in the early 1990s, distinguishes a "gradation of Orients" – that is, a pattern of reproduction of the East-West dichotomy also present within Eastern European cultures and societies. In the case of the former Yugoslavia, this reproduction entailed a prevalent "Western" self-identification in the regions formerly dominated by the Habsburg Empire, which was accompanied by Orientalist representations of the regions that had been part of the Ottoman Empire. Discourses such as the one that emerged in the 1980s, which emphasized a notional Central European identity constructed as fundamentally opposed not only to Russia but also to Eastern Europe, or to the Balkans – also referred to as Southeastern Europe – represent a further example of such "nesting Orientalisms" (Neumann, 1998, 143–160; Todorova, 2009, 140–160).

The Balkanic and Eastern European in-betweenness necessarily leads to a situation in which the West is not simply "an external 'other'" but also "accessible as an internal self-identification" (David-Fox, 2010, 259). Furthermore, the discursive imagination and construction of Eastern European or Balkan societies as being neither fully inside nor fully outside of Europe is also related to the degree to which these societies have historically been seen and have seen themselves as belonging to Europe, which in turn depended on various contingencies. At different moments and in different political contexts, discourses on Eastern Europe (or on various other related geographical concepts, e.g. Central Europe, Southeastern Europe) emphasized either the potential of countries and nations in the region to participate in European culture or, on the contrary, an alleged fundamental incompatibility with the latter.

During the Cold War, for example, an ongoing dichotomization of Western Europe and Eastern Europe – between the supposedly civilized, freedom-loving, liberal and democratic West and the East, whose political system was deemed "totalitarian" and linked to "traditional Oriental despotism" – informed reciprocal representations. The Western discourse on totalitarianism was pervaded by Orientalist stereotypes and appropriated "ideologically familiar elements from the earlier discourse on Western colonialism" (Pietz, 1988). In contrast, the fall of the Berlin Wall and state socialism initially brought with it an "apparent drawing together of Europe" (Hammond, 2004, xi). This seemed to pave the way for a discursive, political, economic and cultural (re)incorporation of Eastern European countries into the broader European family. Yet the process has been neither straightforward nor even. Nor is it irreversible. The initial enthusiasm surrounding the demise of state socialism swiftly gave way to the reproduction of older representations, with the West playing a key role in the making, unmaking and remaking of the region, from both a political and a cultural point of view (Burgess, 1997). Thus, in the early 1990s, and against the background of the war in former Yugoslavia, the "binaristic, hierarchical manner of ordering the continent" seemed to be resurrected, particularly with respect to Balkan countries, which were once more "reviled as an irredeemable other of Western civilisation" (Hammond, 2004, xi–xii).

The borders and boundaries presupposed by the cultural and political ascription of identities are remarkably porous. The aforementioned liminality of Eastern Europe and of the Balkans in particular makes the imagination of symbolic geographies and the delineation of symbolic delimitations a fluid process, never fully entrenched. At the same time, whenever it is put to work, this process functions on the basis of fundamentally essentialist presuppositions and lines of argumentation.

Within Eastern European societies, the demise of state socialism led to the desire for a "return to Europe" and thus to a proliferation of identity and memory discourses emphasizing on the one hand those societies' membership in the "family" of civilized countries and on the other hand their need for political, cultural and moral reforms in order to be accepted into that family (Arfire, 2011). In this context, "Europe" has rapidly turned into one of the most often used clichés in post-1989 newspeak, standing simultaneously for a stereotypical panacea, a symbolic desire and a proud self-assertion of societies in formerly socialist countries. Specifically, this was translated into a swift and highly uncritical embrace of the idea of joining the European Union (EU), seen not only as a political and economic standard to be attained but also as a legitimization of cultural belonging. The EU became a synonym for Europe; joining a political and economic bloc became the way through which a Western cultural identity could be asserted. "Returning" to Europe has been normatively interpreted as one and the same as becoming part of an institution that did not even exist when Eastern European societies were allegedly decoupled from Europe.

Fundamentally, the process of EU enlargement has functioned on the basis of the "post-colonial condition of the European polity" (Arfire, 2011; see also Rigo, 2005). European enlargement, as well as the enlargement of the North Atlantic Treaty Organization (NATO), has been underpinned by a discourse emphasizing the difference between Western Europe (read: proper Europe) and Eastern Europe, with the latter having to emulate the former. During this process, othering discourses have been reproduced within Eastern Europe itself, instantiating Bakić-Hayden's already mentioned "nesting Orientalisms" (Kuus, 2004). In this context, an "East-West slope" has emerged, a trope informed by East-West relationships, closely linked to "coloniality" (Melegh, 2006). The trope refers to a form of domination and hierarchization of populations, according to which the West essentially stands for superior civilization compared to the East. It has had significant implications for "the articulation of identities and political programs" particularly in the context of the post-1989 relationships between West and East (Melegh, 2006, 189). The hierarchization fundamentally underlying such discourses is driven by the notion of Western superiority. It is also accompanied by the idea that the emulation of Western patterns is fundamentally positive (Dupcsik, 2001). Nevertheless, this consideration is to a large extent the expression of a particular political and class ideology, couched in culturalist terms (Cistelecan, 2015).

Yet all these observations should not lead us to dismiss the fact that East-West relationships in Europe are in effect multifaceted and pluridirectional, local and regional dynamics having constantly played an important role in the production of discourses about the Self and the Other (Mishkova, 2008). The East-West dichotomy has not been simply and mimetically (re)produced within Eastern European societies, but rather by dint of complex processes of interaction and transfer. Therefore, analyzing this dichotomy requires a focus on agency and on the contextual function of such (re)productions (Bracewell, 2009). The influence of the West on the East largely informs and regulates the construction of local, Eastern discourses of Self and of otherness, yet the relationship that thereby emerges between Western and Eastern discourses is not one in which the latter are simply mirroring the former. Eastern subjects are not straightforwardly internalizing and reproducing the Western hetero-representations of which they are objects. Any process of mirroring is accompanied by an act of construction, and the analysis of its outcome should take into account the entangledness that informs this complex and often self-contradictory representational web.

Nonetheless, although the internalization of Western assumptions about Eastern Europe is a complex phenomenon in which a series of interests, agencies and discourses intersect, the power relationships between the two parts of the European continent have been essentially and consistently unequal, both before and after the fall of state socialism. This unequally hegemonic nature of the East-West relationship both stems from and influences the dominant images and representations circulating within the region. "Self-Orientalization" and the "internalization" of inferiority complexes are features of a phenomenon called "intimate colonization", which reduces the "meaning of 'civilization' to Western civilization" (Țichindeleanu, 2009). In this context, particularly after 1989 but also at other moments in the nineteenth, twentieth, and twenty-first centuries, Eastern European elites readily participated in such "processes of (self)othering", aiming to impose something like a "westernism-by-design" (Ballinger, 2017, 52).

Concepts such as "self-Orientalization", "intimate colonization" and "westernism-by-design" are fundamentally related to the "self-colonizing cultures" described by Alexander Kiossev (1999). For Kiossev, "self-colonization" encapsulates the Eastern European relationship with the West in the nineteenth century, the era in which Eastern European societies "discovered" Western modernity. He referred to "self-colonizing cultures" as cultures of absence – that is, cultures in which a perception that others (Europe, the civilized world) "possess all that we lack" is widespread (Kiossev, 1999, 115). Kiossev developed this critical framework in the context of an engagement with the development of national identities in nineteenth-century Southeastern Europe, but the ideas underlying his compact argument can be integrated in the study of post-1989 realities as well. Eastern Europe and Russia have repeatedly been (and continue to be) perceived and analyzed by Western observers in terms of the features they allegedly do not possess, or at least not to the same extent as the West: a middle class, liberal capitalism, civil society, freedom and so on. This approach was subsequently also embraced by academic and political elites in Eastern Europe itself, who reproduced the perception of Western Europe as the model to be emulated and the standard to be reached (Adamovsky, 2006; Ballinger, 2017, 52). Thus, significant identity discourses within Eastern European societies, which also possess overt political connotations, enable the interpretation of these societies as "self-colonizing cultures", which tend to embrace foreign (Western) models with "love, ardour, and desire" and largely refrain from showing signs of resistance (Kiossev, 1999, 115). Furthermore, when they nonetheless *do* show signs of resistance, this resistance tends to be expressed mainly by asserting a rigid parochialism or through the embrace of inward-looking nationalist discourses (Cistelecan, 2015, 55).

2.2. West, East, German identity

The German case illustrates the complex and intricate realities obliterated by the discursive homogenization of West and East, as well as the fluidity of the ascriptions and identifications that emerge between the two symbolic and movable poles. It particularly embodies the elective affinities between the colonial mindset and the discursive construction of Eastern Europe. At the same time, it displays significant specificities that must be taken into account when engaging directly with it or with related issues. These specificities are connected with the contested nature of German identity itself, between East and West, and with the role of Central and Eastern Europe as a projection screen for German imperialist and colonialist ambitions.

Said ([1978] 2003) attempted, in his seminal work on Orientalism, to unravel the mechanisms and the underlying rationale of the relationship between Occident and Orient, presenting it as a relationship of power and domination underpinned by a distinct discursive apparatus that emerged in the late eighteenth century and the nineteenth century. Subsequent literature on the cultural construction of Eastern Europe has engaged extensively with the Saidian concept, which became one of the main points of reference for scholars dealing with the topic (Wolff, 1994; Todorova, [1997] 2009). For Said, the development of Orientalism is interwoven with the colonial history of the French and British Empires. Consequently, it is fundamentally a colonialist discursive framework (Said, [1978] 2003; Polaschegg, 2005, 29–30; Marchand, 2009, xviii–xix). In developing his argument, Said did not pay particular attention to the German production of knowledge about the Orient, since he considered it to be only derivative; that is, it simply refined and elaborated "techniques whose application was to texts, myths, ideas, and languages almost literally gathered from the Orient by imperial Britain and France". Nonetheless, according to Said, there was still a particular German "*authority*" over the Orient, stemming from the German belonging to Western culture (Said, [1978] 2003, 19).

The Saidian reading is overly simplistic, for at least two interrelated reasons. First, Germany's belonging to the West has not been always taken for granted. The German relationship with "the West" has constantly been intricate, ambiguous and full of vagaries (Bavaj & Steber, 2015b). Germany has actually been imagined both as a country in the center of Europe and as one that needed "to find a balance between Western rationalism and Eastern mysticism" (Kontje, 2004, 1). German identity discourses in the nineteenth century and the first half of the twentieth century often revolved around the rejection or the negation of the West, where the latter was mostly equated on an ideological level with the Enlightenment and the liberal ideas of the French Revolution. In the early twentieth century, as well as in the context of the First World War, a broad range of both internal and external observers would actually disassociate Germany from the West (Lewis & Wigen, 1997, 59; Bavaj & Steber, 2015b, 17–21; Llanque, 2015). Nevertheless, this German rejection of the West in its liberal guise came together with alternative ideological constructions, which tended to emphasize German exceptionalism and German cultural and civilizational superiority. Ideas of a German Central Europe (*Mitteleuropa*) or the imagination of Germany and of Germans as bulwarks of the Occident and of European culture (under the German aegis) are examples of this ambiguous and strained German affair with the "West" and related concepts (Meyer, 1955; Schlögel, 2002, 14–64; Thum, 2006b, 185; Bavaj & Steber, 2015a; Gassert, 2015; Martin, 2016).[3]

Second, German Orientalism is much more complex than its interpretation as a simple offshoot of British and French Orientalism would have us believe. There is a historically significant tradition of German-language scholarship on the Orient going back to the eighteenth century (Kontje, 2004; Polaschegg, 2005; Marchand, 2009; Wokoeck, 2009). German Orientalist discourses were based on first-hand experience as well as British and French sources. At the same time, such discourses and experiences were already playing an important role in the development of German identity constructions that balanced between Western Europe and the East: "German writers oscillated between identifying their country with the rest of Europe against the Orient and allying themselves with selected parts of the East against the West" (Kontje, 2004, 2–3). Furthermore, the German image of the Orient – somewhat in contrast to the French and British discourses – has often been strongly interwoven with the image of the East closer to home, namely the Eastern part of Europe.

German overseas colonialism had a rather short-lived history, beginning as part of the nation-building project surrounding German unification in the second half of the nineteenth century and coming to an end as a consequence of German defeat in the First World War. At the same time, German pretenses of cultural, economic and political preeminence and competition with colonial empires such as Britain and France led German imperialists to focus on Eastern Europe as Germany's potential colonial space: "The true German counterpart to India or Algeria was not Cameroon: it was *Mitteleuropa*" (Blackbourn, 2006, 322; see also Thum, 2006a). The nowadays dated expression "the German East" (*der deutsche Osten*), whose geography was fluid even when the term was in frequent use, symbolizes this peculiar quasi-colonial German relationship with Eastern Europe (Thum, 2006a). The oscillation between *Mitteleuropa* (Central Europe) and "the German East" (*der deutsche Osten*) is indicative of the existence of different stances with respect to such quasi-colonial and imperialist projections, yet differences are in degree rather than in kind. In the case of the latter of the two expressions, the linguistic appropriation of the "East" indicates its colonialist connotations.

A specific German myth of the East started to emerge at the beginning of the nineteenth century. Its main themes were "an intrinsic eastern disorder, disease, dirt, a deep incapacity for self-rule, which was expressed in the allied phenomena of despotism and slavery; sympathetic encounters; and the assertion of a particular German national calling or mission" (Liulevicius, 2009, 48). German representations of the (European) East have *grosso modo* swung back and forward between the imagination of the East as a space full of opportunities and possibilities and one where dangers lurk everywhere, between *ex oriente lux* and *ex oriente furor*:

> The 'German East' assumed the contours of a mythical landscape, onto which Germans could project their anti-Western and anti-modern yearnings, as well as the notion that they had been summoned from time immemorial to be a colonial power.
>
> (Thum, 2006b, 14; see also Thum, 2006a)

The German myth of the East also played an important role in the configuration of the entangled relationship between the construction of a German national identity in unified Germany and the imperial colonialist ambitions of the latter state, more aptly seen as a "nationalizing empire" than as a nation-state (Berger, 2015). Poland in particular was imagined and constructed as Germany's colonial space in the nineteenth and twentieth centuries (Nelson, 2009; Kopp, 2012). The German imagination of Russia was also closely linked to broader Orientalizing representations of the East and of Eastern Europe (Casteel, 2016). Furthermore, the abovementioned loss of the overseas German colonies as a consequence of the First World War directly contributed to the growing focalization of German foreign policy, with all its racialist and imperialist overtones, on the eastern part of the European continent (Thum, 2006b; Gross, 2015, 27–67). The discursive processes of legitimization that underlay these colonialist projections were largely based on the construction of a German-Slavic dichotomy, with the Slavic Other (mainly represented by Poles and Russians) seen as uncultured, barbaric and backward.

Such representations of Eastern Europe have also been connected to interpretations of medieval and early modern European history as the period in which German colonialism began. These interpretations portray the German-speaking groups in the East (Transylvanian Saxons, Baltic Germans, etc.) as agents of German colonization, endowed with a specific German cultural mission. However, scholarship has also suggested that there were notable differences between the representation of the space east of Germany as a "continental *Lebensraum*" and German involvement in Southeastern Europe, with the latter also being seen "as a place of latent possibilities", readily embracing the path toward a German-forged Europeanization (Gross, 2015, 3). Nonetheless, German historical interest in Southeastern Europe was fundamentally embedded within the "struggle for empire", the competition for global preeminence taking place between European imperial powers (Gross, 2015; Hamlin, 2017b).

The Second World War, and particularly the Nazi war of annihilation in the East, were discursively legitimized at the time as a defense of Europe against the menaces coming from the East (whether Jewish, Slavic or Bolshevik). The colonialistic processes, mechanisms and structures underlying the attempt to build a Nazi empire in Europe are well documented. Such processes, mechanisms and structures were salient in the war against the Soviet Union and in the politics of occupation in Eastern Europe (Lower, 2005; Mazower, 2009; Baranowski, 2011).

Following the German defeat in the Second World War, a recalibration of identity discourses and of politics took place. The historical rejection of the West by Germany has been interpreted as an unhappy deviation from a Western trajectory, replaced post-1945 by an embrace of the West by the Federal Republic. In the wake of German reunification, the "master narrative of the Berlin Republic" has been placing great emphasis on Germany having finally become a proper Western country (Bavaj & Steber, 2015b, 2; see also Winkler, 2006/2007; Berger, 2010). Critical positions with respect to this master narrative refer to post-1989 German–Eastern European relationships (as well as, to a certain extent, to internal German-German relationships), particularly in the context of European enlargement, as a form of "neocolonialism", underpinned by discursive apparatuses of Orientalist and easternist extraction (Kontje, 2004; Best, 2007).

These particularities of German history, of representations of German identity and of discursive and material relationships involving Germany and Eastern Europe suggest that the analysis of the latter "needs to take some inspiration from Edward Said's concept of Orientalism" (Hahn & Hahn, 2008, 431). At the same time, such an investigation cannot and should not be based simply on applying an analytical framework that draws on Saidian Orientalism onto specific German–Eastern European relationships. On its own, such a framework cannot account for the complexity of these relationships. Drawing inspiration from Said does not require the mechanical application of his ideas but rather implies a careful and contextual adaptation, made necessary by the particularities of the connections between Germany and Europe's East.

Furthermore, delineating the contours of the landscape of German–Eastern European relations and of the discourses associated therewith also requires that one refers to the Habsburg past of Central and Eastern Europe. The Austrian imperial legacy is definitely relevant to the configuration of discourses regarding German–Eastern European relations. Scholarly research on the Habsburg Empire has already engaged fruitfully with research paradigms developed within postcolonial studies (Feichtinger, Prutsch & Csáky, 2003). Nonetheless, regarding the Habsburg Empire as a "colonial empire" in the strict sense of the expression would be rather far-fetched (Ruthner, 2003, 114). Concepts accounting both for the ambiguity and complexity of Habsburg politics *and* the empire's policies with respect to its dominions in Eastern Europe, such as "micro-colonialism", "semi-colonialism" or "quasi-colonialism" might be better analytically equipped for a scholarly engagement with Habsburg history (Detrez, 2002). Yet what is at stake is not so much the question of whether it is legitimate to interpret Habsburg history *stricto sensu* as colonial history, but rather the ability to acknowledge the discursive and material expression of particular power relations (Ruthner, 2003, 114). Such power relations are embedded in, for example, the so-called Mitteleuropa discourse that emerged in the 1980s and has continued to be relevant afterward, particularly in the 1990s, a discourse directly drawing on the Habsburg past in Central and Eastern Europe. The abovementioned "nesting Orientalisms" in former Yugoslavia also relied on the construction of a civilizational dichotomy induced by the opposition between the Habsburg and the Ottoman legacies (Bakić-Hayden, 1995).

The features of the West-East relationships in the European context are key for understanding representations of the (Eastern) Self and of the (Western) Other in Eastern European societies. As I will show throughout the following chapters of this book, they offer relevant insights into the phenomenon that I termed philo-Germanism in Romania, in both its historical and its contemporary dimensions. But before laying down the analysis that constitutes the core part of this book, I must outline the background of the German presence in Romania.

Notes

1 The concept of "discursive apparatus" originates, of course, with Foucault (1980, 194–198).
2 The exact quotation in Judit Bodnár's text is "that cast incarnations of modernity as inferior," but the comparative categorization and the hierarchization embedded within discourses on Western-led global modernity and development can make sense only if the "other" modernity projects are regarded as inferior.
3 One should also note here the German antithetic distinction between *Kultur* und *Zivilisation*, where the latter concept is largely rejected in (conservative) German identity discourses, due to its potential universalism.

3 Germans in Romania: A brief historical background

3.1. "Romanian Germans" before 1918

The contours of German–Eastern European relations in general and of German-Romanian relations in particular are very much connected with the historical presence – and its pendant, the contemporary absence – of Germans in this part of Europe. Different interpretations and readings of this phenomenon and of the relationship between Germans and the other national and ethnic groups in Eastern Europe in general and in Romania in particular are linked with different emphases and accentuations in identification discourses and in representations of otherness. Yet whom exactly do we speak about when we refer to the "German minority in Romania" or to "Romanian Germans"?

The expressions "Romanian Germans" (*Rumäniendeutsche*) and "the German minority in Romania" are inscribed within a political constellation fundamentally connected to recent and contemporary history. To a certain extent, both phrasings exclude the pre-1918 history, when most "German" groups understood as constituting the German minority in Romania were actually not living within the Romanian state, a state that anyway exists only since 1859. At the same time, they downplay the relevance of the complex regional allegiances that underpin the identification discourses typical for the various groups of "Germans" in Romania. Moreover, scholarly as well as popular discourses about the German minority in Romania often falsely equate it solely to Transylvanian Saxons (*Siebenbürger Sachsen*) or to Transylvanian Saxons and Banat Swabians (*Banater Schwaben*) only. When referring to Romanian Germans, "one thinks primarily" of these two groups (Totok, 1988, 7). The other "German" groups that live or lived in Romania receive far less attention or are sometimes forgotten entirely (e.g. Göllner, 1979; Wagner, 2000).

Transylvanian Saxons and Banat Swabians are indeed the most-researched and the best-known German-speaking groups in Romania. Nevertheless, the composition of Romania's German minority has been and continues to be more complex, even if its size has dwindled significantly in the past decades. In interwar Romania, Germans lived in "Transylvania, Banat, Sathmar, Bukovina, Bessarabia, and Dobruja, plus some small isolated groups in the 'Old Kingdom' (Regat)" (Castellan, 1971, 52). In post-1945 Romania, despite population movements and the border changes that took place during and immediately after the Second World War, significant numbers of Germans lived not only in Transylvania and Banat but also in the Satu Mare region (Satu Mare Swabians), around Vișeu (Zipser) and in Bukovina and Dobruja (Totok, 1988, 7).

Different surveys and scholarly works make use of various categorizations when referring to the "German" groups in Romania. This shows that the process of scholarly and/or political classification and ascription of groupness to "Germans" in Romania, as with all such processes, is by no means clear-cut. For example, in a short study published in Romania at the end of the 1970s, Monica Barcan and Adalbert Millitz (1978, 39–43) listed eleven German-speaking groups living in the country. They named some of the aforementioned groups, namely the Transylvanian Saxons and Banat Swabians, the Satu Mare Swabians, the Zipser and the Bukovina Germans. In addition, without any mention whatsoever of the Dobruja Germans, they referred to the Durlacher, who settled in the region around Sebeș in 1743; the Bohemian Germans, who lived in the Semenic mountains; the Styrians, centered on Reșița; the Timișoara Germans, who had arrived in Banat from Austria ahead of the Swabian colonization waves; the Landler, who came in the eighteenth century to three villages in Transylvania; and the Swabians, who moved in the nineteenth century to the Transylvanian villages of Aurel Vlaicu (formerly named Binținți/Benzenz in German and Bencenc in Hungarian) and Batiz. In a 1979 edited volume dedicated to the "history of the Germans on Romania's territories" pre-1848, the focus was essentially on Transylvanian Saxons and Banat Swabians; some observations on Satu Mare Swabians, Maramureș Zipser and Bukovina Germans were also introduced, but these can be found on only seven pages out of the roughly 380 of the volume (Göllner, 1979, 321–327). More recently, in a book dedicated to Banat Swabians and the so-called *Berglanddeutsche*, historian Gwénola Sebaux (2015, 195) listed alongside those two communities five other German groups, namely Transylvanian Saxons, Satu Mare Swabians, Carpathian Germans, Bukovina Germans and Dobruja Germans. The website of the German Embassy in Bucharest currently distinguishes between twelve groups of German-speaking settlers who were living on Romanian territory in 1918, when the unification of Greater Romania took place, yet it focuses its short summary of German life in Romania on the Transylvanian Saxons and Banat Swabians. The other ten groups mentioned on the site are Satu Mare Swabians, Bessarabia Germans, Bukovina Germans, Dobruja Germans, Landler, Durlacher, Bohemian Germans, Styrians, Timișoara Germans, and Zipser.[1] The several potential categorizations of Romanian Germans are related to the rather distinct histories of the various German-speaking groups in Romania, but they are also linked to the difficulties inherent in the ascription of ethnic and national identities, as well as the drawing of ethnic and national boundaries. Ethnic, national and religious identifications are in effect (contested) categories of practice: their investigation should try to avoid reifying them further and should not fall into the trap of conflating categories of practice with categories of analysis (Brubaker, 2005, 2006; Brubaker et al., 2006; Brubaker, 2013).

Studies on Germans in Romania, especially but not only those focusing on the pre-1918 period, tend to look at each of the specific groups rather than attempt to integrate these various histories into a coherent whole. Even a work such as *Geschichte der Deutschen auf dem Gebiete Rumäniens* (History of the Germans on the Territories of Romania), edited by Carl Göllner and published in 1979, whose title suggests a potential integrative framework, effectively reinforces the same methodological and analytical separation. However, such an approach is not illegitimate inasmuch it aims to avoid relying on a flawed methodological and at the same time teleological Pan-Germanism *avant la lettre*, doubled by a methodological and no less teleological Romanian nationalism.

Chronologically, the ancestors of the Transylvanian Saxons were the first group to settle on the territory of contemporary Romania. They came to the region in the twelfth century, at the behest of Hungarian king Géza II (1141–1162), in order to settle in the region of Transylvania, at the time newly conquered by the Hungarian Crown. Saxons were not the only population invited to Transylvania for economic and defensive reasons; the Hungarian Crown also invited Szeklers, whose role was to defend the kingdom's borders in the Southern and Eastern Carpathians (Pál-Antal, 2009, 3–4). Under similar conditions, the Spiš region (in contemporary Slovakia) was also colonized with *saxones*, the so-called Zipser Saxons (*Zipser Sachsen*) (Schwarz, 1957, 201). Saxon migration to Transylvania has been interpreted as part of the larger historical phenomenon called *Deutsche Ostsiedlung* (Nägler, 1992, 44–80). A possible translation of the expression is "German settlement in the East", yet the nineteenth-century and twentieth-century political instrumentalization of the "German" presence in Central and Eastern Europe indicate that it is actually meaningful to engage with it as a particular type of colonization, especially on account of its reverberations in modern and contemporary history (Kopp, 2012, 5). In this context, it is also worth emphasizing that the words used in English and in Eastern European languages to refer to the phenomenon belong exclusively to the semantic family of "to colonize" (Irgang, 2012).

Research indicates that Transylvanian Saxons came to Transylvania from different territories, including the Mosel region, Flanders and Luxembourg (Higounet, 1989; Nägler, 1992, 81–114; Gündisch, 1998, 29–33). They came to a scarcely populated region: their being invited in the "land beyond the forests" was meant on the one hand to support its economic enhancement and consequently that of the Hungarian Kingdom and on the other hand to defend the latter's borders, in the Carpathian Mountains. The settlers were enticed to Transylvania through the granting of various privileges. These privileges encompassed administrative, jurisdictional and cultural-religious matters on the territory of the so-called *Königsboden* (Crownland). Thus, the term "Saxon" initially referred to a juridical status (Gündisch, 1998, 30).

Hence, *Saxones* were one of the three legally recognized corporative "nations" in Transylvania, alongside Hungarians and Szeklers. This means that Saxon identity started by being a class identity: the term *natio* "did not automatically encompass everyone of the same ethnic origin but only those persons who possessed special rights and immunities" (Hitchins, 1999, 12). Nonetheless, beginning with the sixteenth century, mainly under the influence of the cultural elite and on the basis of this autonomous status within the Transylvanian region, a specific Saxon group self-consciousness started to emerge (Gündisch, 1998, 89–91). In practice, a "Saxon" ethnicity came into being after the arrival of settlers in Transylvania.

Identity management within the Saxon community and the production and maintenance of group boundaries were done by particular institutions, the most important one being the *Nationsuniversität* (Saxon University), whose leader was the Saxon *Komes* (Count).[2] Starting in the second half of the sixteenth century, the Lutheran Church also acquired a highly important role in this respect, on account of the Lutheran Reformation in Transylvania. As a consequence of the Reformation, in the Transylvanian context, an almost perfect overlapping of the categories "Saxon" and "Lutheran" emerged. Consequently, the Evangelical Church of Augustan Confession in Transylvania became a so-called *Volkskirche* (national church) (Zach, 1998).

Within Transylvania, Lutheranism was one of the four recognized ("received") religions (Catholicism, Unitarian, Lutheran and Calvinist), enjoying "freedom of worship", "equal representation (at least in theory) in all the branches of the central government" and administrative autonomy. The arrangement merely "tolerated" the Orthodox Church, to whom the Romanian-speaking population belonged (Hitchins, 1999, 15–16). The administrative system in Transylvania excluded the largely rural and property-less Romanian population from exercising political rights. However, considering the social context of the period, this discrimination was essentially based on class and status, not ethnicity. At the same time, this particular entanglement of identities and identifications bore the seeds for subsequent discursive conflations of ethnicity and class, especially in the longer term.

Transylvanian Saxons were present in both rural and urban areas. Urban development in the region started in the thirteenth century and took place in "an institutional framework typical for Central Europe", marked by the role played by the Hungarian Crown and by "foreign colonists, especially Germans" (Rădvan, 2011, 126). Saxon settlers in the villages situated in the *Königsboden* were free peasants, who also enjoyed the administrative freedom granted to them by the Hungarian Crown. Their villages supplied Saxon towns with foodstuffs. Furthermore, the strategic location of Saxon towns enabled the development of trade with the Ottoman Empire (Verdery, 1983, 142).

Nurturing regular cultural relationships with the German-language state entities in Europe has been a key element in Transylvanian Saxon history, contributing in time to the emergence and stabilization of what anthropologist Glynn Custred (1992) called a "dual ethnic identity of the Transylvanian Saxons". In particular, studying at universities in German-speaking countries played an extremely relevant role in the development of Transylvanian Saxon cultural and intellectual elites (Armbruster, 1980, 63). For example, Lutheranism was introduced in Transylvania thanks to the efforts of Johannes Honterus, who had studied and worked in Vienna, Regensburg, Krakow and Basel (Gündisch, 1998, 81–87; Custred, 1992, 484).

Starting in the nineteenth century in particular, self- and hetero-identifications of Transylvanian Saxons (as well as of the other German-speaking groups in

Central and Eastern Europe) have been constructed as full-fledged appropriations of, or subtle variations on, the German diaspora theme. Against this background, Transylvanian Saxons have also been analytically conceptualized as a prime example of a "German diaspora" (Custred, 1992, 483; Evans, 2006, 209–227). Nevertheless, such conceptualizations should be taken *cum grano salis* rather than uncritically deployed in historical scholarship, because the use of the term "German diaspora" as a tool for analysis "requires a critical acknowledgment of that concept's twentieth-century derivation from the related concept of the territorial nation-state" (Judson, 2005, 219–220). "Diasporas" and diasporic identities are idioms, stances and claims; they are not bounded entities despite being constructed as such by various ethnopolitical entrepreneurs. Just as in the case of ethnicity and ethnic identity, a distinction has to be made between diaspora as a category of practice and diaspora as a category of analysis, and the two should not be indistinguishably conflated (Brubaker, 2005).

A symbol of the existence of important links between Transylvanian Saxons and the German-language cultural space (duly appropriated throughout history within Saxon identity discourses) was their being called *germanissimi germani* ("very German"), a tag apparently used by Silesian poet and traveler Martin Opitz in the first half of the seventeenth century. The remark would be subsequently modified into *germanissimi germanorum* (which translates roughly as "the most German of all Germans") and instrumentalized both to convey a feeling of superiority and to tie in with a specific type of German identification in Eastern Europe, a not so innocuous discursive shift, with reverberations in the longer term (Möckel, 1977, 63; Dowling, 1991, 343–344; Evans, 2006; Verdery, 1983, 143).

In the second half of the seventeenth century, Transylvania was incorporated into the Habsburg Empire. Around the same time, the advent of the Enlightenment and modernity also significantly affected the institutional life of Transylvanian Saxons. Despite their presumed linguistic and cultural affinities with the authorities in Vienna, the religious cleavage (Catholic versus Lutheran) coupled with the Catholicization tendencies of the Habsburg emperors was a source of friction. In this context, Habsburg rule also led to new processes of "German" migration to Transylvania. Catholic representatives of the state apparatus (bureaucrats, military) settled in Transylvanian towns, whereas Protestants were forcefully deported from Carinthia to Transylvania, more precisely to three villages around Sibiu, in the southern part of the region (Turnișor, Cristian, Apoldu de Sus) (Steiner, 2007). Within the Habsburg Empire, these Protestants, called Landler, were considered to be transmigrants (Beer, 2002; Steiner, 2007, 2014, 243–293). Notwithstanding their small number and their proximity to the Saxon environment, specific Landler identification discourses still exist, based on boundaries with respect to Saxon identification. However, this type of differentiation is functional as such only within the larger group of Romanian Germans, being rather absent when it comes to the way members of these subgroups are perceived by the Romanian population (Bottesch, 2002; see also Girtler, 1992, 1997, 2007).

Moreover, at the end of the eighteenth century, Habsburg Emperor Joseph II (1780–1790) allowed members of other ethnic groups to settle on Saxon lands, granting them full equality. This event has been interpreted as the beginning of modern history for Transylvanian Saxons, since it put an end to the medieval privileges assigned to them upon their arrival to Transylvania, which constituted the crux of Saxon identity (Schaser, 1989; Philippi, 1994, 69). The subsequent severe blow to Saxon attempts to maintain a status quo of assuring their privileges was the establishment of Austro-Hungarian dualism in 1867. The incorporation of Transylvania into the Hungarian part of the empire led to Magyarization drives in general and to the disbandment of the Saxon University in particular.

Thus, starting in late eighteenth century, Transylvanian Saxons gradually lost the underlying tenets of their traditional autonomy, which had constituted the basis on which the particular Saxon ethnic identity had developed. The status of Transylvanian Saxons was in practice downgraded to that of an ethnic minority in the Hungarian part of the Habsburg Empire, a process that was also concurrent with the general upsurge in Europe of national identification discourses. This process also meant that the Lutheran Church in Transylvania remained in practice the only community institution managing the production and reproduction of Transylvanian Saxon identity (Binder, 1988).

Eighteenth-century Habsburg's modernizing endeavors were also of great historical significance to Banat, a region currently divided between Romania, Serbia and Hungary. Following Banat's acquisition after a conflict with the Ottoman Empire, the need arose to transform the border region into an economically viable and militarily secure territory for the Habsburgs. Consequently, the Austrian emperors invited settlers (mostly but not only German-speaking ones) from various parts of Europe to colonize the newly acquired territory. There were three main migration waves: under Charles VI (1722–1726), under Maria Theresa (1763–1771) and under Joseph II (1784–1787) (Paikert, 1967; Senz, 1994, 14–18; Hausleitner, 2014, 23; Gräf, 2018). Although the German-speaking migrants did not come from the Swabian region, the denomination "Swabians" (*Schwaben*) took root. A majority of them settled down in rural areas, and they were hence involved first and foremost in agriculture. Unlike Saxons, who by an overwhelming majority turned to Lutheranism in the sixteenth century, most Swabians in Banat were Catholic. Thus, particularly in the second half of the nineteenth century and in the early 1900s, they were more prone to succumb to the attempts of assimilating them into the Hungarian nation propagated through the Catholic Church. This religious divide has been an important aspect of reciprocal Saxon-Swabian representations and identification discourses.

Another so-called Swabian group, the Satu Mare Swabians, began arriving in the region around Satu Mare – the Hungarian and Ukrainian borderlands of present-day northwestern Romania – in the early 1700s, having come as agricultural workers at the behest of a Hungarian landowner named Károlyi (Senz, 1994, 17; Roşu 2015, 236–237). In a situation similar to that of Banat Swabians, Satu Mare Swabians were systematically confronted with severe Magyarization pressures, particularly between 1867 and 1918. One of the enduring consequences of these pressures is Satu Mare Swabians' peculiar status: members of the group perceive themselves to a large extent even now as ethnic Germans with Hungarian as a mother tongue, a rather sui generis case of a "dual identity" in contemporary Romania (Forstenheizler, 2004; Roşu, 2015; Dácz, 2017).

In the eighteenth century, a process of industrialization also began to take place, particularly in Banat (Rieser, 2001, 62–70). This process brought miners and industrial workers to the region, among them the so-called *Berglanddeutsche* (Lupşiasca, 2013). This industrialization, often strongly connected to the presence of mining, would gain pace in the nineteenth century, in both Banat and Transylvania (Rieser, 2001, 74–84; Verdery, 1983, 141–151). Toward the end of the eighteenth century, settlers from Austria and from the Spiš region (descendants of the abovementioned Zipser Saxons who came to the region in the twelfth and thirteenth centuries) also moved to Maramureş, a region currently in northwestern Romania, bordering Ukraine, where they became active primarily in salt mining and forestry. The Zipser are concentrated in the vicinity of Vişeu de Sus (Scridon & Ilovan, 2015).

Furthermore, in 1775, the Habsburg Empire went on to acquire the region of Bukovina, nowadays divided between Ukraine and Romania. Consequently, German speakers arrived in Bukovina, attracted by the economic opportunities that came together with Habsburg connections. Their de facto privileged position was to a certain extent based on their sharing the official language of the Habsburg Empire. Bukovina Germans were active in agriculture, mining and industry, as well as liberal professions, and they were part of the state apparatus in Bukovina. Unlike in the cases of Transylvanian Saxons and Banat Swabians, the establishment of the Austro-Hungarian Dual Monarchy had no direct impact on them, because the region continued to be ruled by Vienna (Welisch, 1986; Hrenciuc, 2013, 17–34).

Among all these groups, Transylvanian Saxons were institutionally the best organized. Starting in the second half of the nineteenth century, in the face of growing Magyarization (assimilation) pressures coming from the Budapest authorities, important internal conflicts emerged at the level of the Transylvanian Saxon elite. These disputes concerned which political path they should follow. They had two main options: they could choose more openness toward collaboration with the rest of the Germans in the Hungarian part of the Habsburg Empire *or* a focus on exclusively Saxon interests, an option that was translated into an insistence on the reinstatement of the medieval privileges (Möckel, 1994).

Concurrently, following the German unification of 1871, the ideological interest in Germans abroad grew significantly within the German Empire (Conrad, 2010; Manz, 2014; Berger, 2015). In this context and against the backdrop of the nationalizing processes taking place all across nineteenth-century Europe, Germans in Hungary and Transylvania started to be imagined as part of the so-called *Auslandsdeutschtum* (Germanness abroad). The discourse about these Germans emphasized the denationalization attempts of the Hungarian authorities and presented the German minorities as under attack from chauvinistic Hungarian forces and therefore in peril of losing their German identity (Schwicker, 1881, 488–509; Schultheiss, 1898).

Responding to Hungarian pressures toward assimilation and state centralization, Saxon elites increasingly "developed a strong sense of German nationalism"

(Davis, 2016, 44). In exchange, the other German-speaking groups in Hungary, among them Banat Swabians, were "largely indifferent to German nationalism" (Davis, 2016, 46). Particularly in the case of rural Swabians, a sense of "tangible belonging" – that is, a very local understanding of their own identity as opposed to the abstraction of national belonging – was prevalent and implied a particular indifference to "connections to other Germans" (Swanson, 2017; Davis, 2016, 42). This argument can probably be applied to the case of rural Transylvanian Saxons as well. At the same time, Swabian elites, lacking the Transylvanian Saxon history of privileges and of identity-reproducing institutions, displayed a much higher degree of openness toward assimilation within the Hungarian nation. In this context, the acknowledgment by German-minded nationalists in Hungary of the absence of substantial relationships between Transylvanian Saxons and Banat Swabians was connected with the hope that such connections could be developed, following, for example, the case of the village of Benzenz (now Aurel Vlaicu) in Transylvania, which absorbed new Swabian settlers from Banat in the nineteenth century (Schultheiss, 1898, 70; Verdery, 1983, 207).

This short overview of the historical background of the German minority in Romania shows that its presence is mostly related to the Hungarian and Habsburg past of the country's western and northern regions. Nevertheless, German-speaking populations also settled in the Russian Empire, at the behest of Russian czars. Notwithstanding the contemporary geopolitical landscape, statehood and politics of identity, interactions of the Romanian-speaking and German-speaking populations in Bessarabia (currently part of the Republic of Moldova) should also be at least briefly referred to not only when outlining the historical background of the representations of the German minority within Romanian society but also when discussing the post-1989 representations of the Germans in Romania.

Between 1812 and 1842, groups of "Germans" settled in the province of Bessarabia, at that time newly acquired by the Tsarist Empire from the Ottomans. Together with Bulgarians and Gagauzes, they were attracted to the region by privileges granted to them by the Russian authorities, who were eager to transform Bessarabia into an agriculturally productive region (Hausleitner, 2005, 19–25; Schmidt, 2011). After 1841, part of the German-speaking population in Bessarabia would move further south, to Dobruja, attracted this time by promises made by the Ottomans and the desire for better agricultural conditions. Following the Russian-Turkish war of 1877–1878, known in Romanian historiography as the Romanian War of Independence, Northern Dobruja was incorporated into Romania, and Dobruja Germans became Romanian citizens (Petri, 1956; Lascu, 2006).

The state of Romania first appeared on the European map in 1859, following the unification of the principalities of Wallachia and Moldavia: therefore, it is legitimate to speak about the "German minority in Romania" and, to a certain extent, about "Romanian Germans" only when referring to developments and processes that take place after this date. Although the German presence in Wallachia and Moldova can be traced back to the Middle Ages, the "migrations from the German-speaking countries since mid-nineteenth century", together with the concurrent "massive expansion of the European national economies in Southeast Europe and in the Near East for natural resource extraction and the opening of markets", were the main factors contributing to the presence of German communities in post-1859 Romania (Stache & Theilemann, 2012, 20; also Fischer, 1911). Moreover, in the second half of the nineteenth century, cases of Austrians and Transylvanian Saxons migrating from the Habsburg Empire to the Romanian state in search of economic opportunities were also registered (Stache & Theilemann, 2012, 20). The fact that, starting in 1866, Romania was ruled by a German royal family, the Sigmaringen branch of the Hohenzollerns, also attracted Germans to the country.

The rather varied pasts of the groups constituting the "German minority in Romania" attest to their "Germanness" not having been a straightforward, clear-cut, nationally understood identification but rather to a large extent a loosely defined and lax one. A more forthright process of "Germanization" of Saxons, Swabians and the other ethnic groups whose backgrounds I have discussed in the present section emerged only slowly, from the second half of the nineteenth century onward. This was a process of cultural and political coagulation and of imagined "communitization" that qualitatively surpassed the lax "German" affiliation prevalent in the preceding centuries. The unification of the German Empire and its function as a kin state to the German-speaking groups outside its borders, together with the establishment of Austro-Hungarian dualism in 1867, and the dissolution of the Habsburg Empire in 1918, played a vital role in this development (Judson, 2005; Manz, 2014; Berger, 2015).

3.2. Romanian Germans after 1918

At the outbreak of the First World War, despite being part of an alliance with the German and the Habsburg Empires, Romania maintained its neutrality, only to then enter the conflict in August 1916 on the side of the Triple Entente (Hitchins, 1994, 251–291). Against this background, the growing propaganda directed against the Central Powers and the rapprochement with France and the Triple Entente contributed to the deterioration of Romanian-German relations not only in the Romanian state, but also in Transylvania, which was part of the Habsburg Empire (Topor, 2012; Danneberg, 2017). In the latter case, signs of such a deterioration had been visible as early as the turn of the century, in the context of growing national claims on both sides (Danneberg, 2017). Between August 1916, when Romania entered the First World War on the side of the Triple Entente, and 1918, when the war ended, Germans in Transylvania, Banat or Bukovina, citizens of the Habsburg Empire, actually fought against the Romanian army. When entering Transylvania in August and September 1916, Romanian soldiers were perceived by the German-speaking population in the region as invaders. Conversely, the presence of German troops in Banat and Transylvania during the war, fighting against the Romanians, was apparently largely welcomed by the Swabian and Saxon populations (Böttcher, 2009, 265, 308–310).

Nonetheless, at the end of the war, ill feelings toward the Romanian state were pragmatically left aside (Ciobanu, 2013). Representatives of the Transylvanian

Saxons and Banat Swabians eventually consented to the unification of their respective regions with Romania (König, 1979; Gündisch, 1998, 173–177; Ciobanu, 2001, 53–68, 2013, 17–181). A similar course of action was also followed by representatives of other German-speaking groups whom the outcome of the First World War had thrust into an enlarged Romanian state (Hrenciuc, 2013, 39; Ciobanu, 2013, 183–214). These statements of consent should not be interpreted as a unanimous agreement to the political aims implied by the unification of Greater Romania but rather to a large extent as pragmatic acts of lip service, acquiescing to the situation at hand. Furthermore, agreeing to the unification was also linked to the hope that the promises inscribed in the Declaration of Alba Iulia, the symbolic document sanctioning the birth of Greater Romania, would actually be enacted. Such promises included educational and religious autonomy for ethnic minorities, an issue of great interest and relevance to the latter.

The incorporation of Transylvania and Banat into Greater Romania instantly transformed the Transylvanian Saxons and Banat Swabians, together with other German-speaking groups in the newly acquired provinces (Bukovina, Bessarabia), into a minority group within an enlarged Romanian state. The regional breakdown of Romania's German minority according to the results of the 1930 census was as follows: 253,426 Germans in Transylvania, 223,167 in Banat, 75,533 in Bukovina, 81,089 in Bessarabia, 67,259 in Crișana and Maramureș (i.e. Satu Mare Swabians, Zipser), 12,581 in Dobruja and 32,364 in Wallachia and Moldova (Manuilă, 1938, XXXII). Around one-third of the population of interwar Romania were not ethnic Romanians. Thus, although they imagined and constructed Greater Romania as the embodiment of a centuries-old dream of the Romanian people, central authorities in Bucharest were compelled to operate in a de facto multinational environment. In this context, the rejection of regionalist tendencies was shaped according to a French pattern, yet the penchant for treating the members of minority groups as second-class citizens more closely resembles the German idea of nationhood (Brubaker, 1992). Practically, interwar Romanian authorities devised their own method for handling minorities, in effect acknowledging the existence of minority groups but at the same time implicitly or explicitly aiming for assimilating or excluding those groups in the long run.

Thus, state officials administered a political system in which ethnic identity was not fully obscured by citizenship but rather played an important role in the shaping of nationalizing policies, at both the national and the local levels. Ethnic and ethnicized conflicts between the Romanian authorities and the various minority groups living in the country were common in the interwar period. The social and cultural integration of minorities in the newly enlarged state was more of a failure than a success (Livezeanu, 1995; Hausleitner, 2001). The Declaration of Alba Iulia from 1 December 1918 – that is, the programmatic document underpinning the unification of Greater Romania – as well as the subsequent Paris Peace Treaties – might have included generous promises for ethnic minorities, but the policies embraced by the Romanian state did not respect the provisions inscribed in the aforementioned documents. In this context, land reform, the adoption of a new Constitution in 1923, and other legislative measures fomented dissatisfaction

28 *Germans in Romania: A historical background*

among Romanian Germans as well as other minority groups (Gündisch, 1998, 180–185). Authorities in interwar Romania set on a process of Romanian nation-building, disregarding minority claims and demonstrating a preference for the Orthodox religion.

In principle, the enlargement of the Romanian state as a direct consequence of the First World War also created the conditions in which "Germans in Romania" could emerge as a meaningful political category capable of supporting a unifying identity. However, it largely remained the case that "the particular constellation of German speakers in Romania was contingent on new state borders, rather than preexisting ties" (Davis, 2016, 53). Regional, political, religious, social and generational cleavages therefore continued to play a key role in what was now starting to be called the "German minority in Romania", impeding the establishment of a meaningful representative body of Germans in Romania and the success of the attempts to bring to the fore a common identity project. The phenomenon displays interesting similarities to the processes and evolutions concerning the German minority in Poland during the same time period (Chu, 2012a). Although a political body called the Union of Germans in Romania (*Verband der Deutschen in Rumänien*) was founded soon after the end of the First World War, the institution was largely inactive and only achieved limited success in acting as a bridge between Romania's various German-speaking groups (Roth, 1995, 105; Ciobanu, 2001, 166–167). Rather than being a "united institution", it "remained a coalition of smaller regional parties" (Davis, 2016, 56). At the same time, the German Party in the Romanian Parliament was dominated to a great extent by Transylvanian Saxons (Ciobanu, 2001, 173–174).

In the context of Romanian German dissatisfaction with their political status and the policies promoted by the largely traditional conservative elites within the Romanian German communities, and against the background of the growing appeal of Nazism in Germany, a process of "renewal" and right-wing radicalization gained momentum (Böhm, 1985, 1999, 2008). The cultural and political rapprochement to pre-1933, but especially to post-1933 Germany played a vital role in this process, yet it would be a mistake not to acknowledge the fact that the tendency toward and the embrace of fascism also had significant internal motivations and an internal logic, particularly in the case of Transylvanian Saxons. A far-right Transylvanian Saxon movement, emphasizing, for example, the importance of eugenics for the future of the community, started developing largely on its own, albeit with tenets largely compatible with Nazism in the Third Reich (Georgescu, 2016).

Thus, assimilationist pressures, a perceived existential crisis, an embrace of all things German and many things Nazi, as well as intergenerational, political and cultural conflicts, characterized the interwar history of Romanian Germans. In effect, the German minority in Romania in the interwar period (and also afterward) is best conceptualized as a political field – that is, as constituted by a multitude of interwoven stances and positions, which were also emerging in relationship with the fields of the Romanian and German states, the latter acting as a kin state for Germans in Romania (Brubaker, 1996, 55–76; Roth, 1994; Szelényi,

2007; Schüller, 2009; Cercel, 2011, 2017). The multitude of forces vying to gain preeminence among Romanian Germans is well summed up by the title of a work by historian Stephan Olaf Schüller (2009), *Für Glaube, Führer, Volk, Vater- und Mutterland*, which translates to "For Faith, Führer, Nation (*Volk*), Fatherland and Motherland". At the same time, the existence of a significant (mainly Banat Swabian) left-wing opposition voicing criticism against both Romanian state politics and the conservative religious elites from within the community should also be acknowledged, particularly since it has largely been swept under the carpet in historiography, with minor exceptions (Hausleitner, 2014).

The close political and military rapport developing between the Romanian and German states, especially from the second half of the 1930s onward, had significant consequences for Germans in Romania (Haynes, 2000; Lumans, 1993, 107–112). National Socialist policies concerning the *Volksdeutsche* (ethnic Germans abroad), together with the border changes first brought forth by the 1939 Ribbentrop-Molotov pact, contributed to the efficacy of the *Heim ins Reich* (home to the Reich) program, whose aim was to "Germanize" the Eastern territories conquered by Nazi Germany. One of the consequences of this was that German-speaking groups in Bukovina, Bessarabia and Dobruja were resettled in 1940 in the expanding German Reich (Jachomowski, 1984). The program of relocating ethnic Germans from Eastern Europe to the territories newly conquered by the Third Reich had no impact on the fate of Transylvanian Saxons or Banat Swabians, although some efforts in this direction were also made. However, these groups entered into close contact with Nazi ideology and Nazi politics in their own right, a phenomenon also connected with the notable turn toward the far right on the Romanian political scene and, as noted above, with internal Romanian German developments. In November 1940, at the zenith of Nazi power and influence in Europe, Romanian Germans were granted autonomy under the leadership of a newly founded institution, the German Ethnic Group (*Deutsche Volksgruppe*) in Romania. This is the very first case of ethnic autonomy in the political history of the Romanian state. Established under direct pressure from Berlin as an all-encompassing organization for the entirety of the German minority in Romania, the German Ethnic Group was empowered to act as the representative of the minority (Böhm, 1985, 2003). It aimed to be a Nazi-type institution including all ethnic Germans in Romania and made decisive steps in this direction, taking over all German educational, cultural and social institutions in the country. Furthermore, in 1941, Romania officially joined the Axis powers and entered the war against the Soviet Union. Subsequently, following an interstate agreement, around 63,000 Romanian Germans were incorporated into SS units (Milata, 2009; Trașcă, 2013, 499–557). According to historian Ottmar Trașcă (2013, 553), the overall number of Romanian citizens of German ethnicity who were active "in the Wehrmacht, in the Waffen SS, in Organisation Todt, or in other German services during the Second World War . . . lies somewhere above 70,000". This phenomenon was bound to lead to long-term tribulations, not least because on 23 August 1944 Romanian King Mihai I deposed Marshal Antonescu, the de facto leader of the state and of the army, thus allowing Romania to change sides and to declare war on Nazi Germany. In this context, Romanian Germans in the German army fought in the last months of the war against the very state who still counted them among its citizens.

In addition, the Second World War produced another novel situation for Transylvanian Saxons. As a consequence of the Second Vienna Award from 30 August 1940, Northern Transylvania – that is, a surface of 43,591 square kilometers – was ceded by Romania to Hungary (Haynes, 2000, 153). Around 70,000 of the almost 2.5 million inhabitants of the region were Germans (Transylvanian Saxons, Satu Mare Swabians and Maramureș Zipser): this was the first time that Saxons living in the historical region of Transylvania found themselves citizens of two different states. In late summer and autumn 1944, in the context of the Soviet advance toward Northern Transylvania, Saxons from the region fled or were evacuated by the Wehrmacht, most of them ending up in Austria and Southern Germany. This development marks the beginning of the "flight and expulsion" of Germans from Central and Eastern Europe (Kift, 2010, 78). However, at the end of the war, thanks to Stalin's agreement, Northern Transylvania was once again incorporated into Romania (Békés et al., 2015, 18).

As a result of the territorial changes produced both during and as a consequence of the Second World War, including processes of migration involving Romanian German groups (*Heim ins Reich*) and the mass enrollment of Transylvanian Saxons and Banat Swabians in the SS, the end of the conflagration saw Romanian Germans geographically divided, mainly between Romania and Germany (and, to a lesser extent, Austria). Moreover, at the end of the 1940s and in the early 1950s, some Romanian Germans chose to migrate farther, to places such as the United States, Canada, France or Brazil. In the former two cases, these migrants could attempt to join the Transylvanian Saxon and Danube Swabian communities that had formed in the context of the migrations in the interwar period and before the First World War (Maeder, 2011; Vultur, 2012; Frotscher, 2015; Cercel, 2016).

In Romania, in the immediate aftermath of the Second World War and amid the installation of a Moscow-backed regime, Germans still living in the country and German identity itself were subjected to a series of discriminatory measures (Gheorghiu, 2015, 33–169). Romanian Germans were perceived almost entirely as guilty for having sided with Hitler during the Second World War.[3] Consequently, at the request of the Soviets and despite initial opposition from the Romanian authorities, between 70,00 and 80,000 Romanian German men between 17 and 45 years old and Romanian German women between 18 and 30 years old were deported to the Soviet Union to carry out restitutionary labor, a development that came as a severe blow to the community (Weber et al., 1995). Some of the deportees were released in 1946 and 1947, yet they were not sent back to Romania but instead to Frankfurt an der Oder, in the Soviet-occupation zone of Germany. From there, most returnees attempted either to go back to Transylvania or to cross over into the Allied-occupation zone. The great majority of the survivors (around 15% of the deportees died during the deportation) were released in 1949 and sent back to Romania (Beer, 1998, 221; Weber et al., 1995).

Furthermore, the very first measures of agricultural reform (land expropriation) introduced by the new Communist government were explicitly directed at the German population, while in 1945 Germans were also deprived of citizen rights (Beer, 1998, 223–226, 2009; Șandru, 2009). From 1948 onward, these discriminatory measures would gradually be lifted. Nonetheless, anti-German actions (or actions *perceived* as fundamentally anti-German) would continue to take place into the 1950s. They include the deportation to Bărăgan of inhabitants from the Banat villages bordering Yugoslavia (Marineasa & Vighi, 1994, 1996); the so-called writers' trial in 1959, as a consequence of which five Transylvanian Saxon writers were sentenced to a total of 95 years in prison and were not released until 1962 and 1964 respectively (Motzan & Sienerth, 1993); and the so-called Black Church trial in 1958 (Pintilescu, 2008).

However, in an attempt to create a framework that would contribute to the accommodation of Romanian Germans within the Romanian state, the authorities began implementing a series of measures, including the publication of German-language newspapers and the establishment of German-language cultural institutions in communities with sizable German populations. Primary and secondary education in German was provided by the state (Castellan, 1971, 70–71). Romanian German elites could participate in public life in Romania: for example, the Lutheran Bishop, Friedrich Müller, was a member of the National Assembly (Castellan, 1971, 72; Wien, 2002, 249). A tentative state-sponsored manufacturing of a "Romanian German" (*rumäniendeutsch*) identity was in effect a key component of this accommodation offer devised by Romanian authorities. Romanian German cultural and political elites, particularly Romanian German literary critics, also played an important role in this development (Weber, 2010).

At the same time, as already hinted at above, the particular context of the Second World War had given rise to a considerable Romanian German presence outside Romania as well, particularly in the Federal Republic of Germany. Hans-Werner Schuster (2009, 9–10) identified four categories of Transylvanian Saxons in West Germany at the end of the 1940s and the beginning of the 1950s: members of the Wehrmacht and of the SS discharged in West Germany, for whom going back to Romania was to a large extent out of the question; Saxons from Northern Transylvania who had fled or were evacuated by the Wehrmacht in the late summer and autumn of 1944; a small number of intellectuals who had settled in the Reich during the interwar period; and deportees to the Soviet Union who had been sent to Frankfurt (Oder) in 1946 and 1947 and had subsequently managed to move to the Federal Republic. A similar categorization can be employed for the Banat Swabian case as well, although the mass flight from Banat was not such an all-encompassing process as the evacuation and flight from Northern Transylvania (Leber, 2016, 11). The presence in West Germany of members of the other German-speaking groups originating from Romania was largely a direct consequence of the *Heim ins Reich* program mentioned above (Jachomowski, 1984, 202–204).

It was against this backdrop, in the late 1940s and early 1950s, that various elites purporting to speak on behalf of the various German groups originating from Romania founded their own institutions in the Federal Republic, called "homeland associations" (*Landsmannschaften*). In 1957, these associations joined the umbrella organization Federation of Expellees (*Bund der Vertriebenen*), which aimed to represent the entirety of the so-called German "expellees" in the Federal Republic (Ahonen, 2003; Stickler, 2004). Even though Romanian Germans, unlike Germans from countries such as Poland, Czechoslovakia, Yugoslavia or Hungary, were in effect never actually expelled, in the postwar West German context all Germans originating from Central and Eastern Europe and the Soviet Union, irrespective of the subtle or less subtle differences in their postwar fate, were largely subsumed under the politicized category "expellees" (*Vertriebene*). "Expellees" would later become a legal category, to which two other categories were added, namely "resettlers" (*Aussiedler*) and "late resettlers" (*Spätaussiedler*) (Weber et al., 2003, 145–184; Takle, 2011; Nachum & Schaefer, 2018). The latter two categories refer to German migrants from Central and Eastern Europe and the Soviet Union during the Cold War (*Aussiedler*) and in the aftermath of the Cold War (*Spätaussiedler*).

Between the end of the Second World War and 1967, there were no official diplomatic relationships between Romania and the Federal Republic of Germany (Florian, Preda & Trașcă, 2009; Gheorghiu, 2015). This made it extremely difficult for the latter country to act as a kin state for the Romanian Germans living in Romania. The German Democratic Republic did undertake some steps in this direction, but these are still under-researched (Koranyi, 2014; Gheorghiu, 2015, 261–298, 403–421, 527–550; Panagiotidis, 2015). However, not least thanks to pressure exerted by the homeland associations of Romanian Germans in the Federal Republic of Germany on the central authorities in Bonn, a process of Romanian German migration from Romania to the Federal Republic *did* start to take place as early as the 1950s, initially through the mediation of the Red Cross, under the aegis of the process of "family reunification" (*Familienzusammenführung*).

The migration of their co-ethnics to the Federal Republic was a central objective of the homeland associations of Romanian Germans, an objective also embraced in principle by the West German authorities in Bonn. Thus, the postwar history of Romanian Germans is to a great extent the history of a large-scale migration to the Federal Republic of Germany. After the 1967 resumption of diplomatic relations between the two countries, the process of migration intensified and continued essentially unabated until the fall of state socialism in Romania (Dobre et al., 2011). It then reached its peak in the early 1990s, a direct consequence of the opening of borders in the immediate aftermath of the fall of state socialism.

This summary goes some way to expose the paradoxes that informed the postwar history of Romanian Germans. In practical terms, the aforementioned accommodations offered to Romanian Germans by the Romanian authorities provided a framework that contributed to the production and reproduction of a German identity in Romania, yet this identity was to a large extent kept alive solely in order to facilitate the migration and subsequent integration of Romanian Germans in the Federal Republic of Germany (Verdery, 1983, 69). At the same time, although none of the three Romanian Constitutions drafted between 1945 and 1989 called

Romania a "national state" and the existence of minority groups was constantly recognized, state politics continued in many respects to aim toward the assimilation of minorities and thus directly and indirectly pushed them toward migration (Lengyel, 2001). State socialist rule in Romania acquired a distinct nationalist character particularly under Ceauşescu's leadership (Verdery, 1991; Tismăneanu, 2003, 187–232; Copilaş, 2015). Beginning in the early 1970s, politics, discourse and policies implicitly and explicitly aimed at "homogenizing" Romanian society, which in practice was also bound to imply ethnic homogenization. In this context, with the exception of state-sponsored folkloristic approaches, there was no proper place for a real and substantial integration of Transylvanian Saxon or Banat Swabian memories and identities within official Romanian memory and identity discourses, let alone those of other, smaller German-speaking groups. At the same time, this lack of integration is also connected with the particular difficulty of incorporating nationally oriented German memory and identity discourses, such as those with respect to the Second World War, into an anti-fascist framework typical of late socialist regimes in Eastern Europe – that is, significantly tinged by nationalism and burdened by an ambiguous relationship with their countries' own fascist pasts, especially in their last decades (with Romania being a prime example in this respect).

Moreover, the kin-state policies of the Federal Republic of Germany also played a key role in deciding the fate of the German community in Romania. Internal lobbying, a juridical framework that established an entitlement to German citizenship on the basis of a Wilhelminian law (jus sanguinis) and the acknowledgment of the responsibility of the German state for the traumatic events in the recent history of the German communities in Central and Eastern Europe led to the exertion of pressure so that ethnic Germans in this region would be allowed to return "home" (Koranyi & Wittlinger, 2011). Since most of the other German communities in Central and Eastern Europe had been expelled at the end of the Second World War, Germans in Romania, the largest German-speaking community in the region (the Soviet Union excluded) during the Cold War, were among the main beneficiaries of German legislation. The phenomenon known as the *Freikauf* (ransom) of Romanian Germans effectively started in the 1950s but became institutionalized in the 1970s (Dobre et al., 2011; Hüsch, Baier & Meinhardt, 2013). In the last decade of Communist Party rule, around 10,000 Germans a year left Romania for Germany (Dobre et al., 2011). Numbers then exploded in the immediate aftermath of 1989, with around 200,000 ethnic Germans leaving Romania in the early 1990s to become citizens of the Federal Republic of Germany. Narrating the past of the German minority in Romania means in effect narrating its abandonment of the country. This process is best summed up in figures: in 1930, there were 745,421 Germans in Romania, according to the census; 343,913 in 1948; 382,595 in 1966; 332,205 in 1977; 119,436 in 1992; 59,764 in 2002; and, finally, 36,042, according to the results of the census conducted in 2011 (Manuilă, 1938, XXIV; Golopenţia & Georgescu, 1948, 37; Direcţia Generală de Statistică, 1980, 614; Direcţia Generală de Statistică, 1969, 153; Comisia Naţională pentru Statistică, 1992, 38; Institutul Naţional de Statistică, 2003; Institutul Naţional de Statistică, 2011).

3.3. A note on lexical complexity

The equivocal and sometimes indistinct ascription of a German identity to various groups living in Romania is accompanied by a particularly complex semantic landscape revolving around the term "German" in Romanian (Romanian: *german*). The connotations of the latter term are far from straightforward. It can refer to German citizens, and during the Cold War, it referred to citizens of both the Federal Republic of Germany and the German Democratic Republic. At the same time, it can and does refer to members of the German-speaking groups who have lived, for longer or shorter periods of time, on Romanian territory. It can even designate the nomadic Germanic tribes from the Middle Ages.

Furthermore, the Romanian language has two synonyms translatable, in English, with the word "German": *german*, of Latin origin, and *neamț*, of Slavic origin.[4] This complex linguistic conundrum is illustrated, for example, by someone like Gheorghe Șincai, an eighteenth-century Romanian historian and philologist from Transylvania, who used both *german* and *neamț* when referring to Germanic migrations from the beginning of the Middle Ages, even if he did not appear to equate *sas* (Saxon) with *german* or *neamț* (Zăloagă, 2004, 211). Historically, *german* or *neamț* also referred to things pertaining to the Habsburg Empire. In the nineteenth century, in the principalities of Moldova and Wallachia, *austriac* (Austrian) and *german* were used indistinctly (Marieș, 1996, 207). The existence of supplementary words denominating the various German-speaking groups in Romania, such as *sas* (Saxon) or *șvab* (Swabian), further complicates the semantic landscape.

This semantic and lexical complexity was and is bound to have consequences on the images associated with the "German" and with the "Germans" circulating in Romanian society. For example, in historian Valeriu Leu's analysis of the representations of the "German" in notes found in Romanian books in Banat from the end of the seventeenth century to the eighteenth century, he argued that:

> Speaking sometimes about the "German", sometimes about the "German king" and sometimes about the "German empire", the notes preserve the meaning of a collective term, which, however, did not refer to the German population of Banat, but to the authorities, to the lordship, to the administration, simply to the state! All these at once and at the same time!
> (Leu, 1996, 241)

Representations of Germanness in Banat at the end of the eighteenth century and the beginning of the nineteenth century were shaped along the same lines, the Habsburg Empire being fundamentally perceived as a "German" empire (Leu, 2018, 40). The multiple valences of what "German" can stand for in the Romanian context enable the development of a complex representational landscape:

> the German is *par excellence* represented twofold in Romanian writings: on the one hand, as an inhabitant of the German-speaking space, and on the other

hand as a member of the German population in Romania. Two images of the German are thus born, each showing specific traits and constantly influencing each other, both positively and negatively.

(Eiwen, 1998, 264)

The two images referred to by literature scholar Daniel Eiwen are indeed the main images associated with Germanness in the Romanian context, but as I have suggested above, the representational landscape is more complex still, because it can also include other referents, such as things that are Austrian, Habsburg and so on. Moreover, between 1866 and 1947, the Romanian royal family was of German origin, namely the Sigmaringen branch of the Hohenzollern family. The reign of Carol I, which lasted from 1866 to 1914, is largely seen as having brought modernization to Romania and having fundamentally contributed to the consolidation of its social, cultural and political links with Western Europe (Binder-Iijima, Löwe & Volkmer, 2010). The constant interference and reciprocal influence of the various imagined referents captured within the term "Germans in Romania" on one another is one of the phenomena that informs the subject matter of this book. An analysis of how the German minority has been represented in post-1989 Romania must take these intricacies into account and remain sensitive to the complex interweaving of ideas attached to even apparently simple conceptions of Germanness.

Notes

1 "Ausführliche Informationen zur Geschichte der deutschen Minderheit in Rumänien," www.rumaenien.diplo.de/Vertretung/rumaenien/de/06-Kultur-Bildung/seite__minder heiten.html (accessed 20 September 2017).
2 The term *Universität* did not refer to an institution of higher education of Transylvanian Saxons but rather to the totality of Transylvanian Saxons.
3 All these anti-German measures also entailed that trying to adopt other identities, most often Romanian, could be positively consequential for Transylvanian Saxons, Banat Swabians and the others if they wanted to avoid being singled out as Germans. The case of those Banat Swabians who in the immediate aftermath of the Second World War resorted to the Alsatian and Lorrainian origin of their ancestors to assert a French identity is telling in this respect (Vultur, 2012). Marriages of convenience with Romanians were also a means through which Germans could escape the deportation, and indeed, some made use of it.
4 For a concise explanation of the denotations of the two terms, see Ion Bogdan Lefter, "Imaginea germanului în civilizaţia românească şi în literatura română," *România literară* 42, 25 October 1995.

4 The Self and the Other

4.1. Romanian identity between East and West. Romanian-German reciprocal representations

Modern Romanian political and cultural history has been informed by the constant attempt to cope with tensions and frictions arising at the intersection of structural constraints, geographical location, desired self-images and external, ascribed identities. Starting with the emergence, in the eighteenth and nineteenth centuries, of a Romanian national consciousness, the representation of Romanianness and Romanian identity as caught between the Orient and the Occident acted as a recurrent fad and obsession feeding into discourses, institutions, politics and policies, as well as images of the Self and of the Other (Mihăilescu, 2017).

The origins of the top-down intellectual process of Romanian national identity-building are roughly traceable back to the eighteenth century, at the crossroads of the emancipatory project of the Enlightenment and its ethnicizing, backward-looking, Herderian tendencies. Romanian identity constructions and political projects have never fully overcome the contradiction arising from these two impulses (Karnoouh, 2008; Mihăilescu, 2017). Thus, discourses and debates on Romanian identity have been forced to engage endlessly with seemingly unresolvable questions about cultural and political belonging and about being situated, symbolically and physically, between East and West, where West has been understood to mean Europe and East has been perceived variously as the full rejection of Europe or as a flawed and incomplete version of it. Concepts such as "the West", "the Occident" and "Europe" have played a key role as points of reference for the configuration of Romanian identity discourses and politics of identity, of Romanian symbolic geographies and of the imaginaries and binary oppositions associated therewith. In this context, the dichotomy between West and East, between the Occident on the one hand and the Orient or the Balkans on the other hand has come together not only with inferiority complexes associated with Romanian identity being perceived as an Eastern or Balkanic identity but also with a never-ending quest for a Romanianness living up to the European and Western standards (Djuvara, 1989; Hitchins, 1994, 293–334, 1996; Antohi, 1999; Mitu, 2001; Cioroianu, 2002; Spiridon, 2004; Popovici & Pop, 2016; Mihăilescu, 2017; Naumescu, 2018). Against this background, the Orient and the Balkans have often been represented in cultural and political discourses about Romanian identity as the "genetic and historical antidote of Romanian Europeanization" (Spiridon, 2004, 81).

Questions and dilemmas related to the Romanian relationship with the West and with Europe are thus constitutive of the process of development of a modern Romanian national identity in the eighteenth and nineteenth centuries. Yet especially in the Transylvanian context, discourses that can be regarded as incipient forms of ethnic identifications started developing earlier, in direct relationship with the legal administrative system of the Principality of Transylvania. Discursive manifestations of "ethnic prejudices" (as well as of "patriotic feelings") can be found as early as the fifteenth and sixteenth centuries (Almási, 2010, 125–126).[1] Concretely, Saxon authors tended to play up "the importance of Saxons in Transylvania" while also asserting Saxon superiority over the other "nations" in Transylvania and particularly over the Wallachs, who were in effect not a legally recognized "nation". Moreover, remarks by various external observers could be and were brought to the fore to emphasize and construct the representation of Saxon superiority in Transylvania. These processes of derogatory othering had particular political and economic motivations, which were discursively legitimized and naturalized by reaffirming cultural(ist) arguments and essentializations (Almási, 2010).

Historian Adolf Armbruster (1980) reviewed in extenso Romanian-Saxon interactions and reciprocal images as represented in historical chronicles authored between the fifteenth and nineteenth centuries. He noted for example that Transylvanian or Moldovan chroniclers such as Nicolaus Olahus (1493–1568), Miron Costin (1633–1691) or Nicolae Costin (1660–1712) particularly emphasized the civilizational calling, the prosperity and the degree of development of Transylvanian Saxons (Armbruster, 1980, 21, 268–270). Even though his tendency to employ national identity as an analytical device in shedding light on phenomena taking place in a period when this had not yet been configured on the same terms as in recent history can definitely be called into question, Armbruster's study has the merit of emphasizing the rather numerous, albeit not always consistent and substantive, premodern Romanian-Saxon intellectual encounters. In this context, it must also be stressed that research on Romanian-Saxon relations and interactions and on the reciprocal representations of Romanian and Saxon otherness suggests that before the eighteenth century these representations were not informed by East-West dichotomies. The antagonistic construction of the Wallach Other in the late Renaissance presages the subsequent Euro-Orientalist dichotomies, and yet it was not delineated according to an East-West scheme (Armbruster, 1980; Almási, 2010). This is yet another indication that there is no essential and unchanging reality connected with such oppositions and that they should be contextualized and historicized, even as they are investigated in their *longue durée*.

In Armbruster's study on Romanian-Saxon interactions and encounters, he also acknowledges the breakthrough moment brought forth by the Transylvanian School (*Şcoala Ardeleană*), the most important and influential cultural movement addressing issues related to Romanianness in the eighteenth century and first half of the nineteenth century (Armbruster, 1980, 29–37; Stanciu, 2010). Under its aegis, Romanian-language intellectuals in Habsburg Transylvania discursively imagined and constructed (or discovered/rediscovered, as some would argue) the idea of the modern Romanian nation, an idea that conjoined the "Orthodox sense of community" with the special value granted to the region's Roman heritage (Hitchins, 1999, 41). Vying for political legitimacy, which in the case of the Romanian population translated into the quest for equality in rights with Hungarians and Saxons, representatives of the Transylvanian School "emphasized the Latin identity of Romanians in order to enhance their cultural and political prestige in Europe" (Neubauer & Cornis-Pope, 2006, 255). This striving for social emancipation also underpinned the decision of a part of the Orthodox Church in Transylvania to undertake, in 1697, the Union with Rome, whose direct consequence was the birth of the Uniate Church (Hitchins, 1999). Furthermore, top-down processes of imagining the Romanian nation were both concurrent with and closely linked to similar processes impacting on the other ethnic groups living in Transylvania. Transylvanian Saxon narratives about the past were also implicitly or explicitly aimed at the strengthening of Saxon legitimacy in the face of the dissolution of the class/corporate structure of the Transylvanian state (Armbruster, 1991; Szegedi, 2006; Mitu, 2016; Török, 2016).

The discursive construction of Romanian self-identification in Transylvania entailed the development of particular stances and positions on the complex Transylvanian web of ethnicities and nations. In this context, preoccupied by issues regarding Romanian identity and the place of the Romanian population in Transylvania, the aforementioned Transylvanian School, through its representatives, dealt at length and in a critical manner with ethnic otherness and its relationship with Romanianness. Hence, Hungarians, Slavs, Jews, Roma and of course Saxons, were objects of interest for Romanian-language Transylvanian intellectuals active in the eighteenth and nineteenth centuries. The contours of the representations of the Romanian Self, as they can be grasped for example from the discourses disseminated by Transylvanian intellectuals in the eighteenth and nineteenth centuries, were to a not insignificant degree a reaction to the representations by external observers of Romanians that were disseminated through various channels (Mitu, 2001). In effect, self-identification discourses have constantly been interwoven with internal representations of otherness and with external representations of Romanianness. This recognition must be taken into account beyond mere acknowledgment and analytically integrated whenever scholars engage with such topics.

Historians of the Transylvanian School paid particular attention to the "Saxon phenomenon within the ethnic, political, religious and social landscape of Transylvania" (Armbruster, 1980, 30). The interest for Saxons went significantly beyond the clerical religious frameworks on which chroniclers had relied in previous centuries. It was also closely connected with specific social and political developments taking place at the time in Transylvania (Armbruster, 1980, 35–36). In the political context of the eighteenth and nineteenth centuries, marked by intensified conflict and competition, anti-Romanian stances disseminated by Transylvanian

Saxon elites were entangled with Romanian representations of the Saxon population as being fundamentally opposed to Romanian interests and therefore keen to denigrate and slander the Romanians (Mitu, 2001). Nonetheless, such Romanian representations of Saxons coexisted with essentially more positive and appreciative ones beholden to a civilizational and hierarchical understanding of the world that was in effect a key component of the social philosophy of the Transylvanian School (Mitu, 2016, 80–81). For example, Ioan Budai-Deleanu, one of the main representatives of the movement, referred to Transylvanian Saxons as occupying the highest place among the nations in Transylvania on an imagined cultural/civilizational ladder (Hîncu, 1998, 81). Romanian "cultural backwardness" and self-stigmatization were important issues informing the discourses of Romanian-language Transylvanian cultural elites in the eighteenth and nineteenth centuries (Mitu, 2001). The strong preoccupation with questions related to Romanian identity unfolded within an intellectual landscape largely shaped by tensions whose representational horizon was one in which distinct traces of self-Orientalism and intimate colonization can be detected (Mitu, 2016).

At the same time, drawing on the constant communication and knowledge transfer between the German-language cultural space and Transylvanian Saxon political and religious elites, a phenomenon whose origins reach significantly further back in time (Armbruster, 1980, 63; Custred, 1992), eighteenth-century and nineteenth-century Saxon representations of alterity made significant use of discourses and cultural constructions relying on Orientalizing frameworks. Ideas of Saxon superiority in Transylvania, discursively legitimized through references to an alleged civilizational role, were disseminated by Saxon elites (Mitu, 2016, 101–102). An insightful and comprehensive analysis of Saxon-Roma relations and of Saxon representations of the Roma (*Zigeuner*) in the eighteenth and nineteenth centuries indicates the existence of relevant points of convergence with German Orientalist discourses. The Roma were exoticized in ways similar to the exoticization of the Oriental Other (Zăloagă, 2015). Saxon representations of the Roma population can also be placed within the broader context of pre-WWI German and Hungarian discourses about the Roma in Hungary. A closer look at such discourses reveals that they address competing – Hungarian and German – modernization projects and "civilizing missions", which are best understood when they are considered to be part of the Hungarian-German competition for political and cultural preeminence. This competition largely took place in the context of the Magyarization pressures directed against the German-speaking groups in Hungary (Davis, 2017). In a similar vein, scholarship looking in depth at the historical construction of Romanian otherness within Hungarian-language cultural products demonstrates that Hungarian representations of Romanians have been largely indebted to the "imagination of Eastern Europe by Westerners" and are a "very broad extension of this representation" (Mitu & Mitu, 2014, 33).

Starting in the eighteenth century, identity-building processes loosely linked with the political and economic processes unfolding in Habsburg Transylvania but also displaying significant variations due to differences in political contexts began to take place on the other side of the Carpathians, in the principalities of

Wallachia and Moldova. Formally under the suzerainty of the Ottoman Empire, Wallachian and Moldovan elites took to embracing various Europeanisms/Westernisms implanted onto a cultural life that largely stood under Greek and Turkish influence (Djuvara, 1989; Drace-Francis, 2006). Thus, the period between the end of the eighteenth century and the beginning of the nineteenth century is the period in which straightforward positive references to European civilization emerge in Romanian cultural products (Drace-Francis, 2013, 139) and in which the discursive distinction between things Romanian and things European starts gaining momentum.

An emphasis on the difference between "Europe" and boyar Ienăchiță Văcărescu's own country of origin is for example visible in Văcărescu's observations during his diplomatic trip to Vienna as an official representative of Wallachia at the end of the eighteenth century. However, Văcărescu did not betray any feeling of inferiority with respect to the "Europeans" whom he met on his journey to Vienna (Dascălu, 2006, 26–32). The same cannot be said for Dinicu Golescu, a Wallachian boyar wearing an attire of Ottoman origin, who traveled to Western Europe in the first half of the nineteenth century, some decades after Văcărescu. We know about his encounter with otherness in its Western guise from the book he wrote on this occasion, a publication that would secure him a key place in Romanian cultural and literary history. *Însemnare a călătoriei mele* (Accounts of my travel) recounts his journey of discovery, from Wallachia to "Europe", a journey that took place in the 1820s (Golescu, [1826] 1990). In it, Golescu uses his own astonishment when faced with the features of European 'civilization' in order to emphasize what he had come to perceive as the shortcomings and backwardness of his country. His observations are a prime example of the intrinsic relationship between discourses of otherness and self-identification discourses. They are largely informed by apparent inferiority complexes that are produced and reinforced through the comparison of his Wallachian homeland to what he sees throughout his journey westward. This permanent act of juxtaposition leads toward "a plea for a general reform of domestic institutions in a 'European direction'" (Drace-Francis, 2013, 135). Thus, Golescu's visible fascination with "Europe" and the political character of his work make *Însemnare a călătoriei mele* an Occidentalist manifesto in favor of "Eurotopia" (Drace-Francis, 2013, 135–159).

Starting his journey in Bucharest, the boyar Golescu passed through Brașov (Kronstadt in German, Brassó in Hungarian) and Țara Bârsei (Burzenland in German, Barcásag in Hungarian), in effect the first town and region he encountered after crossing the border from Wallachia to Transylvania. There, he praised Saxon diligence and order, remarking that "a stranger, as soon as he enters their villages, would recognize their industriousness and the rightful character of their laws for the happiness of the nation" (Golescu, [1826]1990, 5–6). However, despite his overall positive assessment of localities inhabited mainly by Saxons and also by Hungarians, Golescu did not describe anything as "European" "until at least halfway through his description of Vienna" (Drace-Francis, 2013, 152).

Given the argument that I advance in this book – that contemporary Romanian philo-Germanism is a self-Orientalized and self-colonized assertion of a yearning for Europe – two aspects of Golescu's observations need to be emphasized. First, the prestige associated with Transylvanian Saxons (as well as with Banat Swabians) was seen as a counterpart to the poor economic and cultural state of Golescu's native Wallachia. Second, the unclear status of Transylvania, different when compared to his home country and yet not necessarily straightforwardly "European", anticipates subsequent identification debates regarding the cultural belonging of Romania's different regions and illustrates the liminality and in-betweenness that are key markers of the symbolic geographies put to work in describing regions and countries in Eastern Europe. The self-Orientalizing innuendos and assertions in Golescu's chronicled journey, while representative of their epoch, are also another indication of the usefulness of analyzing Romanian cultural history in general, as well as politics and identity discourses in particular, within a framework that allows for a critical engagement with the East-West dichotomy in its various forms and guises.

In roughly the same period as Golescu, German travelers to the two Danubian Principalities, united into one state in 1859, also tended to configure their discourses in noticeably Orientalist and easternist terms. For example, when Richard Kunisch, "a German travel writer and folklorist with distinct Romanian leanings", wrote in 1861 about a visit to Romania, he situated the country within an "undifferentiated *Orient*" (Hamlin, 2010, 424–425). In a similar fashion, in a poem about her first meeting with King Carol, Romania's future queen, Elizabeth of Wied, who was also a prolific poet author under the pen name Carmen Sylva, referred to the country as a "fairyland in the Far East" (Eiwen, 1988, 34).

It is by no means surprising that the predominant representations of the Romanian population present in German-language cultural products from the late eighteenth century to the early nineteenth century belonged to a large extent to the broader set of representations within Western societies, namely that of underdeveloped Eastern and Southeastern Europe. Cultural historian Klaus Heitmann (1985, 300) spoke of a complex of representations, universally valid in the countries in Western and Central Europe, putatively much more developed on a political level, much more industrialized and much more urbanized, about the still archaic-agrarian societies from the developing countries in Eastern and Southeastern Europe.

Nonetheless, although Klaus Heitmann's observation is generally valid, it would have been better qualified by an analysis that also considered the particularities of German representations of Eastern Europe in the context of specific German political and economic interests in Eastern Europe and of the related German–Eastern European and German-Romanian entanglements that developed particularly after the German unification of 1871. A recent analysis focusing on German-Romanian relations in the second half of the nineteenth century and during the First World War shows for example how German Orientalizing and easternist representations of Romania and of Romanians were linked to the construction of a Romanian dependency on the German economy and that fluctuations in such discourses were always connected with particular political and economic developments and goals (Hamlin, 2017b).

German observers of developments taking place in nineteenth-century Romania also noticed and emphasized the allegedly peculiar intermingling between European models and Europeanizing attitudes on the one hand and Oriental mores and habits on the other. However, a closer look at their discourses and representations reveals that "as the nineteenth century advanced, German travel writers increasingly added a wrinkle to their understanding of Romania as Orient" (Hamlin, 2010, 425). This process of nuancing, in effect an external discursive construction of Romanian in-betweenness and liminality, was concurrent and tightly bound up with the development of the political and economic interests of the German Empire in Southeast Europe in general and in Romania in particular (Gross, 2015; Hamlin, 2017b).

In Wallachia and Moldavia, the nineteenth-century cultural, political and economic rapprochement with Western Europe was accompanied by a distancing with respect to the Ottoman Empire. It also implied the strengthening of ties with Czarist Russia, although this phenomenon was not wholeheartedly embraced by the elites in the two principalities. Wallachia and Moldavia united in 1859, under the leadership of prince Alexandru Ioan Cuza. In 1866, Cuza was forced to abdicate. The throne was then offered to the Prussian prince Charles of Hohenzollern-Sigmaringen (Carol I), under whose rule Romania also became nominally independent from the Ottoman Empire, a direct consequence of the Romanian War of Independence, known in English-language historiography as the Russo-Turkish War of 1877–1878. Romania is not the only Southeastern European country whose independence from the Ottoman Empire and entry into a Western European orbit was associated with the investiture of a German royal family. Bulgaria, Greece and Albania were also ruled for shorter or longer periods in the nineteenth and twentieth centuries by royal families of German origin. Alongside the Habsburgs, such dynasties were agents of Westernization (Ingrao, 2008, 60). This phenomenon largely indicates the importance of Western (in general) and German (in particular) power interests in the region and suggests that reading German politics toward Southeastern Europe at the end of the nineteenth century and in the first half of the twentieth century as a form of (informal) imperialism is legitimate (Gross, 2015). Furthermore, the appointment of Western royals to the thrones of Eastern European countries can also be interpreted as an instantiation of the phenomenon that Bulgarian cultural theorist Alexander Kiossev (1999) called "self-colonization". Within self-colonized cultures, the image of the Western Other as possessing all that "we" lack is predominant. What better way to attempt to get out of this apparent cul-de-sac, what better way to endeavor to fill the absence of everything Western, than to import Western rulers, in the hope that they will make their subjects Western as well?

The attempted Romanian top-down embrace of Europeanism was buttressed and informed by a growing economic and political dependence on foreign capital and by the country's transformation into a semi-periphery of Western capitalism (Chirot, 1976; Murgescu, 2010, 113). At the same time, the desired Europeanization was materially connected to a cultural and intellectual rapprochement toward France and French culture (Eliade, 1898). Romanian Francophilia, prevalent among a significant part of the emerging bourgeoisie in the young Romanian state, was also straightforwardly configured according to self-Orientalizing claims. In a classical text on French-Romanian relationships, French influence in Romania was described as a phenomenon supposedly unknown to history: "a civilized people helping a backward people to enter the path of historical life and to form an original civilization" (Eliade, 1898, III). After 1866, the political and cultural Francophilia that many of the Romanian elites were embracing was prone to come into conflict with the German political, military, cultural and economic orientation of the royal family. Anti-Germanism and Francophilia were particularly visible during the Franco-Prussian War of 1881, for example (Kellogg, 1995, 77). In this context, criticism directed against the Hohenzollern royal family was often framed as anti-German and Francophile. But not all elites welcomed the process of Europeanization – understood as the uncritical championing of Western models and the attempt to apply such models in Romania – unequivocally. The conservative grouping Junimea, under the influence of its *spiritus rector*, Titu Maiorescu, was largely critical of the conceptualization of Westernization as the wholesale import of foreign institutions and models. For them, this type of Westernization was regarded as a "form without substance" (Hitchins, 1994, 55–67). In the way that they shaped their criticism, members of Junimea, who exerted an important influence in both culture and politics, as well as some of their subsequent followers, were influenced by German philosophy and social thought (Hitchins, 1994, 60; Dascălu, 2006, 9).

The growing imperial German political and economic interest in Southeast Europe and Romania was culturally framed by a reliance on discourses aiming to legitimize the German role in the region. Largely informed by hierarchizing, Orientalizing and easternist representations of the autochthonous populations, such discourses were a key component of the process of imagining the German speakers living outside the borders of the German Reich as a German "diaspora" endowed with a cultural mission (Manz, 2014; see also Conrad, 2010). This process gained in intensity after German unification in 1871. The emphasis on tropes such as the *Pionierarbeit* (pioneering work) and *Kulturarbeit* (civilizing work) undertaken by Germans in Romania, be they Germans from the Reich or Transylvanian Saxons, was almost *sine qua non* in texts addressing the topic (see for example Fischer, 1911; Kaindl, 1911). Along these lines, the perspectives of Germans from the Reich and of Germans living in Eastern and Southeastern Europe were very much intertwined.

By resorting to Orientalizing and easternist narratives and discourses that relied on the hierarchized differentiation between East and West but that were also underpinned by an implicit and explicit discursive construction of the liminality characteristic of representations of Southeast European societies, Romania could also be imagined under the aegis of progress, more precisely as capable of attaining progress by means of German involvement in the country. This involvement could be both economic (via foreign German capital or via the German minority), and political (via the Hohenzollern royal family). Thus, German discourses linking the development of Romania with the presence of a Prussian royal family on the country's throne should also be understood as a means of legitimizing German imperialist claims in Eastern Europe (Heitmann, 1985, 277; Hamlin, 2017b). Practically, the liminality and the in-betweenness bestowed on Romania by virtue of the way its geographical location was culturally and politically interpreted made it to a certain extent possible for Romania and Romanians to be constructed as well-suited to Europeanization (if only with the help of Westerners in general and of Germans in particular). Allegedly, Romanians (or rather some Romanians) could therefore actually become more Occidental through the contribution of those situated on a higher position on the civilizational ladder. In order for this to happen, however, the Western/German agents of Europeanization needed some local allies. Consequently, Romania's supposed "Europeanized elite" "was shown as engaged in a process of transforming Romania, enriching and civilizing it", whereas "those left behind economically were presented as cultural laggards" (Hamlin, 2010, 428). The discourse of culture and Westernization effectively shrouded the class divisions that were at that time deepening/becoming increasingly entrenched in the context of the process of capitalist modernization. Cultural and culturalist discourses were apt to obscure social and economic divisions.

Asserting the existence of a German superior model to be emulated by the Romanian population became a fundamental component of the discursive apparatus governing Romanian-German relationships, both concrete and symbolic. For example, in a 1911 text about Germans in the Romanian Kingdom authored by a certain Emil Fischer, a Transylvanian Saxon medical doctor practicing in Bucharest (Hienz, 1998, 70–79), discursive tropes underlining a perceived innate German superiority were put to work within anti-assimilationist lines of argumentation. The text also emphasized Romanian inferiority:

> Germans will be of particular use to this country, as long as they maintain their particularities. The more authentically German they remain, the better for the country and the people of Romania; it speaks for itself that they will be a guiding example only as long as they do not become Romanians.
> (Fischer, 1911, XIV)

Fischer also directly indicates in his argument that Romanians should try to emulate the Germans in order to climb the civilizational ladder.

Fischer's interpretations of German history in Romania and his (normative) representations of German-Romanian relations were not warmly received in Romania. In a response to Fischer's book, a certain Vladimir Mironescu (1911) lambasted the derogatory representations of the Romanian population present in the work. Nonetheless, one should also note that discourses fundamentally similar to Fischer's could also be found in works authored by Romanian observers. Transylvanian pedagogue Ioan Pop Reteganul (1900) provides an especially striking example in this respect. In the early 1900s, Pop Reteganul gathered a collection of moralistic parables meant to contribute to the education of the "people". Therein, he wrote of Saxons in extremely laudatory terms, seeing in them a model worthy of emulation. The title of the section directly dealing with the Saxon population, "Să luăm pildă" (Let's take example), speaks for itself. According to Pop Reteganul (1900, 18–22), one could see "wonders" in Saxon villages, and the gardens maintained by Saxons were "heaven on earth". Hence, Romanians, whose villages and gardens were, one is led to deduce, far from remarkable, had a lot to learn from their Saxon neighbors. At the same time, Saxons were also portrayed as victims of the Jews. Pop Reteganul argued that the latter had allegedly "caught too deep roots amongst" the former. The fact that positive representations of Germans were placed in a straightforward relationship with disparaging and xenophobic views of other ethnic or religious groups, in this case Jews, indicates the relevance of broader networks of representations of alterity. The production of representations of (ethnic) otherness is interwoven with representations not only of the Self but also of *other* Others.

Nineteenth-century and early twentieth-century Romanian discourses emphasizing German civilizational ascendancy were not limited to Transylvanian Saxons. For instance, according to Romanian writer Ioan Slavici ([1930] 1994, 222), cultural superiority was also a trademark of Banat Swabians. Slavici remarked in his memoirs (published after his death, in 1930) that Swabians were "better-off, better dressed, culturally superior", and had "thriving villages, cattle and horses of the best breed, well established churches and schools". In *Mara*, a novel authored by Slavici and first published in 1894, which depicted a love story between a Romanian girl and a Swabian boy, the complex rendering of Romanian-Swabian relations touches on the main issues informing these relations, namely cultural conflict, economic frictions and economic partnership. At the same time, the fact that the settlement of Swabians in Banat was not informed by a medieval legislation regulating rigidly hierarchized relationships between groups might have actually contributed to the existence of fewer frictions between Romanians and Swabians, as compared to the case of Romanian-Saxon interactions in Transylvania (Leu, 2018). However, for economic and political reasons, advancing on the social ladder was associated by Romanians in Banat with appropriating German culture, a phenomenon also illustrated in Slavici's aforementioned *Mara* (Eiwen, 1988, 50–53).

Many further instances of Romanian authors directly engaging with or referring to German otherness could also be brought to the fore here, but the examples discussed are sufficient to demonstrate that the post-1989 positive representations of Germanness in Romania that will be addressed in the subsequent chapters of this book did not appear from thin air but rather have an older genealogy. Existing scholarship has already examined both the representation of the German Other in Romanian culture/literature and the representation of the Romanian Other in German-language cultural products (Eiwen, 1988; Dascălu, 2006; Heitmann, 1985). These studies review a great number of works and hence offer a comprehensive inventory of such representations. However, for the most part, they do not attempt to go beyond an essentially descriptive approach, although to a certain extent, they *do* imply that the analysis of Romanian representations of Germanness from the eighteenth and nineteenth centuries onward could actually unfold within a theoretical framework informed by concepts such as self-Orientalism and self-colonization. It is thus particularly worth emphasizing that the positive image of Saxons in Transylvania (or of Swabians in Banat) has historically tended to be accompanied on the one hand by the assertion of a hierarchical relationship between Saxons and Romanians and on the other hand by the assertion of rather disparaging discourses about other ethnic groups. However, bringing to the fore these older genealogies should not lead to the fallacious inference that representations of alterity are in any way immutable or stable. We should be wary of reifying contingencies, discursive constructs and categories of practice, even as we note that there is a broader history of self-Orientalizing Romanian identity discourses that is linked with an appreciation of things Western in general and of things German in particular.

4.2. Conflicting symbolic geographies

At the outbreak of the First World War, Romania adopted neutrality, despite having been part of a formal alliance with the Central Powers since 1882. In August 1916, under the leadership of King Ferdinand I, the nephew of Carol I, Romania's ruler since 1866, who had passed away in 1914, the Romanian state took the further steps of denouncing its association with Germany and Austria-Hungary and entering the war on the side of the Entente, against its erstwhile allies. In this context, Romanian Francophilia could easily function as a discursive legitimization of such a choice, especially since the embrace of the new alliance was relying on a public rejection of political and cultural philo-Germanism.

Certainly, there were also dissenting voices: in spite of a largely Francophile public opinion, some intellectuals and politicians in Romania adopted philo-German positions during the war, making use of varying lines of argumentation. In a similar fashion, in Transylvania, there were Romanian intellectuals who were torn between their allegiance to the Romanian kin state and that to the Habsburg Monarchy (Boia, 2014). Yet the hegemonic stances and attitudes were rather Francophile and anti-German.

The unfolding conflagration brought the Romanian army close to catastrophe. Despite a short-lived successful military campaign in Habsburg Transylvania, by December 1916 the Central Powers had come to occupy the regions of Wallachia and Dobrudja almost in their entirety, forcing Romanian authorities to retreat to Iași, in Moldova, and to continue to govern what was in effect only a rump state (Torrey, 1992, 463). Hetero-representations, identity ascriptions and symbolic geographies are always fluid and prone to change. In the context of the events and developments taking place during the First World War – more specifically, in the context of the German occupation of a large part of Romania – German representations of Romania were based on the construction of a German-Romanian relationship in accordance to strongly colonialist discourses and practices. This suggests a degree of transformation with respect to the prewar period and an increased resemblance to what historian Vejas Liulevicius (2009) called "the German myth of the East":

> Before the war, Germans largely celebrated Romania as an example of progressive development. Germans gradually moved Romania from a paradigmatic example of the Orient to a liminal state between Orient and Occident and finally to a proto-Occidental state, the 'gateway' to the West in the words of one traveller. During the war, by contrast, Romania became a deeply problematic land with a staggeringly ignorant peasantry dominated by a feminized and decadent elite. The only hope seemed to reside in the innate good nature of Romanian peasants and a small cadre of conservative politicians.
> (Hamlin, 2017b, 16)

During the occupation by German and Habsburg troops, the Central Powers "treated Romania as Pandora's box", marking it "as a colonial territory", in an effort "to assert that Eastern Europe was not Europe" but rather "something else, Asia, the Orient" (Hamlin, 2017b, 13). At the same time, German discourses about Romania tended to link the defects, vices and shortcomings of the former almost-European ally turned enemy with French influence rather than with the Ottoman past and with the British Queen Mary rather than with the German King Ferdinand (Hamlin, 2010, 2017a, 2017b).

However, despite the disastrous Romanian military campaign and the signing of a peace treaty with the Central Powers in May 1918, the end of the First World War actually saw Romania on the side of the winners and Germany on the side of the losers. The last-minute Romanian victory in the war led to the annexation of Transylvania, Banat, Bukovina and Bessarabia by the Romanian state, which became the so-called Greater Romania. This also meant that Transylvanian Saxons, Banat Swabians and other German-speaking groups were turned into citizens of an enlarged Romanian state almost overnight. The new political configuration was bound to lead to symbolic and concrete antagonisms, not least considering that it was the consequence of a war lost by the German and Habsburg Empires, the two states to which especially Saxons but also the other German-speaking groups in newly enlarged Romania felt culturally and politically close (Davis, 2011, 2016).

The ongoing Transylvanian Saxon cultural rapprochement toward the German-language cultural space had been accompanied, from the end of the nineteenth century onward, by a political rapprochement toward the German Reich as such. This went hand in hand with particular self-representations whose main traits were connected with the civilizing role, the "calling" or the "mission" of the Transylvanian Saxons in Eastern Europe. The aforementioned "myth of the German East" was particularly important to the self-identification discourses of Transylvanian Saxons (and of other German-speaking groups), that tended to greatly emphasize their role as defenders of an Occident informed by the superiority of German culture. Elites increasingly forged Transylvanian Saxon values and identity discourses in accordance with what they perceived as "Western" or "Occidental" values and identities, where both "Western" and "Occidental" were, from their point of view, rather synonymous with "German" (Roth, 1998; Davis, 2011, 2016; Mitu, 2016). In this context, Saxon and German representations of Romanians and of Romanian institutions, especially of the ones outside Transylvania – that is, on the other side of the Carpathians – were largely configured according to a pattern indebted to Orientalist and easternist frameworks, a mixture of condescending and empathetic views (Heitmann, 1998, 34–37). Integration and cooperation attempts usually concerned the potential development of "Transylvanism" and thus showed, in some cases, a distinct potential openness toward Transylvanian Romanians, yet this did not come together with a similar openness toward Romanians in Wallachia or Moldavia (Davis, 2011; Kührer-Wielach, 2014). Nevertheless, at the end of 1918, faced with the impending unification of Greater Romania, Transylvanian Saxon elites, as well as various more or less representative assemblies speaking on behalf of the other German groups that were about to become citizens of the enlarged Romanian state, officially embraced the cause of Greater Romanian statehood.

The management of Transylvanian Saxon identity and the production and reproduction of Transylvanian Saxon identification discourses appertained to political, economic and religious elites: "predominantly Lutheran clergy and professionals" (Davis, 2016, 41). Following the de facto disbanding of the Saxon University in the second half of the nineteenth century, the Lutheran Church had officially remained the main (if not the sole) institution responsible for the production and reproduction of Saxon identity. This makes the positions disseminated by its leaders an extremely relevant source for understanding the symbolic and cultural framing of the concrete political, social and economic frictions associated with the Romanian state incorporating Transylvania.

Lutheran elites in Transylvania were also directly involved in the production of historical knowledge about the Saxon past. This means that works of historiography authored by key religious figures and published at the beginning of the twentieth century can provide important insights into Transylvanian Saxon views of the Self, nourished and disseminated by elites, and into the associated paternalistic, condescending and fearful representations of the Romanian population and of the Balkans/Orient as a whole. Such discourses both resorted to and reinforced symbolic geographies of an Orientalist and easternist nature. I will introduce this topic by referring to two significant Transylvanian Saxon historiographic works and two literary products from the first half of the twentieth century, and I will demonstrate how they situated Transylvanian Saxon identity, and representations of otherness, within a horizon informed by the tentative essentialization of West-East dichotomies. This ultimately somewhat hesitant process of essentialization is fraught with tensions and frictions that are particularly illuminating.

In 1916, Friedrich Teutsch (1852–1933), at the time bishop of the Lutheran Church in Transylvania, published the first edition of a study titled *Die Siebenbürger Sachsen in Vergangenheit und Gegenwart* (The Transylvanian Saxons in the Past and in the Present). Starting in the foreword, Teutsch (1916, IX–XI,

1924, V) put forward a series of positive Transylvanian Saxon self-stereotypes, portraying them as a "people of colonists", "conveyer(s) of high culture" and "educator(s) of the environment", compelled to cope with the difficulties of a harsh and unfriendly ambience. German settlement in Eastern Europe is presented as "the real 'achievement' of the German Middle Ages" (Teutsch, 1924, 7). The East-West dichotomy marks the framework of Teutsch's argument from the very beginning of the book, functioning as an interpretative key underlying the entire representation of Transylvanian Saxon history and Transylvanian geography. Transylvania is physically "almost unapproachable from the East", and the cultural influences on the region came "only from the West or from the South". The Christianization of the region made it part of the "Occidental, predominantly German culture". For the Lutheran Bishop, even the atmospheric conditions (*Witterungsgang*) sanctioned Transylvania's belonging to the West (Teutsch, 1924, 3–5).

The emphasis on Transylvania's Occidental affiliation, understood as directly due to the presence of Saxons, is a recurrent theme throughout the book and contains something of a normative dimension. In Teutsch's rendering of Saxon history, Transylvania oscillates between straightforwardly belonging to the West (thanks to its Saxons) and being liminally situated between the Orient and the Occident. One finds an inconsistent use of symbolically geographic ascriptions related to Transylvania, a permanent fluctuation between West and East, between Occident and Orient. This suggests that the Occidental/Western cultural belonging was not fundamentally perceived as being a default characteristic of Transylvania but rather understood as something almost always in danger, to be fought for at important moments. Teutsch emphasizes particular instances in Transylvanian history in which only the Saxons strove to keep the Western affiliation alive (Teutsch, 1924, 192).

In Teutsch's narrative, the history of Transylvanian Saxons is fundamentally the history of a group continuously having to cope with a multitude of threats in order to survive. These menaces are largely a result of the location of Transylvania at the crossroads of Orient and Occident. The perils for Transylvanian Saxons, which ultimately endangered their very survival in the "far East" (Teutsch, 1924, 49), were often seen as coming from the Orient:

> They could not recognize the dual danger, that in those times was coming from the Orient: to begin with, the Romanians (Wallachians) settling at the borders of the Saxon region, against whose unculture Saxons first defended themselves with fire and the sword; and the Turks, who would be a scourge upon the country for three hundred years.
>
> (Teutsch, 1916, 35)

A second, augmented edition of the work would only be issued after the end of the First World War and after the incorporation of Transylvania into Romania, more precisely in 1924. In it, Teutsch eliminated the word "unculture" (*Unkultur*) and replaced it with "attacks" (*Angriffe*) (Teutsch, 1924, 34). Teutsch's criticism was also directed against the Habsburg and especially Hungarian state authorities and their policies that undermined the survival of the Transylvanian Saxon group, but such criticism did not rely to the same extent on the cultural and culturalist argument employed to emphasize the civilizational cleavage between Romanians and Saxons. Furthermore, in Teutsch's understanding, the Saxons also fared significantly better when compared to the other German-speaking groups in Hungary. Hence, the Lutheran Bishop emphasized that in the nineteenth century they were still able to put to work their ancient "spirit of colonists" (*Kolonistengeist*) despite pressures and difficulties, in marked contrast to the Swabians, whose settlement in three Transylvanian villages did not lead to the "best experiences", because they supposedly "lacked the spirit of sacrifice" (Teutsch, 1924, 346–347).

The Romanian population was largely regarded by Teutsch as an uncultured rabble, who only stood to gain from their interactions with Saxons: "Whoever wants to see the influence of Saxon life on the Romanians only has to compare the cultural state of the latter in *Sachsenland* with that of those in Romania or in Maramures; two worlds apart" (Teutsch, 1924, 329). Furthermore, in Teutsch's interpretation of the Transylvanian Saxon past and present, Romanians were perceived as a danger mainly because of their high birth rate and their migration to Transylvanian Saxon areas, phenomena leading to a change in the ethnic landscape that was detrimental to the Transylvanian Saxon population (Teutsch, 1924, 113, 138, 164, 202). The settlement of Romanians in Saxon villages was regarded as playing a direct role in the "disintegration" (*Zersetzung*) and "downfall" (*Untergang*) of the Transylvanian Saxon people (Teutsch, 1924, 202). Thus, in spite of their shared rejection of Hungarian state policies and particularly of Magyarization (assimilation) pressures in the nineteenth century, the Romanian-Saxon relationship continued to be one largely informed by enmity due to socio-economic reasons (Teutsch, 1924, 266, 280). This enmity emerged regardless of what Teutsch saw as Saxon superiority and in spite of the role of Transylvanian Saxons as "instructors" (*Lehrmeister*) of the other "peoples" (*Völkerschaften*) lucky enough to live around them (Teutsch, 1924, 329).

In another book with a similar topic, first published before the First World War, and then republished after 1918, Friedrich Müller-Langenthal (1884–1969) delineated the contours of an almost symbiotic relationship between Transylvania and Transylvanian Saxons, which was at the same time also strongly informed by the East-West dichotomy. Müller-Langenthal was also an important religious figure of the Transylvanian Saxon community. At the time of publication, he was headmaster in Sighișoara (Schäßburg in German, Segesvár in Hungarian). He would subsequently become the bishop of the Lutheran Church in Romania (1945–1969) (Wien, 2002, 26, 211–273).

In his *Siebenbürger Sachsen und ihr Land* (Transylvanian Saxons and Their Country), Müller-Langenthal argued that Transylvania, lying as it did at the "cultural border between West and East", could be called "the Eastern Switzerland" (Müller-Langenthal, 1922, 9). For Müller-Langenthal, even the climate suggested that Transylvania was the meeting point between East and West, although this meeting is symbolically regarded as a conflictual one: "the eastern and the western climates fight continuously for hegemony (*Vorherrschaft*)" (Müller-Langenthal,

1922, 10). In an adverse environment, having to face "un-German ethnic components" and "the juggernaut of Magyarization", Saxons nonetheless represented a superior culture and stood for "Western cultural evolution", their duty being that of "functioning like the sourdough of cultural work" in an environment in which the neighboring countries were "unorderly and culturally poor" (Müller-Langenthal, 1922, 22, 17, 35, 32). Thus, according to Müller-Langenthal (1922, 16), "the superiority of Western culture can be appraised in its fullest significance by looking at its impact on the countries in the East, which are lagging behind".

At the same time, Saxons were also supposed to be "the main defenders of the border to the South-East", to fulfill "the duty of guard in the East" and to constitute the "vanguard of the party steadfastly attached to the West" (Müller-Langenthal, 1922, 38, 46). The Romanian population is a marginal presence in Müller-Langenthal's account. Nonetheless, when Romanians do make an appearance, they are presented as taking over Saxon lands or seen, in light of their high birth rate, as a "radical danger to Saxonness", a fear that echoes those of Teutsch (Müller-Langenthal, 1922, 80, 120). The modern Saxon-Romanian relationship is presented as a "vital struggle for space" (Müller-Langenthal, 1922, 122). This is associated with a belated acknowledgment of the class-based character of the labor relations connecting Saxons and Romanians: "On average, the Romanians were, as opposed to the autochthonous, land-owning German population, a social underclass of day laborers and subsistence farmers" (Müller-Langenthal, 1922, 120). The future bishop also commented on the compatibility between Saxonness and capitalism, claiming, on the basis of a supposed Saxon tendency toward internal equality, the existence of a long-held animosity and distrust toward capitalism within the Saxon community. Nevertheless, in what is an add-on to the first edition of the book, Müller-Langenthal (1922, 115–116) changed his tune and attempted to argue that it was Transylvania's incorporation into the largely agrarian Greater Romania in particular that had aided the development of the capitalist institutions of the Transylvanian Saxons.

These two works, authored by high-ranking religious figures in the Transylvanian Lutheran Church, indicate that the accommodation of Transylvanian Saxons and of Transylvanian Saxon identities and interests within Greater Romania could not be a smooth process and was bound to lead to strife and dissension. The shift in the political frontier may have changed economic relations, but it did not annul the perceived existence of a cultural boundary, which was also related to particular social conflicts. Historian Sorin Mitu (2007, 64) summarized the significance of the change of power in Transylvania (an argument that can be extended to the cases of Banat and Bukovina as well):

> After 1918, through its integration into the Romanian kingdom, mostly inhabited by adherents of the Orthodox faith, Transylvania was administratively moved from one region to another: from Vienna-oriented Central Europe, it swayed towards an Eastern Europe plotting a course amid the backwash of Moscow and towards the Balkans impregnated by the Oriental dilatoriness of Istanbul.

Mitu's wording should not to be taken at face value as an analytical assertion, because to a certain extent, it is paradoxically a reproduction of Orientalist dichotomies. However, it does indicate in effect how the political transition was perceived by Transylvanian Saxon elites and within the broader Transylvanian Saxon community (and to a not insignificant extent also by Romanian elites in Transylvania).

Transylvanian Saxons might have seen themselves as defenders of Western civilization at the gates of the East, but from a national(ist) Romanian perspective, the incorporation of Transylvania at the end of the First World War led to the transformation of a natural frontier – the Carpathian Mountains – into an integrative natural element. What used to divide was now bound to unite the Romanians living on both sides of the mountain chain. The Carpathians played an important symbolic role in narratives of Romanian unity. In a variety of Romanian historiographic discourses and representations, the separating mountain chain is transformed into a uniting one (Boia, 2001, 59). Conversely, the Carpathians had a radically different function for Transylvanian Saxons: they were imagined as the natural frontier separating West and East, Occident and Orient, Europe and the Balkans. One can actually speak of a particular Transylvanian Saxon cultural fetishism whose object was the Carpathian Mountains. This proclivity is especially visible from the nineteenth century onward: the foundation and ongoing activity of the *Siebenbürgischer Karpatenverein* (Transylvanian Carpathian Association) are proof of the symbolic appropriation of the Carpathians within Transylvanian Saxon self-identification discourses (Wedekind, 2004; see also Roth, 2013, 376–493).

Two literary works from the interwar period illustrate the double role of the Carpathians for Transylvanian Saxon self-identification: both as natural borders and as symbolic boundaries with respect to the Eastern world. I refer to *Die Stadt im Osten* (The Town in the East) by Adolf Meschendörfer, published in 1931, and *Zwischen Grenzen und Zeiten* (Between Borders and Eras) by Heinrich Zillich, published in 1937. Both Meschendörfer and Zillich were important Transylvanian Saxon cultural figures, who also acted as de facto ethnopolitical entrepreneurs. Meschendörfer (1877–1963) was a writer, as well as teacher and headmaster at various German-language schools in Transylvania, including the Honterus Gymnasium in Brașov, one of the most prestigious educational institutions of the Transylvanian Saxons. Between 1907 and 1914, he edited a German-language cultural magazine called *Die Karpathen* (The Carpathians) (Sienerth, 1994). Zillich (1898–1988) was a journalist and writer active as a German-language intellectual in interwar Romania. Adhering to Nazi ideology, he moved to Germany in 1936. However, his political career effectively reached its peak after the Second World War, when he became one of the most important figures within the Homeland Association of Transylvanian Saxons in the Federal Republic of Germany (Böhm, 2006, 60–76).

Both novels directly address the transition from Hungarian-administered to Romanian-administered Transylvania, seen as a movement – an unwanted one, that is – from the West to the East. The fact that the cultural and geographical references in *Die Stadt im Osten* and in *Zwischen Grenzen und Zeiten* are rarely, if ever, Romanian serves to confirm the fact that Transylvania's incorporation into the Romanian state was perceived as an unnatural process. In Meschendörfer's symbolic geography – as we find it delineated in the pages of his novel – Kronstadt (Braşov) is located decidedly closer to towns such as Munich or Strasbourg than to Bucharest, or to whatever might lie on the other side of the Carpathian Mountains, whether in the Kingdom of Romania or beyond it. The emphasis Zillich places on the constant cultural communication with the German-speaking space ensures that the horizon inscribed in his Transylvanian Saxon symbolic geography went beyond Transylvania. In *Zwischen Grenzen und Zeiten*, he grants more attention to what lies on the other side of the Carpathians, yet only in order to emphasize difference. At one point, Lutz, the biographical alter ego of the author, asks his Romanian friend, "The ones behind the mountains – what do we care about them!?" (Zillich, 1937, 52). Within Transylvanian Saxon imagination, the eastern world beyond the mountains is able to take on the features of a terra incognita, at times exotic and appealing precisely because of its difference. Romania is also the place where women become prostitutes, as it appears to happen with one of the novel's female characters (Zillich, 1937, 547). During the First World War, the German occupying troops also associated Romania with sexual promiscuity, a typical Orientalist trope (Hamlin, 2010).

For both Meschendörfer and Zillich, the West (almost synonymous with Europe) was inextricably related to Germany and Germans. The German role in and influence on the making of the West were seen as quintessential: in their view, Germans made the West Western. Against this background, the transition to Romania was perceived as a move toward the East:

> Here, the West was reigning: security, law and *Heimat*. Now, the unknown East is coming. Now, we have become something completely novel, we have become Germans from abroad. Do understand that! We are sitting in a centuries-old German tower and unknown life is flowing by it.
>
> (Zillich, 1937, 604)

The threatening and unknown East was embodied by the enlarged Romanian state, coming to clench Transylvania and potentially alter the Westernness of Transylvanian Saxons. In having their direct relationship with the Occident cut, Saxons were increasingly turning into Germans abroad. This indicates an imagined recalibration of the relationship with the German Reich, the beginnings of which can, however, already be found in the pre-WWI period. Zillich dealt extensively with issues of cultural geography in his *Zwischen Grenzen und Zeiten*: in doing this, he both took for granted and discursively reinforced the symbolic division between East and West. At one point, one of the characters in Zillich's novel makes an excurse through Hungarian history, connecting the Europeanness of Hungary with the medieval summoning of German settlers. The latter were able to bestow on Hungary the "radiant Occidental civilization" (Zillich, 1937, 202). This historical digression also includes a straightforward circumscription of Europe as a cultural space ending in Transylvania: "We have come to this country to defend the borders. Whose borders? Europe's borders" (Zillich, 1937, 202). At a later stage in the novel, the same character describes the border in the vicinity of Kronstadt as "the border to another world" (Zillich, 1937, 298). The Romanian state is perceived as another world, un-Western and hence un-European. Zillich also addresses the occupation of Kronstadt by the Romanian army during the First World War, a phenomenon that allegedly forced three quarters of the Saxon population of the town to flee. Not only did the occupation entail the appointment of a new Romanian mayor by Romanian authorities, not only were the decisions taken by the authorities allegedly communicated in Romanian only and not in German and Hungarian to the inhabitants, but even the bells of the Black Church, a key architectural and religious Saxon symbol, ceased to toll (Zillich, 1937, 415).

The town in the East in Meschendörfer's novel is the same Kronstadt, a city whose role in Transylvanian Saxon symbolic geographies was and is particularly important because it lay extremely close to the mountainous border separating Transylvania and Wallachia. In Brașov, as elsewhere in Transylvania, Romanian-Saxon conflicts had historically contained an important geographical dimension: Saxon homes and businesses were located in the centers of Transylvanian towns, whereas Romanians and others mainly lived on the periphery, with city centers being at first de jure and then de facto mostly off-limits to them. This division was particularly salient (and at the same time visibly under threat from around the beginning of the nineteenth century) in Brașov.

In *Die Stadt im Osten*, the yearly Romanian feast called Junii Brașovului (Brașov's Youngsters) plays a central role. Describing it allows Meschendörfer to expose the tensions that existed between Romanians and Saxons. The narrator in *Die Stadt im Osten*, an alter ego of the author, is fascinated by the festivities yet at the same time emblematically frightened. Traditionally, the feast marked a day of the year on which the Romanian population, usually not allowed to inhabit the walled town of Kronstadt, could enter it in a ritual celebrating youthfulness and power. Thus, the festivity signaled a symbolical appropriation and assertion of power over the town and took on a somewhat portentous quality. Meschendörfer (1931, 293) notes rhetorically, "And if the monstrosity inscribed in the old legend should somehow come to pass! If the Romanian riders should succeed in entering the inner town and circling the old Saxon town hall three times, then the city would belong to them!" He is bewildered by the Romanian costumes, "a piece of rampant folk phantasy", as the "colored Orient gleams from each of them" (Meschendörfer, 1931, 294). The contrast to the frequently referenced black attire of the Saxon officials in the Black Church is striking, marking the dichotomy of West and East as a dichotomy between sober rationalism and seriousness (Lutheranism) on the one side and Oriental color and exoticism on the other side.

In Meschendörfer's understanding, demography is a threat: the growing Romanian percentage of the population is worrying for the Saxons. We have already seen that important religious and political figures such as Teutsch and Müller-Langenthal shared similar fears. Romanian characters are almost absent from

Meschendörfer's novel, despite the fact that its storyline is set at the end of the nineteenth century and the beginning of the twentieth century (Lăcătuş, 2009, 73–79). Romanians appear only as exotic and marginal figures, who threaten the Transylvanian Saxon high culture and civilization of Kronstadt. The author is writing from the position of a representative of an "island" of culture in the East. The last pages of the 1931 edition offer the perspective of Transylvanian Saxon self-victimization, under the influence of the unfulfilled promises of the Declaration of Alba Iulia in 1918. The "world powers" are accused of forgetting this Transylvanian Saxon island, which is striving to cope with the threats coming from the Romanian authorities. The Saxons are represented by Meschendörfer as being in peril. After almost four hundred pages in which Romanians are in effect barely present, the writer strongly deplores the fate of the Transylvanian Saxon minority in the newly enlarged Romanian state. All Saxons want is to "remain German" – and if not, "may the storm flood take us all" (Meschendörfer, 1931, 371). Conveyors of culture in the east, the Saxons are about to lose their identity *because of* the east. In Meschendörfer's geography, Kronstadt has been a town in the east, an island of Germanness in the east, yet precisely this geographical location, this proximity to the east and to all the dangers embedded there, make it so easily penetrable and its Germanness so fragile.

The symbolic border lying in the vicinity of Kronstadt and dividing Transylvania from the Ottoman-influenced Romanian principalities plays a key role for both Meschendörfer and Zillich and for their characters, as the Romanian world beyond the mountains is, in both cases, radically different and of little interest, at least until 1918. However, this world is represented as slowly catching hold of the Saxons and pressuring them into assimilation, which is perceived as the transformation of high culture into confusion and unculture. The erasure of the symbolic Carpathian border, a political event that followed the annulment of the physical *Königsboden* border during the Habsburg reign in Transylvania, brought with it, for Meschendörfer and Zillich, a decoupling from the political and cultural world whose orbits were Vienna or Berlin, hence the "we discourses" emphasizing an "island" mentality – that is, one of alienation and an identity in peril.

Notwithstanding some of the (significant) differences between them, the identity discourses and symbolic geographies proposed by Meschendörfer and Zillich were meant to convey the message of Transylvanian Saxons as civilizing colonizers and defenders of Europeanness in a rather inferior environment, one which was aiming in the long run at their assimilation. The cultural connections with Germany and the German-language cultural space contributed to the enhancement of a specific set of symbolic geographies and to the reinforcement of the typical positive stereotypes associated with Saxonness. Furthermore, the readership of both Meschendörfer's and Zillich's works was mainly German. Neither author had been translated in Romanian at the time, yet they were present on the German book market during the Nazi period. Zillich eventually settled in Germany, where he would act as an advocate of a conservative and Nazi-oriented understanding of Germanness. After the Second World War, he was active in the Homeland Association of Transylvanian Saxons in Germany and became one of the main Transylvanian Saxon ethnopolitical entrepreneurs in the Federal Republic.

An internal tension is, however, detectable in all these discourses. *Either* Transylvanian Saxons stand for the West and, by means of a metonymy, the whole of the region they colonized (Transylvania and by extension the entire Hungarian kingdom) belongs to Western – that is, European culture – *or* Saxons have been instructors conveying high culture and civilization to the uncultured East, particularly to the Romanians (but to a certain extent also to the Hungarians), yet end up in peril of being suffocated by the very same – essentially un-European – East and of losing their identity. The latter understanding actually requires that Transylvania's Western character *not* be taken for granted. The East-West tension ensuing out of such Transylvanian Saxon discourses in effect indicates the liminality and in-betweenness that characterize representations of Eastern Europe in general.

The incorporation of Transylvania into Romania also led to the publication of a text with clear political aims, distinctly aimed at a Romanian audience, which was meant to act as a prop within an argument whose goal was that of securing collective rights for the Saxons. *Ce sînt și ce vor sașii din Ardeal?* (Who are the Transylvanian Saxons, and what do they want?) appeared in 1919, shortly after the unification of Greater Romania. The brochure had no official author, yet historian Vasile Ciobanu (1991) has convincingly showed that the one who wrote it was Emil Neugeboren, a Transylvanian Saxon who had previously been a member of the Hungarian Parliament.

The publication of the text in Romanian, which included a preface authored by well-known Romanian historian Nicolae Iorga (in effect, a text written in 1909 and republished on this occasion), was intended to indicate the existence of a Romanian-Saxon compatibility on the basis of which Romanian-Saxon intercommunication in general and the accommodation of Saxon interests in Greater Romania in particular were deemed possible. However, this compatibility was directly linked with the representation of a hierarchized civilizational relationship that reinforced the idea of Saxon superiority: "All those who know the Saxon people know that it is a very precious element, that it has a glorious and hard-working centuries-long history and that it can serve as model of order and good habits" (Neugeboren, 1919, 9). The text described the twelfth-century Saxon colonization as providing the legitimacy for their rights and argued that it was on the basis of these rights that they had developed an appreciation of "freedom and a democratic way of thinking", comparable only to that of the Swiss people (Neugeboren, 1919, 13). Furthermore, in a *captatio benevolentiae* aimed at the new authorities, Neugeboren emphasized the pro-Romanian stances of Transylvanian Saxon historical figures such as Stephan Ludwig Roth or Daniel Roth, who in the nineteenth century had envisaged that Transylvania at some point would become part of a Romanian state. At the same time, in Neugeboren's representation of Transylvanian Saxons, which was aimed at a Romanian audience and had clear political goals, Saxons appeared in toto as members of the middle class. Supposedly lacking both an aristocracy and a proletariat, Saxons were bound by an internal class cohesion (Neugeboren, 1919, 22).

The Self and the Other 57

Arguing that the well-off Saxon peasants have always been guiding examples for Romanian and Szekler peasants, Neugeboren made a plea in favor of a form of agricultural reform that will not affect the interests of the former. In effect, also spurred on by the competition with the "much more fertile land of Wallachia and Moldova", Saxon peasants could become an important factor in the development of agriculture in Greater Romania (Neugeboren, 1919, 28). When discussing Saxon industry and trade, Neugeboren highlighted the advantages that integration into the enlarged Romanian state could provide:

> The domicile of Saxons moved from the periphery of a State into the center of their new homeland and the passes in the Southern Carpathians no longer stop the free transit of raw material and finished products. Now, all the Saxon traits that push them towards work in industry and trade, can develop unhindered, and the beginning which was made in this field can continue in full freedom.
>
> (Neugeboren, 1919, 30)

On the one hand, such a view is at odds with the representation of Transylvanian Saxons as a bulwark of the Occident and with the Carpathians as representing a physical and cultural boundary of Germanness. On the other hand, presenting the unification of Greater Romania and the integration of Saxons into the new state as a potential success story with an emphasis on free trade and free markets suggests the birth of a new discursive strategy. Neugeboren emphasizes the bridge role that Germans in Transylvania play in their belonging to the middle class and their capitalist credentials, which would allow them, as long as they are supported by Romanian state politics, to "walk as a good example in front of their fellow citizens" (Neugeboren, 1919, 50).

In the preface to this Transylvanian Saxon attempt to cultivate Romanian goodwill, Nicolae Iorga emphasized the civilizing role of the Transylvanian Saxons in Transylvania and their influence as models for ethnic Romanians. The passage below is often quoted in texts on and by Transylvanian Saxons, as it has actually turned into an important self-identification (!) marker within the Saxon community, a development that suggests the compatibility of Romanian representations of Saxons and of Saxon self-representations:

> to have brought superior culture, to have founded urban life on both sides of the Carpathians, to have definitively settled the life of the entirety of Transylvania in fixed forms, to have connected West and East all the way to the Danube and to the far-away "Tartar", Greek and Turkish countries, by means of commercial relationships, to have fruitfully exerted Western influences upon the oldest Orientally colored Romanian art, to have helped the success of Romanian national language upon the medieval cultural form of Slavonian language.
>
> (Iorga, 1919, 4–5)

The Oriental versus Occidental dichotomy is conspicuous, and the entire text by Iorga essentially praises Saxon influence on Romanian culture in Transylvania. Orientalizing and easternist tropes are straightforwardly brought to the fore, but at the same time, the liminality and in-betweenness of Eastern Europe also enable referring to the existence of mutual influences. The Saxon colonization of Transylvania is coded in a fundamentally positive manner, presented as disseminating elements of a "higher culture" to this "corner of the far wild East". Nonetheless, according to Iorga, "the blossoming of Saxon culture" would not have been possible "in the absence of a propaedeutic local civilization, as well as of its natural carriers" (Iorga, 1919, 4). Thus, the Romanian historian manages to link Romanian self-emancipatory claims with the positive reading of Saxon colonialism, in a mix of conservatism, ethnonationalism and self-colonization. Iorga imagined an alliance between the Latin spirit of Romanians and the German spirit of Saxons, as well as a common mission of the two, that of mediating between East and West. At the same time, the Romanian historian clearly attributed to Transylvanian Saxons an educational role, seen as underlying and informing their relationship to the Romanian population. He understood the historical Saxon-Romanian relationships in Transylvania as unequal, the former being representatives of a higher culture and disseminating it to the latter. Furthermore, he posited that the Saxon input to Romanian culture consists mainly in their influence toward the acclimatization of a series of traits that are in effect symptoms of Western modernization: urbanization, social and institutional stabilization and contributing to the development of the Romanian vernacular.

In 1920, Liviu Marian (1920), a Bessarabian Romanian member of parliament, dedicated a succinct booklet, written in a similar vein, to the Germans in this region, which had been part of the Russian Empire up to the end of the First World War. The structure, the message and the rationale of Marian's text are largely akin to the aforementioned *Ce sînt și ce vor sașii din Ardeal*. Acknowledging the risk of being considered a "Germanophile", Marian argued that the Romanian state should not fall into the political trap of oppressing minorities and sketched a positive picture of Bessarabian Germans. According to him, the Germans in Greater Romania, but especially those in Bessarabia, embodied the "civic virtues" that the Romanian state needs, since they are "industrious, hard-working, capable, honest and patriotic elements" (Marian, 1920, 5). These characteristics, combined with a location particularly favorable for agriculture, led to their "blossoming economic situation, rightly envied and yearned for by the other inhabitants" (Marian, 1920, 12). Strongly anti-Russian, Marian lambasted the migration policies of the Russian czars, which were meant, in his view, to restrict the influence of the local Moldovans. Nonetheless, his criticism fell short of being directed against German migration. On the contrary, when addressing the issue of German migration to Bessarabia, he embraced a radically different position, asserting that the Russian czars should actually be thanked "for receiving German colonists on the territory of Bessarabia" (Marian, 1920, 14), as the latter had, from the very beginning, provided a role model for the "scarce and uncultivated locals". "Assiduous, smart and disciplined", these colonists "truly knew how to civilize the lands where they settled". As a consequence, their communes are "thriving, rich, clean" (Marian, 1920, 15). This made them, and here Marian drew a straightforward connection with Transylvanian Saxons, "the only immigrated foreigners from whom our people and our country could profit, without being alienated, aggrieved or even denationalized" (Marian, 1920, 15).

Marian made an explicit plea for an alliance between Romanians and Germans against the "expanding Slavism", also arguing that the unification of Greater Romania saved the latter "from slavery or even from certain death" (Marian, 1920, 4, 15). He locates the legitimacy of this alliance in the shared anti-Bolshevism and Europeanness of the two peoples (Marian, 1920, 15–16). The political, anti-communist message, is particularly salient. Since they own land – and for Marian, Bessarabian Germans deserve this because they work the land with love and skill – theft, robberies or murders "by means of which one can get rich out of someone else's wealth" are not to be found in their villages (Marian, 1920, 22). The fear of Bolshevism and of the abolition of private property triggers Marian's argument, yet for him Bessarabian Germans and Romanians can fight together against this danger. At the same time, the eulogy that Marian delivers of the orderly and clean character of German villages, where there is supposedly no poverty because "labor is a virtue appreciated by all" and "idling around a vice despised by all", indicates the normative and civilizational aspect implied by the positive image of Germans in Bessarabia and the ideological horizon within which this image is situated. Bessarabia was indeed associated with poverty and backwardness, but by emphasizing German well-being in the region, Marian also suggested that the appropriation of German virtues was both necessary and possible and that it would enable the local Moldovan population to reach a similar level of progress, something that Bolshevism allegedly could not have done.

The interventions by Iorga and Marian can be referred to in order to bring a nuance to the assertion made by historian Sacha Davis (2016, 48), who argued that in the interwar period, "Romanian politicians were unmoved by appeals to German 'cultural superiority'", and they "viewed German speakers as an unthreatening minority". The representations of Transylvanian Saxons and Bessarabian Germans found in the texts by Iorga and Marian, both of whom were active as politicians, resort to tropes of German cultural superiority, aiming to discursively put this superiority to work in the context of the newly enlarged Romanian state. Considering the period in which they were published and the fact that they were authored by intellectuals turned politicians, the two texts can be read on the one hand as a form of bidirectional *captatio benevolentiae* – toward both the new authorities and German elites in Romania – and on the other hand as aimed at a Romanian readership unacquainted with the ethnic realities of the newly acquired provinces. In both cases, Germanness was equated with a series of positive attributes.

When addressing the representations of Germanness in interwar Romania, one must not omit Lucian Blaga, a philosopher and diplomat who systematically expounded on aspects related to Transylvanian Saxons in his work on cultural philosophy and cultural theory. In a book that historian Keith Hitchins (1994, 309) called "the most important philosophical investigation of Rumanian traditionalism undertaken in the inter-war period", Blaga attempted to draw links between space and culture (in a very ethnicized and essentialized understanding of the latter term). In doing so, he developed the concept of a so-called mioritical space (*spațiu mioritic*), supposedly peculiar to Romanian geography, informed by the oscillation between plains and hills.

In order to substantiate his argument, Blaga juxtaposed the Romanian use of space to the Saxon use of space in Transylvanian villages, arguing that the two stood for different "unconscious horizons". Houses in Saxon villages suggest the "rings of a collective unity", whereas houses in Romanian villages are defined by the distances between them (Blaga, [1936] 2011, 168). Characterized by different "matrix-spaces", Romanians and Saxons are "two types of people, who live in the same landscape, but in different spaces", thus rendering effectively impossible the "useless and unfruitful irony of a so-called 'Transylvanianism', common to the ethnic populations living one next to each other in this landscape" (Blaga, [1936] 2011, 174). If the Romanian spirit is marked, for Blaga, in an interpretation that would subsequently have a long and successful career in Romanian intellectual debates, by fatalism in the face of destiny and death and by the supposedly untranslatable word "dor" (*yearning*), then Saxons in Transylvania stand for the "spatial vision" of the "Western Europeans", which embodies "the gothic spirit, the mystique of unfettered freedom and the valiant and engineer-like spirit of a gigantic fight with nature". This "ample organic and unconscious framework" had been brought by the Saxons "precisely eight hundred years ago, from the banks of the Rhine" (Blaga, [1936] 2011, 66). The Romanian-Saxon dichotomy is also visible, for Blaga, in the relationship with nature. Saxon houses suggest the "presence of a collectively channelled human energy", which aims to "impose a primordial plan on nature", whereas Romanian houses seem to be located at random, although they actually "emerge organically out of the landscape" (Blaga, [1936] 2011, 246). Behind the gates of the houses built by Saxon colonists, one can expect to see a "threshing machine", whereas behind the gates of Romanian houses, you can expect to find "Muma Pădurii", a (female) mythological figure of Romanian folklore, supposed to live in forests. Mastering nature under the aegis of order versus living in an organic communion with nature, rationality versus superstition, constructing one's own destiny versus embracing fatalism and colonization versus indigeneity: in his dichotomic presentation of the Romanian and Saxon "unconscious horizons", Blaga resorts to a metaphysical vocabulary that ties in seamlessly with the unbridgeable oppositions implied by Orientalist, easternist and colonial discourses. In Blaga's understanding, cultures are clear-cut units, living almost parallel lives one next to the other. Processes of communication, knowledge transfer, acculturation, assimilation or métissage seem completely irrelevant. A naturalized, almost racialized, East-West dichotomy permeates his theorizations:

> The Westerner, no matter whether he lives in the mountains or in the plains, on the Continent or on an island, in Europe, in America or in Australia, in

temperate areas, in the Tropics or in the Subtropics, will remain, through his attitudes and initiatives, in the same infinite horizon as his country of origin.
(Blaga, [1936] 2011, 69)

The rhetoric of Blaga is largely symptomatic for the broader political and cultural milieu of the period, marked by essentialized understandings of national and ethnic identities. Political and cultural elites in the interwar period dealt extensively with what it means to be Romanian, self-representations communicating as usual with representations of otherness. At the same time, beyond cultural discourses, interwar Romania was, at the political level, the site of a state-sponsored process of nation-building, which was also attempting to legitimize itself by asserting essentialized and largely exclusionary understandings of Romanianess (Livezeanu, 1995; Hausleitner, 2001). The final and tragic outcome of this process were the policies of ethnic cleansing and genocide directed against Jews and Roma during the Second World War.

The perception that Romania's territorial integrity was threatened by its revisionist neighbors (e.g. Hungary, the Soviet Union and Bulgaria) and by the minority groups unhappy with their status in Greater Romania was widespread. Young intellectuals turned toward the far right and anti-Semitism. The likes of Mircea Eliade, Emil Cioran or Constantin Noica were openly in favor of the Iron Guard, Romania's own far-right movement, or of Nazi Germany. However, on a discursive level, the xenophobia that was a key aspect of the nationalism they promoted was not necessarily directed against the German community in Romania. This is why, in one of his interwar xenophobic outbursts, historian of religions Mircea Eliade could go as far as to single out "Swabians" as the only "allies" of Romanians among the several other "foreign" ethnic groups in the country (Volovici, 1991, 123). In the 1980s, Emil Cioran, whose destiny, like Eliade's, lay outside Romania from the early 1940s onward, deplored in his personal correspondence with Wolf von Aichelburg, a Transylvanian Saxon writer, the Saxon migration from Romania, stating that it was having a heart-breaking effect on him. For Cioran (1995, 268) – who originated from Rășinari, a village inhabited mainly by Romanians yet lying in the immediate vicinity of Sibiu, in a largely Transylvanian Saxon environment – the Saxon population was an oasis of morality in the Balkans: he even reminisced about writing something of the sort in the 1930s.

Against this background, in the buildup to the war and during the war, symbolic geographies and identity discourses in Romania tended to emphasize a supposed cultural and political Romanian-German compatibility. From a Nazi perspective, the Second World War was to a large extent presented as an act of defense of European culture and civilization (Miloiu, Dragomir & Ștefănescu, 2007; Martin, 2016). This tied in particularly well with representations of German cultural superiority that were very much embraced within German communities in Eastern Europe, such as Transylvanian Saxons. At the same time, in Romania, the Romanian-German alliance in the Second World War was also represented as part of a larger struggle for the defense of Europe against eastern Bolshevism (Giurescu, 1941; Miloiu, Dragomir & Ștefănescu, 2007; Case, 2009). Despite this constructed anti-Soviet Romanian-German compatibility, Romanian-German frictions and Romanian German self-representations emphasizing cultural superiority and Romanian backwardness and underdevelopment played an important role in, for example, the mass enlistment of Saxons and Swabians in the SS rather than in the Romanian army (Milata, 2009).

4.3. The Cold War

Romania's change of sides in August 1944, the defeat of Nazi Germany and the radical social transformations that the imposition of a Soviet-backed socialist regime brought along were bound to impact both official and unofficial representations of Germanness in Romania. Discourses about Transylvanian Saxons and the other German-speaking groups in Romania as defenders of Europe and disseminators of civilization to the backward East were even more at odds with the new political situation than they had been at the end of the First World War.

Officially, in the final stages of the war and in the immediate aftermath of the conflagration, Romanian Germans were largely equated with Nazis. The 1943 mass enlistment of Romanian Germans in the SS directly contributed to the imposition of this equation. This also meant that the German community was the target of distinct retaliatory measures, such as the January 1945 deportation to the Soviet Union of Romanian Germans for "the reconstruction of the country" (up until 1949) and the land reform in March 1945, two measures that took effect while the war was essentially still ongoing (Weber et al., 1995; Şandru, 2009).

Nevertheless, starting in the late 1940s and the early 1950s, Romanian authorities devised measures meant to accommodate the German community in Romania and to contribute to its integration into the new political and social order. Specifically, the state had a German-language cultural and educational offering meant to cater to the particular needs of the German minority in relation to socialist Romania, but also to the particular needs of socialist Romania in relation to its German minority. This offering was accompanied by attempts to discursively construct a "Romanian German" identity, a process also embraced by some of the Romanian German cultural and political elites in Romania during state socialism (Weber, 2010). Such identification discourses were largely devoid of the culturalist and civilizationist outlook that had informed Romanian-German entanglements and representations of Germanness in Romania before the end of the Second World War.

At the same time, the postwar history of Romanian Germans has been fundamentally marked by the physical separation of the Romanian German communities by the Iron Curtain. This division shaped the contours of an identity crisis and had inevitable consequences for the tropes and myths underlying the identification discourses of Romanian German groups, particularly of Transylvanian Saxons (De Trégomain, 2003, 2006; Koranyi, 2008). In West Germany, Romanian Germans organized under the aegis of the so-called *Landsmannschaften* (homeland associations), along the lines of their regional affiliations from Romania (Transylvanian Saxons, Banat Swabians, etc.). The identity discourses promoted by the luminaries of these associations displayed marked continuities with the conservative, nationalist and even Nazi identifications promoted before and during the Second World War. Furthermore, the conservative anti-communism underlying the East-West division during the Cold War could easily nurture identification discourses and representations emphasizing the allegiance of Transylvanian Saxons, Banat Swabians and the other Romanian German groups to Germany, to Europe in its Western-centered understanding and to the anti-communist Occident.

The main issue animating postwar Romanian German history in all its dimensions was the question of migration. A potential return to the homeland was envisaged in the early aftermath of the Second World War. The so-called *Recht auf Heimat* (right to the homeland) was also largely supported by the much more numerous (and also more vocal) associations of German expellees in West Germany, originating from Western Poland or the Sudeten region of Czechoslovakia. Such visions were nonetheless soon given up, and the homeland associations of Romanian Germans started to lobby for the migration of the co-ethnics still in Romania to the Federal Republic, in the name of family reunification, although there were also important dissenting positions, especially in the Transylvanian Saxon case (Weber et al., 2003, 517–625).

Moreover, particularly in the immediate aftermath of the Second World War, discussions about the overseas migration of Romanian Germans were also common. In this context, in 1950, Heinrich Zillich (1950, 27–28) pleaded before an audience of Transylvanian Saxons in West Germany against overseas migration on the basis of the Transylvanian Saxon belonging to the "wonderful Occident", a Eurocentric construction that did not seem to include North America. In the same speech, Zillich also referred to Kronstadt as the "the most Southeastern town of Europe". Both the representation of an incompatibility between Germans in general and Saxons in particular as representatives of Europe in the Southeast and the representation of the Romanian state as something other than Europe tied in well with typical Cold War dichotomies emphasizing the alleged un-Europeanness of communism.

The Cold War Transylvanian Saxon conflict between those pushing for Romanian German migration from Romania to West Germany and those upholding the opposite option, that of supporting Saxon (and by extension German) permanence in Romania, was also a conflict between different identification discourses and perspectives. The perception of a German, as well as European, belonging of Transylvanian Saxons was a *sine qua non* of both stances and positions. However, according to those who largely pleaded for migration, Germanness and Europeanness could no longer be maintained in the context of the division of the European continent and of Romania's membership in the socialist bloc. Such representations could also tie in with symbolic geographies of an older extraction, emphasizing a number of almost essentialized cultural and civilizational tensions related to the German presence in Eastern Europe/at the borders of Europe. For example, in a pamphlet published in 1976 on Transylvanian Saxons under Communist rule, the author Hans Bergel, one of the main supporters of migration from Romania and also editor in chief of *Siebenbürgische Zeitung*, the official newspaper of the Homeland Association of Transylvanian Saxons, provided an extensive list of abuses and discriminations against his co-ethnics. Among the consequences of the Romanian anti-German policies, Bergel noted the "increasingly more evident loss of the genotypical feature of Saxons, namely the Western European-Occidental component, that is gradually disappearing in favor of the Eastern European-Balkanic one". Bergel saw a tragedy in this, not only for the Saxons on whose behalf he purported to speak but also for the Romanian population, since it deprived the latter of the presence of a "cultural force" that "had animated and influenced the culturally and politically fruitful development of the Romanian people" and that could do the same in the future (Bergel, 1976, 13–14).

Those who advocated in favor of the "remain" option acknowledged the challenges that the new political conjuncture represented yet suggested that leaving Romania would in effect be a defeat and a symbolic abjuration of Saxon and German identity in Transylvania. Nonetheless, their discourses were constructed around a line of argumentation emphasizing the duty of Saxons with respect to the fundamentally Saxon/German/European culture that their ancestors had constructed, despite all the hurdles and difficulties that came from the East.

A third type of identity approach is the aforementioned attempt to construct an overarching "Romanian German" identity, meant to reconcile the apparent Romanian-German opposition and, to a certain extent, also to move away from the conservative, *völkisch* and sometimes even Nazi connotations to which both camps in the so-called migration conflict were in effect indebted, although they employed them differently. Despite the apparent progressive attitude inscribed in this attempt – which also made Romanian German identity appealing for young left-leaning German-language writers and intellectuals in Romania critical of the Nazi and conservative past of their parents[2] – the processes of folklorization of ethnic identities, typical of the nationalist turn taking place in Romania in the 1970s and 1980s in particular, took its toll and made the identity discourses promoted by these writers and intellectuals recede in the background.

Within this apparent diversity of Romanian German identification discourses, the position of the Homeland Association seems to have prevailed, at least if we consider the actual trajectory of migration of Romanian Germans from Romania to the Federal Republic. This so-called migration of "ethnic unmixing" unfolded throughout the entire period of the Cold War, but after taking place either illegally or through the mediation of the Red Cross in the 1950s and early 1960s, it clearly gained in intensity following the official reinstatement of diplomatic relations between Romania and the Federal Republic of Germany, which happened in 1967 (Brubaker, 1998; Weber et al., 2003; Cercel, 2017; Florian, Preda & Trașcă, 2009; Dobre et al., 2011).

Under the rule of Nicolae Ceaușescu – and particularly from the mid-1970s onward – state ideology in Romania followed a distinctly nationalistic and authoritarian path (Verdery, 1991; Copilaș, 2015, 149–234). The consequences of this nationalism for the relationship between the Romanian state and its German minority, as well as for discourses on Romanian identity and German otherness – or, vice versa, on German identity and Romanian otherness – were ambivalent.

On the one hand, the discursive imagination of a socialist nation referred to a history of struggles against social and national exploitation, in which Saxons and Swabians allegedly took part alongside Romanians and the other "co-inhabiting nationalities" (Copilaș, 2015, 214). On the other hand, Romanian ethnic nationalism, coupled with the steady process of migration to the Federal Republic of Germany, was conducive to de facto assimilationist pressures on Romanian Germans that functioned as another argument in favor of migration. The mixture of nationalist ideology and delusional dictatorship reinforced a climate of distrust among Romanian Germans, the origins of which were, however, also much older. What anthropologist Steven Sampson (1984) called "national integration through socialist planning" – that is, the so-called systematization of villages, which was one of the key top-down modernization projects of Ceaușescu's regime – was a process that took a heavy toll on ethnic minorities, particularly in Transylvania. Yet "the preference for modernizing Saxon villages" was for some observers "based partly on the Saxons' traditional propensity for hard work, sobriety, thrift and community effort" (Sampson, 1984, 115). At the same time, the process of village systematization was interpreted at least within the Transylvanian Saxon community as an attack on Saxon identity and also on the fundamentally European character of the German past in Western Romania (Bergel, 1976; McArthur, 1981, 161–162; Sampson, 1984, 228–230).

The national ideology discourses promoted under Ceaușescu aimed to assert, both internally and externally, a proud Romanian identity, and they stood in a relationship of implicit and explicit dialogue with representations of "Europe" or concepts with related denotations – that is, the "West" or "civilization". So-called protochronism, a phenomenon that played a key role in the cultural politics of the Ceaușescu regime in the 1970s and 1980s, referred to the idea that "developments in Romanian culture" "had anticipated events in the better-publicized cultures of Western Europe" (Verdery, 1991, 167). Thus, it was in effect not a rejection of a European Romania but rather an attempt to "raise Romania's image in the esteem of the world", an endeavor "clearly symptomatizing the plight of subaltern cultures dominated by metropolitan centers" (Verdery, 1991, 168).

Combined with Ceaușescu's megalomania and against the backdrop of dire economic shortages, protochronism rapidly took the form of extreme exaggerations. However, even these exaggerations functioned (and continue to function) as nationalistic discursive units only with overt references to Europe. For example, theories about the existence of an ancient "Dacian civilization" acknowledge "Europe" as the contemporary standard of civilization, and appropriate it by tracing the genealogy of this civilization to the Dacians, and from there to contemporary Romanians. According to some of these theories, Europe itself originated on the contemporary territory of Romania and Dacians spoke Latin or a similar language long before the Romans. It is therefore not a rejection of Europe but rather an attempt to intellectually and discursively annex it. For extreme protochronists, what was at stake was not showing how European Romania is but rather showing how Romanian Europe is. Such theories could also be particularly useful in the development of anti-Hungarian arguments in the apparently never-ending political and cultural conflict over Transylvania, emphasizing the indigenous (hence European) character of Romanians, as opposed to the "Asian" origin of the Huns as ancestors of Hungarians.

It would be too simplistic to single out the ideology of Romanian nationalism under Ceaușescu or the supposed rejection of totalitarianism and desire for freedom typical of Romanian Germans as causes of migration, even if some popular discourses about Romanian and Romanian German history in the twentieth century attempt to do this. Romanian German migration took place against the backdrop of a multitude of interrelated issues, not least economic ones, particularly in the context of the crisis of the late 1970s and 1980s. The German legislative framework, welcoming toward Germans from Central and Eastern Europe, also played a vital role in this respect.

Officially, the Romanian authorities were critical of Romanian German migration to West Germany, but at the same time, Securitate documents show that this migration was an important source of much-needed foreign currency, particularly during the economic crisis that began at the end of the 1970s (Dobre et al., 2011). This process of migration led to the development of particular ideas about West Germany, since Germans who migrated would often come back to visit their relatives and friends after they received West German citizenship. This contributed to the reinforcement of the Romanian Occidentalist fascination with West Germany. Items brought from West Germany by Saxons and Swabians in their trips to Romania (e.g. Neckermann catalogs) were seen in Romania as a symbol of capitalist luxury (Petrescu, 2008, 215–217; see also Koranyi, 2008). The envisaged possibility to legally migrate to West Germany was one of the main factors that contributed to the preservation of markers of German ethnicity in Romania, despite an overall decline in the centrality of German ethnic identity in social life (McArthur, 1981; Verdery, 1985). Furthermore, this possibility presumably also made German ethnicity to a certain extent attractive for people who by means of origin, language knowledge and so on could choose between several ethnic identifications.

4.4. Other "Others"

The analysis of the representations of Germans and of the German minority in post-1989 Romania can only gain in depth if situated in a broader setting. This implies engaging with the wider network of representations of ethnic otherness because even briefly addressing representations of other Others can highlight the apparent peculiarity of the Romanian German case. It can also anticipate the gains to be derived from the analytical juxtaposition of representations of the German minority with perceptions and representations of other ethnic groups in post-1989 Romania, an approach that I will resort to at times in the subsequent chapters.

Lucian Boia (2001, 170–174) emphasized the existence of "three sensitive files" belonging to what he calls Romanian consciousness, namely "the Gypsies, the Hungarians, and the Jews", often represented in Romania through a xenophobic lens. The construction of a Romanian national identity in Transylvania, due in part to the efforts of the aforementioned Transylvanian School, involved adopting particular stances with respect to the other ethnicities with which Romanians were in contact (Mitu, 2001). For example, the movement emphatically rejected the supposed influence of the Slavs on Romanian identity, as this would have been at odds with the emphasis placed on the Roman origin of Romanians (Hitchins, 1999). A politically connoted Russophobia has been characteristic of representations of Russia and of Russians in Romanian culture over the past two hundred years (Ivanov, 2004, 117), although some nuances should also be taken into consideration, at least when it comes to the official images of Russia during the first decades of state socialism. In the post-1989 context, the targets of xenophobic representations have continued to be mainly Russians, Jews, Hungarians and Roma (Grancea & Ciobanu, 2002, 365–367).

Important Romanian works of literature, history and philosophy written at the end of the nineteenth century and the beginning of the twentieth century are illustrative of the xenophobic character of representations of Jews and of Jewishness (Turliuc, 2004, 155–182). A comprehensive inventory of the historical representations and perceptions of Jewish traits in the Romanian sociocultural setting would also show that the stereotypes and clichés associated with Jewishness are not devoid of paradoxes and contradictions. However, in spite of such paradoxes and contradictions, the hegemonic representations of Jewishness in the Romanian context have been largely imbued with anti-Semitism. Moreover, despite the wide-scale disappearance of the Jewish minority in Romania, as a consequence of both the eliminatory anti-Semitism culminating in the Holocaust during the Second World War and the subsequent migration of Romanian Jews to Israel that took place during the Cold War, anti-Semitic representations continue to freely circulate in the Romanian public space.

"The slow and widening accumulation of stereotypes, distortions, pictures and slogans" related to Jews (Idel, 2009, ix) has been analyzed by cultural historian Andrei Oișteanu (2009) in a comprehensive study. The murderous and genocidal character that this anti-Semitism took on in various moments throughout Romanian history stands in direct relation to the politicization of representations of the ethnic (or religious) Other, but this is an issue that Oișteanu does not engage with in depth and whose investigation would require much more historical contextualization than his *longue durée* approach allows. In his approach, Oișteanu (2009, 5) has also emphasized the relevance of "ethnic comparison" – that is, of showing the similarities, dissimilarities and the connections and entanglements between representations of different ethnic Others in the same setting. Oișteanu's work has also indicated that historical anti-Semitism in Romania can be linked to the broader Central European context. Yet not only historical but also contemporary Romanian anti-Semitism can be integrated in a wider context. Nowadays, anti-Semitism is often related to the rehabilitation of anti-communist figures in Central and Eastern Europe, being thus an element within conservative and nationalist positions in several countries in the region, Romania included (Shafir, 2018).

Despite a general absence of comprehensive studies regarding the image of the Hungarian Other within the Romanian-speaking world, the constructed antagonistic relationship between the two nations, visible in identity and memory discourses, is based on the overall representation "of a permanent confrontation between Romanians and Hungarians, seen as a main element of their history" (Mitu, 2006, 239; see also Miskolczy, 1999). Historical representations of Romanians within Hungarian society have also acknowledged this confrontation, yet apparently not to the same extent as the other way around. The construction of the Romanian Other in Hungary is very much related to the (desired) Western self-understanding that has been historically prevalent within Hungarian society and to what Maria Todorova ([1997] 2009) would call liminality. Hungarian representations of Romanians also clearly indicated a civilizational hierarchy placing West above East and hence Hungarians above Romanians. They are therefore often connected with the self-assertion of a Hungarian Western identity. Such a hierarchy partially stems from a colonialist mindset but was at the same time illustrative of the urban-rural binome typical of the Enlightenment body of thought. Thus, representing the Romanian population as "noble savages" or as peasants stubbornly refusing to embrace progress was very much linked to wider representations of rurality during the period of the Enlightenment. Worth underlining in this context is that the confrontational aspect underlying reciprocal Hungarian-Romanian representations should not be considered to be an immutable characteristic over the course of history. In various contexts, often where representations of Slavic otherness as a threat took precedence, Romanians were also imagined as potential allies of Hungarians (Mitu & Mitu, 2014).

Alongside Hungarians, Jews and Germans, the Roma have been the most significant ethnic Other for Romanians, particularly against the backdrop of the disappearance of Jews and Germans from Romanian society in the past eighty years. Romanian history has been largely written without the inclusion of the Roma population as actors therein (Achim, 2004, 1). This means that the history of the centuries-long slavery of the Roma in Wallachia and Moldova is most often written out and not confronted in scholarship and even less so in public debates. When moving away from nationally oriented approaches, studies on Transylvanian history *do* address the broad web of Romanian-Saxon-Hungarian entanglements, but they still largely omit the Roma (Roth, 2003). Writing a history of Romania that would include the interethnic and intersocial entanglements that Roma were part of is still a desideratum waiting to be fulfilled.

Shannon Woodcock (2005) critically analyzed the relationship between the representations of the Roma and modern Romanian identity in her unpublished doctoral dissertation, seeing in the Roma population a "catalyst" for the antonymic framing of Romanian national identity discourses. Woodcock's examination is a comprehensive study of the historical entanglements between representations of the *Țigan* Other and Romanian identity discourses. There is also an ever-increasing body of literature that focuses on the image and representations of the Roma in post-1989 Romania. Such literature emphasizes, for example, the constructed "semantic oppositions" between Romanians and Roma and underlines the representations of the latter as having a wild and uncivilized character (Hasdeu, 2008). Particularly in postsocialism and in the context of the European integration project, the *Țigan* Other remained "a central site of contestation" in Romania (Woodcock, 2007). The nominal conflation of Roma and Romanians by external observers is a particularly sensitive (and thorny) topic within Romanian society. This penchant for drawing strict ethnic boundaries between Romanians and Roma indicates on the one hand a process of racialization of the Roma identity by the Romanian majority and on the other hand the largely negative representations of Roma within Romanian society, which by and large amount to Romaphobia.

As historical examples suggest, Germans have to a large extent functioned for Romanians as a European Other worthy of being emulated or, in any case, as a representative of a different culture endowed with positive characteristics. It would definitely be wrong to argue that Germans, be they Transylvanian Saxons or Banat Swabians, be they German speakers from the rest of the Habsburg Empire or from the German Reich, were fully spared the hetero-ascription of negative ethnic markers by Romanian observers. However, compared to the other ethnic Others significant in the Romanian context, Germans appear to have fared significantly better. Such strong implicit and explicit positive and Europeanizing dimensions are not to be found in Romanian representations of other Others with whom Romanians also closely interacted.

Juxtaposing representations of German otherness with representations of other Others in the Romanian context enables a deeper understanding of the former. It is useful to shed light on the interconnections between different hetero-representations while also bringing to the fore that such hetero-representations are related not only to discourses on the Self, but also to the broader landscape of discourses on other Others. Thus, as this book will also show, specific representations of otherness often acquire greater meaning when conjoined not only with self-identification discourses but also with representations of other Others. The multiethnic Romanian setting and the existence of several historical encounters with a series of Others, alongside the historical encounters with Germans, gave birth to a multitude of representations of alterity, which mutually inform and complicate one another.

Notes

1 Historian Ioan-Aurel Pop (1998) goes so far as to argue that there was a medieval Romanian nation, on the basis of what he calls "Romanian medieval solidarities".
2 Richard Wagner, "Cărțile 'pline' și cerul 'gol'," interview by Rodica Binder, *Observator Cultural* 317–318, 20 April 2006.

5 "A valuable and unmistakable contribution to the life of Romanian society"

5.1. Nationalism, minority politics and Europeanization in post-1989 Romania

Particularly in the wake of the Helsinki Accords of 1975, the discriminatory treatment of ethnic minorities in Ceaușescu's Romania, and especially of the Hungarian and German communities in Transylvania and Banat, was among the main accusations leveled against the regime. Thus, criticism was framed by distinctly resorting to discourses and arguments that emphasized the regime's assimilationist policies and the human rights abuses perpetrated by the Romanian state (e.g. Bergel, 1976). It was against this background that the Romanian authorities that emerged after the revolutionary turmoil of late 1989 were practically compelled to address the political and legislative legacies of state socialist rule, not only in terms of Ceaușescu's dictatorship in general but also with respect to its effects on the majority-minority relationships and on minority politics in particular. In this context, it is telling that the first visits of high-ranked foreign officials to Romania were those of Gyula Horn and Hans-Dietrich Genscher, the ministers of Foreign Affairs of Hungary and the Federal Republic of Germany respectively, the two countries acting as kin states for the Hungarian and German minorities in Romania (Novák, 2013, 56–57; Ciobanu, 2016, 307).

At first glance, the new authorities appeared willing to undo the political legacy of the preceding decades by making radical changes and embarking on a new type of minority politics. Programmatic documents sketched out by the new elites who were about to take power were made public during the final days of 1989 and seemed to critically acknowledge and reject the nationalistic policies embraced under Ceaușescu (Shafir, 2000, 102). Point 7 of the Declaration read on 22 December 1989 on state television on behalf of the National Salvation Front (NSF) asserted the "respect for the rights and liberties of national minorities and the guaranteeing of their full equality in rights with Romanians".[1] The same idea was then reiterated in a more clear-cut manner in the NSF declaration issued on 5 January 1990. The latter statement straightforwardly condemned the treatment of ethnic minorities under the previous regime and openly asserted an intellectual indebtedness to the 1918 Declaration of Alba Iulia. It guaranteed the individual and collective rights and liberties of national minorities. Furthermore, the Front proclaimed that such a clause would subsequently be inserted into the new Constitution. Last but not least, it announced that a minorities' law would be drafted no later than six months after the validation of the Constitution.[2]

Nonetheless, the overt reference to the 1918 Declaration of Alba Iulia seems to have acted as a self-fulfilling prophecy. Looking closely at the two declarations reveals marked similarities not only as regards their tenets and their outlook but also as regards their lack of effectiveness. In December 1989, the NSF promised to grant collective rights to the ethnic minorities in Romania, a gesture of goodwill and healing in light of the nationalistic ("homogenizing") ideology and politics that had been prevalent under Ceaușescu's rule. Similarly, the Declaration of Alba Iulia, issued on 1 December 1918, had stipulated that ethnic minorities would be granted collective rights. Nonetheless, the interwar Romanian authorities eventually failed to put into practice the generous promises inscribed in the Declaration of Alba Iulia.[3] Consequently, especially for minority groups such as the Hungarians and the Germans in Transylvania, the Declaration of Alba Iulia can be regarded as symbolizing an unfulfilled pledge. In a similar development, the apparently liberal and generous stipulations inserted into the NSF Declaration from 5 January 1990 were not matched by the subsequent minority politics of the Romanian state: "the idyll was short-lived" (Shafir, 2000, 102). The National Day of Romania was set on 1 December, but what is celebrated is the act of unification rather than the Declaration as such. The tension that arises upon a closer investigation of the Declaration, namely that between the promises with respect to the recognition of collective rights for ethnic minorities included in the text and the official position of the Romanian state of not acknowledging collective rights, has not been openly addressed.[4]

The paradigm that has been embraced by Romanian authorities after 1989 is that minority rights should be regarded in both theory and practice as individual rights. According to this interpretation, by being conceptualized as a subspecies of human rights, minority rights can be applied only to individuals and not to groups.[5] Commenting on the concept of collective minority rights, Romania's first post-1989 president, Ion Iliescu (1995, 133), called it a "pseudo-legal concept, aiming to remove the problems associated with national minorities from the human rights field and to transform them into a purely political weapon". This interpretation has been in effect largely shared by all Romanian political actors.

Therefore, in spite of the apparent minority-friendly stances that the power shift initially seemed to bring along, the approach of Romanian authorities rapidly took a different path. At both the discursive and the material level, nationalism strongly informed the incipient transition toward capitalism, neoliberal democracy and free market rule. Various groups appropriated, in different social contexts, the national idea that had previously been promoted, particularly during the final decades of Communist Party rule (Verdery, 1991, 1996). Thus, as regards nationalism and minority politics, there have been notable similarities between Romania under Ceaușescu and post-1989 Romania. One could go even further and trace a direct continuity in policy all the way to the interwar period. This embrace of nationalism also had a meaningful impact at the level of foreign policy: "when Romania applied for Council of Europe membership (just three months after its revolution), it was put under exceptionally intense scrutiny", due to concerns surrounding the status of human rights in the country, including the situation of its ethnic minorities (Ram, 2009, 180). Thus, in the 1990s, there was significant European pressure on the central government in Bucharest to improve the situation of minorities (Bell, 1996, 505).

Among the symptoms (as well as causes) of the so-called politics of intolerance in Romania in the aftermath of the fall of state socialism one can note the emergence of the nationalist movement Vatra Românească (The Romanian Hearth), the violent and deadly Romanian-Hungarian clashes that took place in Târgu Mureş in March 1990, and the participation in government between 1992 and 1995/1996 of xenophobic nationalist parties such as Greater Romania and the Party of the Unity of the Romanian Nation (Gallagher, 1995). The Hungarian minority was largely seen as the threatening Other with respect to Romanian nationhood and Romanian national statehood. Discourses about a potential "Hungarian danger" or about "Hungarian separatism" with regard to Transylvania circulated broadly. Racist views of the Roma, perceived in part as those to blame for "the effects of market reforms", were widespread (Verdery, 1996, 99). Moreover, the dissolution of state socialism further entrenched, in mass media but also on the political stage, the "anti-Semitism without Jews", whose origins could, however, be traced to the pre-1989 period (Shafir, 1991; Eschenazi & Nissim, 2004, 317–349). In this context, the most pertinent insight, valid particularly for the first postsocialist decade, is that "the post-Ceauşescu Romanian regime . . . continued a nation-state strategy inherited from the previous regime" (Csergő, 2002, 27). This general observation allows me to emphasize, through contradistinction, the peculiarity of the phenomenon that I describe as philo-Germanism without Germans.

The national elections in Romania that took place in 1990 and 1992 were won by the de facto continuator of the former Communist Party, which renamed itself the Party of Social Democracy in Romania (PSDR) in July 1993. Between 1992 and 1995/1996, it ruled in a coalition with one nominally socialist and two openly nationalistic parties. Nevertheless, in spite of the overt nationalism expressed by the main political forces in Romania, the country's new Constitution guaranteed the right to a parliamentary seat for all national minorities. In 1990, eleven representatives of minority groups entered Parliament on the basis of this principle of parliamentary representation for minorities, which establishes a rather symbolic electoral threshold for the latter. These seats have been "intended to compensate minority organizations that were not successful in crossing the electoral threshold" normally needed to get into Parliament (Protsyk & Matichescu, 2010, 32). In contrast to this expectation, the Democratic Alliance of Hungarians in Romania (DAHR) has consistently managed to garner the votes required to enter Parliament starting with the first post-1989 democratic elections held in Romania.

The existence of the positive discrimination proviso is often put forward in order to convey the image of a state friendly and well disposed toward minorities. In 1993, a Council for National Minorities was established, consisting of representatives of minority groups, although relations between state authorities and the Hungarian minority continued to be particularly strained. The vocal demands of the latter's representatives for "cultural autonomy" did not fare well in a context in which the hegemonic discourse in Romanian society was clearly nationalistic and centralistic (Ram, 2009, 182; Csergő, 2002, 10). The principle of parliamentary representation for ethnic minorities in Romania has favored the smaller minorities in the country; indeed, it was most likely adopted in order to provide a counterweight to the Hungarian presence in Parliament (Alionescu, 2004, 63). Currently, there are eighteen ethnic minorities represented in the Romanian Parliament, seventeen of which make use of the positive discrimination reservation. One of these seventeen is Romania's German minority.

A significant change in Romanian-Hungarian political relationships, with consequences for minority politics as well, came in 1996, when a rather motley coalition that vocally pushed for neoliberal reforms succeeded in winning the elections and also co-opted the DAHR to form the government (Pavel & Huiu, 2003, 319–322). This governmental shift also ran parallel to a policy change taking place within the DAHR, as its leaders started to advocate for more openness to bargaining and reaching compromises with majority political actors (Toró, 2016, 91–94). Thus, starting with the elections of 1996, the practice of co-opting the DAHR in various governmental coalitions in Romania or of securing the parliamentary support of the DAHR by the parties in power has been repeated several times.

The most salient political goals of the coalition that won the 1996 elections were accession into the EU and joining NATO (Pavel & Huiu, 2003, 319–322). The two objectives were largely regarded as being part and parcel of one and the same larger political project, namely Romania's formal recoupling to Europe and to the West, the so-called return to Europe. Thus, even if initially the "economically liberal turn" chosen by the new authorities "plunged the country into a deep recession", leaving the government "on the brink of declaring a state of emergency", Romania dove headfirst onto its path toward being integrated into the EU and NATO (Ban, 2013, 7). The official invitation to open accession negotiations came in 1999 (Phinnemore, 2010, 292). The subsequent return to power in 2000 of the ex-Communists, rebranded this time as a party close to Third Way social democrats, did not alter the political path set by the previous government. Thus, the integration into the EU in particular "saved" the liberal project in Romania "from implosion", a project that was then continued and further entrenched after the elections of 2004, which were won by an ideologically radicalized liberal-conservative coalition (Ban, 2013, 7).

The assimilation of European minority rights standards was presented as a key prerequisite of the return to Europe, as part of the symbolic, ideological and legislative package that had to be embraced (albeit sometimes grudgingly) in order to facilitate this return and to become part of the European Union. In 1993/1994, Romanian authorities nominally agreed "to protect minorities on the basis of the principles of Recommendation 1201" of the Council of Europe so that the country could become a member of the European body. The first co-optation of the DAHR to government, "which enabled subsequent significant reforms, was probably also in part the result of Romania's EU membership objective" (Ram, 2009, 188). Through its mechanisms, the Council of Europe also highlighted the anti-Roma racism in Romania (Ram, 2009, 187). In this context, issues related to the discrimination of the Roma minority in Romania began to be granted significantly more attention, at least on the discursive level, starting with the second half of the 1990s (Ram, 2009, 182).

Hence, the main impulses toward concrete legislative changes in Romanian minority politics and other closely related fields were directly connected with the political goal of joining the EU and with the requirements entailed in this objective. Joining the EU depended on abiding by the so-called Copenhagen Criteria, which also specifically included clauses related to minority protection and minority rights. This meant that from being clearly nationalistic-oriented in the early 1990s, the Romanian authorities slowly changed their approach, moving toward the accommodation of minority demands and needs, under the influence of and conditioned by the process of so-called Europeanization (Dobre, 2004). From the early 1990s up to 1995, Romanian minority politics were characterized by inertia – that is, "lack of change or even resistance to EU required change". A second period then followed, from 1996 to 2000, which was "characterised by a mixed nature of change and transformation according to the EU conditionality". The third period, starting in 2000, was interpreted in 2004 by political scientist Ana Maria Dobre (2004, 646) "as the beginning of a transformation within the political setting and its relevant policy choices". This latter periodization can surely be extended to at least 2007, the year in which Romania officially joined the EU. In essence, it was under external pressures and in order to prove their European political identity that Romanian authorities met particular legislative and policy demands related to minority protection.

The incentives underlying the accommodation of some key demands of the representatives of the Hungarian minority, including demands regarding issues such as anti-discriminatory legislation and the use of language in both education and public administration were important components of the process of European integration (Ram, 2009, 183). Steps taken in order to address the problems faced by the Roma population have also been directly linked with the same process. The "dramatic shift" implied by the EU accession decisively "affected the dynamics of nationalism and minority rights" in the country (Smith, 2016, 433). The pressures and political criteria associated with European integration in terms of minority rights have contributed to significant legislative and policy changes theoretically designed to facilitate the development of minority identities (Ram, 2003; Sasse, 2006). Following the series of measures issued in the first decade of the 2000s aimed at the accommodation of national minorities and given the complexity of these measures, at the end of the last decade, Romania was optimistically seen as occupying a leading position on the international and European scene in this respect, going from "laggard to leader" (Salat, 2008, 9; Ram, 2009).

Nonetheless, there have also been voices suggesting that the conditionality implied by the process of European integration was more than once overlooked in Romania's relationship with the European Union (Phinnemore, 2010).

Furthermore, despite this apparent accommodation of the interests of minorities in Romania, anti-Hungarian and anti-Roma discourses and policies have continued to surface recurrently, both on the local and national levels. The liberal optimism visible in analyses from the late 2000s and early 2010s might have been somewhat premature, although some voices continue to emphasize the "spectacular minority regime" functioning in Romania (Salat & Novák, 2015, 63). Following the EU accession, pressures related to minority politics actually dwindled, not least because there is practically no political nor institutional leverage to be used anymore in this respect. This might also explain why the political strategy of the DAHR increasingly moved away from the attempts to exert international pressure (Kiss & Székely, 2016, 606). The problems faced by the Roma population are far from being solved. Prejudice and discrimination continue to substantially inform the social and economic status of the Roma. The absence of a well-organized political representative body speaking on behalf of the Roma in Romania also plays a role (Ibryamova, 2013). Thus, despite Romania having joined the EU, the integration of the Roma seems on many counts to be more of a failure than a success (Fleck & Rughiniş, 2008; Ibryamova, 2013).

Hungarians and the Roma are the two most numerous minorities in Romania, which explains why these two minority groups have been in the foreground of Romanian minority politics after 1989. According to the official results of the 2011 census, there are about 1.2 million Hungarians in Romania: around 6.5% of the entire population of the country. In the same census, around 620.000 Romanian citizens self-declared as Roma, thus representing about 3.3% of the population of Romania (Institutul Naţional de Statistică, 2011). However, in the case of the Roma, figures are heavily contested, various estimations suggesting that the number of the Roma in Romania is actually much higher.

Scholarship engaging with minority politics, and often looking particularly at the aforementioned two cases, indicates that the European dimension should be taken into account as an analytic field unto itself when undertaking research on minority-related issues in post-1989 Central and Eastern Europe, Romania included. It also shows that the often-applied "analytic triangle", the theoretical framework developed by Rogers Brubaker (1996, 55–76) for the analysis of nationalism and minority politics, can be refined. In specific, the triadic nexus consisting of nation-state, kin state and minority – conceptualized as interwoven political fields developing processual relationships with each other – should be expanded into a quadratic nexus by adding the field of "Europeanization/Westernization" into the analytic landscape. This latter field can account for the relevance of the aforementioned international organizations, in this case particularly the Council of Europe and, from the end of the 1990s onward, the European Union (Smith, 2002). Furthermore, in the case of the Roma, in the absence of a kin state to lobby on their behalf, one can in effect speak of an analytic triad, only that this has been constituted through the interactions and entanglements between the field of the Romanian state, the field of the Roma minority in Romania and the "Europeanization/Westernization" field, including mainly European institutions and other European member states.

76 *"A contribution to Romanian society"*

In the same vein, research that has focused on the role of Germany as a kin state for German minorities in Central and Eastern European countries after the fall of state socialism in particular has also noted the entangled relationship between German kin-state politics and processes of Europeanization in the said countries:

> The democratization of the formerly Communist societies in Central and Eastern Europe opened new opportunities for Germany's external minority policy. Greater possibilities to support the German minorities in their host-states, the need to do so in order to halt the mass exodus of ethnic Germans, and the genuine interest of the former Communist countries in improving their relationship with Germany, which was seen as an important stepping-stone towards accession to the EU and NATO, complemented each other in a unique way.
>
> (Cordell & Wolff, 2007, 309; see also Wolff, 2006)

This means that the emphasis on the role of Europeanization – that is, of the "return to Europe" as a project translated as political integration into the EU, with reverberations and effects on the level of both minority politics and identity discourses – is also legitimate when looking at the representations of the German minority in post-1989 Romania.

5.2. The Romanian-German Treaty for Friendly Cooperation and Partnership in Europe

The fall of state socialism created opportunities for the new political organization and representation of ethnic minorities in Romania (Bárdi, Gidó & Novák, 2014). In late December 1989, German elites in Romania made use of the first signs of regime change to set up an organization meant to represent the German minority (Ciobanu, 2016, 303). The rapidity with which Germans in Romania, first and foremost Transylvanian Saxons, organized themselves, can be understood if we take into account the rich political and institutional tradition of the community. Furthermore, considering the Romanianizing policies carried out by Romanian authorities in the last decades of state socialism and the migration of Romanian Germans to the Federal Republic that was both a cause and an effect thereof, the urge to create an ethnic organization to represent Romanian Germans in Romania can be seen as an attempt to overpower the nationalistic tendencies that permeated a significant part of the Romanian social and political life in the aftermath of the 1989 regime change (Karl, 2006; see also Karl, 2011). Against the backdrop of the experiences of authoritarian governance under the Ceaușescu regime, the participatory objectives of the Democratic Forum of Germans in Romania as the representative body of the ethnic Germans were listed in January 1990 in a memorandum sent to the Council of the NSF.[6]

In the context of the ongoing, and at the time very intensive, dissolution of the Romanian German communities in Romania, the question was whether the foundation of the Forum stood for a "prospect for the future" or a "conjuration of the past". The answer probably lies somewhere in-between (Philippi, 2010, 23). The far-reaching propositions advanced by the Forum in January 1990 aimed to countermand the nationalizing measures that had been taken in the final decades of state socialist rule. Specifically, the Forum pleaded for the right to self-determination in cultural matters, a say in education policy, the introduction of the history of Germans in Romania as a subject of study in German-language schools, measures to address the need for young German specialists in order to be able to provide German-language graduate study, the establishment of cultural institutes dedicated to the German minority in Sibiu and Timișoara, state subsidies aimed at preserving German culture and identity in Romania, the use of German toponyms in German-language media, the reintroduction of a German-language program on state television and, last but not least, the resale of expropriated properties that belonged to members of the German minority to their former owners.[7] In these ways, the founders of the Forum aimed to push back against the consequences of decades of state-sponsored nationalism under state socialism and to establish a framework for the preservation and development of a German social, cultural and economic life in Romania.

The process of Romanian German migration to the Federal Republic was already in full swing by the time state socialism collapsed in Romania. In the immediate aftermath of the 1989 revolution, the dilemma that continued to inform the differing political and ideological positions developing within the German community in Romania was whether to stay or to leave, although the possibility to return was now also on the table (Gabanyi, 1991). Of the three options, the second was the one chosen by the overwhelming majority. In the first two years following the fall of the Iron Curtain, around 150,000 ethnic Germans from Romania migrated to Germany.[8] The mass departure of Germans from Romania for the Federal Republic was also linked to the nationalistic atmosphere in Romania and distrust toward the new Romanian authorities. Considering their nationalist and communist credentials, the latter were perceived as trying to perpetuate the former regime. Nonetheless, it must also be emphasized that in the context of the dire economic situation in the region, the early 1990s saw a mass migration of Romanian citizens (and Eastern Europeans in general) to Western Europe, irrespective of ethnicity.

Against this background, the Forum found itself in a rather tricky situation. The mass migration of Romanian Germans would have realistically implied its own demise. Since any organization exists only through its members and since the members of the Forum were the ethnic Germans in Romania, by supporting migration, the Forum would have in fact supported its own loss of membership and potential voter base. The more Germans left, the more the Forum was doomed to resemble a "conjuration of the past" without any prospects for the future. Therefore, the Forum was, from the very start, an organization aimed mainly at creating incentives for those ethnic Germans wishing to stay in Romania, even if this meant placing itself in an awkward position with respect to the majority of Romanian Germans. Fundamentally, the Romanian German representatives who gathered within the Forum were supposed to support the "remain" alternative and to sustain the development of Transylvanian Saxon and Banat Swabian culture in Romania, under the aegis of the newly acquired freedoms. Nonetheless, the migration-ready Romanian Germans expected the representatives of the German minority in Romania to do everything possible in order to facilitate migration. The Forum was in effect perceived by many of those in Romania whom it purported to represent as an institution that was supposed to facilitate emigration visas, a representation at odds with the fact that the Forum mainly wanted to support the German minority *in* Romania (Lupșiasca, 1993, 73). In this context, Germans wishing to leave Romania did not necessarily perceive the Forum as an organization standing for their interests (Durst, 1993).

In early 1990, Romania's new president, Ion Iliescu, seemed confident that Germans would be able to send their representatives into Parliament without having to rely on the aforementioned positive discrimination proviso. During one of the March 1990 sessions of the Council discussing the parliamentary representation of ethnic minorities, Ion Iliescu said to Florin Cioabă, representative of a Roma organization, "We are discussing article 4 here, but this does not raise a problem for Roma, Hungarians or Germans".[9] Iliescu was suggesting that the size and the political mobilization of the German minority would enable it to get the number of votes necessary to go beyond the standard threshold for political parties. However, when voters eventually went to the polls, the reality on the ground turned out to be rather different. The results of the May 1990 elections show the marked absence of any sustained German political mobilization. The Forum received only 38,768 votes for the Chamber of Deputies and 19,105 for the Senate (Preda, 2013, 70). Most Germans in Romania were more preoccupied with organizing their departure and with trying to envisage a future in the Federal Republic of Germany. However, there were also several additional factors that prevented the Forum from faring well in the 1990 elections, among them the absence of an office in Bucharest and the organization's failure to gain the confidence of Banat Swabians, who perceived the Forum as a "Saxon" institution (Karl, 2006; see also Karl, 2011).

In theory, both Romania and the Federal Republic of Germany attempted to counter the migration frenzy among Germans in Romania. German minister of Foreign Affairs Hans-Dietrich Genscher paid an official visit to Romania in January 1990 (Ciobanu, 2016, 308). In his address to the crowd gathered in Sibiu on 16 January 1990, Genscher acknowledged the responsibility of the German state for the situation of the German minority in Romania, stating that the responsibility of the German federal government was to do everything possible to improve the situation for those wishing to stay in Romania but at the same time also for those who decided to move to Germany. He promised that Germany's doors would always remain open to those wishing to migrate, thus presumably (and ineffectively) hoping to halt a presumed mass migration of Romanian Germans.[10]

The visit of Hans-Dietrich Genscher was followed on 24 January 1990 by the establishment of an *Immediatkommission* (a commission communicating directly with the head of government) in Sibiu, designed to swiftly address issues related to the German minority in Romania on behalf of the German government (Philippi, 2010, 24). For their part, the new Romanian authorities made a show of their willingness to grant particular attention to the issues related to the German minority. The first post-1989 prime minister, Petre Roman, founded the Governmental Commission for the Stabilization of the German Minority in Romania, which was, though rather inefficient, nominally active for two years. Nonetheless, the concept of "stabilization" was regarded with skepticism by elites within the Forum: "The spokespersons of the Forum have always emphasized that it is too late for a 'stabilization' of the situation at hand, that now it should be much more about emboldening the remainder of the minority to a new beginning" (Philippi, 2002, 23–24).

Given the numerous setbacks regarding the general framework of Romanian minority politics at the time, Romanian Germans and their representatives in the Forum did not have particular reasons to be optimistic about a German future in Romania. The murderous interethnic Romanian-Hungarian clashes that took place in Târgu Mureș in March 1990, anti-Roma violence and the descent of rioting miners from the Jiu Valley on Bucharest (the so-called *mineriade*) throughout 1990 and into 1991 contributed to the rather pessimistic atmosphere of the period. Furthermore, the perpetual postponing of the parliamentary debate on a minorities law and the absence of official investigations into the migration that had taken place during the Ceaușescu regime, together with the difficulties encountered by ethnic Germans in accessing reparations, suggested a growing gap between the goals and objectives of Romanian Germans and the position of the Romanian state. In May 1990, in the immediate aftermath of the first postcommunist elections, an official declaration was issued by the Forum, stating among other things, "we have to say that the expectations we were then [December 1989] nurturing were fulfilled only to a very small extent".[11]

Against this background, a Romanian-German rapprochement nonetheless took place at the state level. It materialized in 1992 in the signing of the Romanian-German Treaty for Friendly Cooperation and Partnership in Europe. It was the first post-1989 bilateral treaty signed by the Romanian authorities that included provisions and guarantees regarding the rights of individuals belonging to a minority group, as two of its articles dealt directly with the German minority in Romania. Its Preamble explicitly states that "the German minority in Romania has brought and continues to bring a valuable and unmistakable contribution to the life of Romanian society", on the basis of which it "constitutes a natural connecting bridge between the two peoples". "The wish to keep this historical contribution viable, for the common good" was also part of the underlying rationale of the Treaty, as expressed in its Preamble.[12]

The Treaty continues to provide the general framework governing bilateral Romanian-German relationships and the policies concerning the ethnic Germans who live in Romania. The two articles related to the German minority in Romania are Articles 15 and 16. According to Article 15, the guiding legal standards on minority protection are those set out at the Conference for Security and Cooperation in Europe from July 1990. The Romanian state affirms that it will protect the identity of persons belonging to the German minority in Romania and will support the latter's furtherance through concrete measures. Moreover, the Romanian state also acknowledges and facilitates the furtherance measures undertaken by the German state in favor of the German minority in Romania. During the Cold War, such a proviso would almost certainly have been perceived as an attempt to interfere in Romanian internal affairs. The Treaty thus marked a clear change in the Romanian approach toward its relationship with the Federal Republic of Germany. At the same time, considering that it was one of several similar agreements between Germany and Eastern European countries, the Treaty also reinforced the particular German interest in and feeling of responsibility toward its relationship with Eastern Europe, and it must therefore also be understood as a direct continuation of the West German *Ostpolitik* initiated at the end of the 1960s (Cordell & Wolff, 2007).

The tenor of the Treaty is not only minority-friendly but also clearly situated in a Europeanizing horizon. "Europe" is already present in the official title of the act: "Treaty between Romania and the Federal Republic of Germany on Friendly Cooperation and Partnership in Europe". A plethora of further references to "Europe" are strewn throughout the text. The Preamble places the signing of the Treaty in the broader context of "historical changes in Europe", which encourage the two sides to undertake "decisive steps" in order to definitively overcome the "division of Europe" and to create "a just and durable peace order in Europe". The document asserts the common responsibility of both countries for "building a new, free Europe, united by human rights, democracy and the rule of law", as well as the "creative contribution of both peoples to the common cultural heritage of Europe". The Preamble also explicitly mentions Romania's aspiration toward becoming a member of the Council of Europe and the rapprochement toward other European institutions. The text of the articles themselves further reinforces the European outlook of the Treaty.[13]

The first paragraph of Article 15 states that the legal norms to be applied by the two "contracting parties" are "the standards on the protection of minorities contained in the Document of the Copenhagen Meeting of the Conference on the Human Dimension of the CSCE, from 29 June 1990". The latter document included wide-ranging provisions on national minorities.[14] At the time, these provisions went beyond "the current international provisions with a binding force in this area" (Andreescu, Stan & Weber, 1995, 9; see also Wright, 1998, 4). Drawing on this, scholars actually noted soon after its signing that "one might come to the conclusion that the Romanian state is willing to grant to the German minority in this country such opportunities as it would deny the Hungarian minority" (Andreescu, Stan & Weber, 1995, 9; see also Bell, 1996, 501). The differences in the Romanian treatment of its Hungarian and German minorities were also noted by Romanian German journalist and political activist Horst Weber, who remarked that the Treaty enabled the German federal government to initiate measures and programs in favor of the German minority in Romania, while a German-Romanian governmental commission oversaw the implementation of these programs:

> Such a 'positive discrimination' of a minority is without comparison in Romania. To the other minorities and the respective kin states that asked for

the same right – first and foremost Hungarians –, it was explained that it would be an intrusion in the internal affairs of Romania (a formulation formerly dear to Ceaușescu).

Romanian Germans can only appreciate such a special treatment. But if this is not generalized upon all minorities, one can only conclude that a conjunctural interest (related to the relationships to the European great power that is Germany) lies above empathy with respect to minorities and the sense of justice.

(Weber, 1993, 12–13)

On the basis of the Treaty, a mixed intergovernmental Romanian-German commission was set up. It convenes on a yearly basis to discuss issues affecting the ethnic Germans living in Romania. Striking in view of the Romanian reticence regarding the interference of foreign states in internal affairs, which was still very much permeating Romanian political life in the early 1990s, particularly at the level of the parties in power, is the following stipulation present in the Treaty: "Romania will allow and facilitate the measures of promotion from the Federal Republic of Germany in favour of the German minority in Romania". Thus, one can conclude that Romanian authorities officially acknowledged that Germany's role as a kin state for its German minority legitimizes its open involvement in the social and cultural life of Romanian citizens of German ethnicity.

Adrian Năstase, minister of Foreign Affairs at the time when the Romanian-German Bilateral Treaty was signed, published a multi-volume work about his stint as Romania's external representative, substantially based on his ministerial diary of that period. In the fourth volume of this publication, Năstase details his first visit to Germany, in April 1991, when he met Hans-Dietrich Genscher, Horst Waffenschmidt and Franz Kroppenstedt, the latter two being at the time secretaries of state in the German Ministry of Internal Affairs (Năstase, 2007, 311–325). As one might expect, their discussion touched on the issue of the German minority, with Năstase underlining Romania's that the Germans continue to live in Romania. At the same time, he stated that the only "realistic way" to convince these people to remain in Romania was to raise the standard of living of Romanian Germans; in view of this objective, he looked for (financial) support from the German government (Năstase, 2007, 317–319). Concluding that it would be appropriate to set up an intergovernmental commission to deal with the German minority and, through common projects, to try and improve its standard of living, Năstase delineated the overall context and the possible implications of such an enterprise from the Romanian point of view:

> [. . .] a very important thing for us is to explain that we cannot have two democratization gears, one for the majority and one for the minorities. We have made a special effort to grant a special status to the ethnic Germans, although this could have created difficulties for us as regards other ethnic groups. It is obvious, if we can discuss openly, that in our relationship with Hungary, the question of the Hungarian minority has a political dimension.

> What we agree now with you acquires the value of a precedence case, and that can be dangerous for us. Nonetheless, we have made special efforts, both as regards education in all forms, accepting teachers from Germany, and also the idea of a consulate in Sibiu. These are things what we do in good faith and with the desire to help a particular process.
>
> (Năstase, 2007, 321)

The Romanian-German Treaty was signed at a time when Romanian authorities were highly sensitive to the issue of minority rights, particularly with respect to the Hungarian minority. For example, attempts of the Hungarian state to open a consulate in Cluj-Napoca or to push for the Romanian state-sponsored foundation of a Hungarian-language university in the same town were seen as interferences in Romania's internal affairs and were met with fierce political opposition. The German state opened consulates in Sibiu and Timișoara as early as 1990, whereas the Hungarian consulate in Cluj-Napoca opened only in 1996.

In this context, alongside Năstase's negotiations with German officials, a statement by Traian Chebeleu, at the time state secretary and chief of staff in the Ministry for Foreign Affairs and subsequently advisor to President Iliescu, indicated the different perceptions of minorities within Romanian society and of their potential political effects. When questioned on the status of minorities in Romania and about possible similarities between the Hungarian-Russian Statement on the Rights of National Minorities, issued in November 1992, and the Romanian-German Treaty of April 1992, Chebeleu retorted,

> [In the Treaty,] there are the practical stipulations through which concrete measures on behalf of the German government in view of the preservation of the German minorities [sic] are sustained, together with its endorsement as regards the reorganization of social, cultural and economic life under the new circumstances in Romania. This practical stipulation has an objective basis, as you know, due to some policies and causes that we should not comment upon here. In the meantime, the German minority shrank, so that today it is less than a third of its size during the years preceding the Revolution. The German minority enriches Romanian life from a cultural point of view, but also from other points of view – spiritually, even politically. We have an interest in preserving and consolidating the German minority and the cultivation of its traditions in Romania. This is the meaning of the practical stipulation in the Treaty with Germany. As regards our relationship with Hungary, the issues are not to be treated in the same way, neither in principle, nor in practice.[15]

Political analyst Valentin Stan (1995, 45) was the first to draw attention to Chebeleu's assertion, remarking on the hierarchical difference that it entailed. Năstase's aforementioned comments, issued in front of official representatives of the Federal Republic of Germany, indicate the same pattern of thought, according to which the German minority in Romania occupies a positive special place within

Romania's ethnic landscape, being thus more valuable than the other minority groups and particularly than the Hungarian minority.

The Romanian-German Treaty is the only bilateral treaty signed by Romanian authorities that acknowledges the right of another state to carry out measures in favor of the minority living in Romania. The Romanian-Bulgarian Treaty, signed in January of the same year, included no references to rights of individuals belonging to the respective minorities, despite the fact that there is a Romanian minority in Bulgaria and a Bulgarian minority in Romania (Andreescu, 2004, 149).[16] Furthermore, the Romanian-Hungarian and Romanian-Ukrainian Treaties, two of the domestically and externally most contentious bilateral treaties ratified by the Romanian state after 1989, signed in 1996 and 1997 respectively, would include provisions relating to minorities, yet these provisions would strongly assert the obligations of the state on whose territory the minority group resides to carry out measures for the protection and promotion of its identity.[17] Potential kin-state rights in this respect are not stipulated.

The Preamble of the Romanian-Ukrainian Treaty contains no reference to the Ukrainian minority in Romania or to the Romanian minority in Ukraine and to their contribution to the two societies. The Preamble of the Romanian-Hungarian Treaty includes a general reference to "national minorities as an integral party of the society they live in", asserting that their protection is strongly linked with European cooperation and peace and thus regulated through the international protection of human rights. An emphasis on the positive agency and contribution of a distinctly named minority can be found only in the Romanian-German Treaty, where the "German minority" appears as a both historical and contemporary (collective) subject capable of actively bringing a positive contribution to Romanian society, as long as the necessary conditions are created. There have been several other bilateral treaties signed by Romania in the 1990s, that include references to minorities and minority rights, such as the Romanian-Yugoslav (Serb) Treaty, the Romanian-Croatian Treaty, the Romanian-Polish Treaty or the Romanian-Slovak Treaty. Yet none of these bilateral treaties signed by Romanian authorities and including references to minorities and minority rights has any clause comparable to the one in Article 16, paragraph 1 of the Romanian-German Treaty, which distinctly recognizes that the Federal Republic of Germany is entitled to act as a kin state in relation to the German minority in Romania. The Romanian-Croatian Treaty and the Romanian-Slovak Treaty include a clause according to which the exercising of the right to association by persons belonging to national minorities should not be used against the interests of the other party.[18] A clause emphasizing the obligation of minority members to be "loyal" to the state whose citizens they are is included in the Romanian-Ukrainian, Romanian-Slovak and Romanian-Croatian Treaties. In contrast, the Romanian-German Treaty states that the measures convened by the two states in order to ensure "the preservation of the German minority in Romania" and to support the "reorganization of its social, cultural, and economic life" should not disadvantage other Romanian citizens.

Relationships between nations are largely utilitarian, with "friendship" and related discourses functioning rather as a "tool of public relations and spin"

(Devere, Simon & Verbitsky, 2011, 65). Closely analyzing the language of treaties can enable the deconstruction of such discourses. In the case of the Romanian-German Treaty of 1992, the overt references to Europe and the emphasis on the important and valuable role of the German minority in Romania indicate the (instrumental) equation of Germanness in Romania with Europeanness, in both its symbolic and political dimensions. Other bilateral treaties signed by the Romanian state also have a Europeanizing tenor, but they never distinctly name particular minorities as collective agents bringing a valuable contribution to Romanian society. The Romanian acknowledgment that the Federal Republic of Germany has in effect the right to act as a kin state for the German minority was most assuredly utilitarian, but it also highlights the symbolic and political rapprochement to Europe as a key aspect of this utilitarianism. At the same time, it does not say much about what exactly the two sides meant when referring to Europe: it might very well be that their understandings differed. A more thorough investigation of the contours and shapes of the Europeanness inscribed in Romanian heterorepresentations of Germanness, as well as of their interactions with German representations of the Self and of the Romanian Other, can furnish relevant insights in this respect.

5.3. Economy: expertise, technocracy and management

Particularly in the early 1990s, but also afterwards, discourses about the German minority in Romania tended to emphasize the problems it faced, which were seen in connection with both pre-1989 and post-1989 Romanian state politics. Their underlying argument was that the German-friendly discourses of Romanian authorities were far from being matched by appropriate political and legislative measures. At the same time, when acknowledged by Romanian German political and cultural elites, the existence of a mainly discursive tendency that ascribed a preferential place to Germans within Romania's minority landscape was linked with the fact that positive representations of Germanness in Romania could play an instrumental role in the politically and economically important relationship between Romania and the Federal Republic of Germany. In effect, (political) appreciation for Germans did materialize in particular initiatives, such as the signing of the Romanian-German Treaty for Friendship and Cooperation in Europe or the foundation of the Commission for the Stabilization of Romanian Germans. The latter was theoretically active in the early 1990s, although without any tangible results. The initiative was actually perceived as little more than an attempt to attract much-needed capital from the Federal Republic to Romania (Weber, 1993, 9).

Instrumental self-representations have also been cultivated within Romanian German discourses that style Romanian Germans as usable in order to attract economic capital and various aids to the country on the basis of their links with German-language countries. For example, an open letter criticizing the anti-German discriminations in the application of the Law on Land Resources, which was addressed to Romanian authorities by the Democratic Forum of Germans in April 1992, argued that these discriminations render impossible the "capitalization on behalf of this country of the multiple opportunities that precisely our nationality offers us".[19] Highlighting the existence of particular (economic) opportunities, presented as practically embedded within the very belonging to the German nationality, also ties in well with emphasizing the cultural and civilizational dimension of the Romanian German input to Romanian society as a whole.

Recognizing the role of the Federal Republic of Germany as the external kin state acting on behalf of Romania's German minority, the Forum attempted from the very beginning of its existence to present itself and to act as an intermediary between Romania and the Federal Republic, hence capable of contributing to the attraction of much-needed foreign capital, and helping the economic development of Romania in general and of Romanian Germans in particular. Its first program, published on 19 January 1990 in *Hermannstädter Zeitung*, listed the four areas in which it aimed to be active. These areas were politics, society, economy – discursively framed as "sustaining economic invigoration" (*wirtschaftsbelebend*) – and culture. Four points were subsumed under the category "the economic domain": they concerned the possibility for Romanian Germans to set up private enterprises and cooperatives; "accepting foreign economic help for a reconstruction, or reorganization of agricultural or manufacturing, as well as industrial enterprises in the form of private businesses or cooperatives", also on the basis of the fact that such economic assistance "would contribute to the Romanian economy as a whole"; developing a Romanian German bank (*Geldinstitut*); and restoring the former collective properties of Romanian Germans and their institutions.[20] The issue of property restitution in particular would go on to remain one of the main points of contention and dissatisfaction in relationships between Romanian Germans and the Romanian authorities at both the local and the central levels (Verdery, 2003; Koranyi & Wittlinger, 2011, 109).[21]

An electoral leaflet of the Forum, issued in March 1990, in the context of the campaign for the elections that were to take place in May of the same year, ends with the following call: "*The entire country* needs our vote, so that economic competence for individuals as well as for free groups becomes again profitable in the future (*damit sich wirtschaftliche Tüchtigkeit für einzelne wie für freie Gruppen in Zukunft wieder lohnt*). **We stimulate economic reconstruction**" (Philippi, 1993, 19, both emphases in the original). A statement put forth by the Forum on 9 July 1990 reads:

> Without capital and economic assistance (*Kapital- und Wirtschaftshilfe*) from outside, the agony of the economy will be prolonged, and the state of general anarchy will become unbearable. . . . We believe that the process of democratization in Romania does not have to be pressed ahead only from a political point of view, but also has to be bolstered economically; accordingly, measures of economic assistance from abroad can be used in order to help the country on its way to Europe.
> (Demokratisches Forum der Deutschen in Rumänien, [1990] 1993, 48–49)

Such assertions illustrate the construction of a discursive link between economic development brought by German entrepreneurship and German competence on the one hand and symbolic and political integration into Europe on the other. Slogans used by the Forum in the electoral campaigns in the early 1990s underline this link: "We help open windows towards Europe" or "We can transform any desert into a blossoming garden. We just have to want it" (Baier, 2010, 29).[22] The representation of the Romanian Germans as a "bridge" – between Romania and Germany, as described in the text of the Romanian-German Treaty of 1992, or between Romania and Europe, as one can encounter in other discursive contexts – is inscribed within the same representational apparatus. In the early 1990s, Paul-Jürgen Porr (1993, 90), currently president of the Forum, emphasized that hoisting the European flag in the neat aula of the Forum was not a random occurrence but rather a proof of the "bridge" function of the institution (and hence of the Romanian Germans on behalf of whom it purports to speak). The underlying rationale of such representations is that Germans in Romania are by default closer to Europe than Romanians are: yet if the necessary conditions are created for the former to be able to put their German entrepreneurship and know-how to work, they can actually contribute to bringing that Europe closer to Romania and to Romanians.

The Romanian-German Treaty includes a clause concerning the support granted to the German minority in Romania in the reshaping of its economic life. The Forum – despite theoretically not being a political party – has always had a well-delineated economic policy, which holds that particular economic measures are apt to support the production and reproduction of a German identity in Romania (Ciobanu, 2016, 340). Its electoral program from 1992 emphasized that through

> its local economic committees as well as through the Foundation for International Cooperation in Banat and through the Saxonia Foundation in Transylvania, the Forum offers advice and supports private start-ups belonging to Germans and negotiates for them foreign material aid under favorable terms.
> (Weber, 1993, 65)

In the same vein, it underlined how it helps German farmers to acquire land and set up agricultural associations, provides these with seeds and agricultural equipment, and endeavors to build up a small processing industry with foreign support (Weber, 1993, 65). According to its Statute, adopted in 2001, one of the five working commissions of the Forum is the Economic Commission.[23]

Five economic foundations (*Wirtschaftsstiftungen*) were set up in the 1990s: Saxonia, Banatia and Sathmar in 1991; Transcarpatica in 1995; and Bukowina in 1997 – all of them with financial support coming from the German state. A recent temporary exhibition on the German minority in Romania, organized by the Forum and the German Embassy in Romania, explicitly addressed these programs of business development (*Wirtschaftsförderung*), arguing that they play a particularly important role in contemporary German identity and Romanian-German entanglements: "Exemplary for the good cooperation between the

German minority and the Federal Republic of Germany is the work of the five economic foundations whose structure corresponds to that of the regional fora of the DFDR" (Demokratisches Forum der Deutschen in Rumänien, 2014, 74). Those who profited from the economic development programs promoted by these foundations were mainly "persons starting up new businesses and small entrepreneurs who wanted to consolidate their company or to preserve and boost their competitiveness" (Demokratisches Forum der Deutschen in Rumänien, 2014, 75). Against this background, the much-touted bridge function acquires a straightforward economic dimension, the German minority in Romania becoming a "mediator in the economic relationships between Germany and Romania". This process of mediation is then seen to contribute to the consolidation of the economic and social structures of the German minority in Romania, thus becoming an important element in the production and reproduction of a German identity in Romania (Demokratisches Forum der Deutschen in Rumänien, 2014, 78). At the same time, the presentation of the activities of the foundations stresses that they sponsor applications from all Romanian citizens. This then leads to the "strengthening of the prestige of members of the German minority: regional and local forum branches increasingly enjoy the support of the beneficiaries from the ranks of the majority population" (Demokratisches Forum der Deutschen in Rumänien, 2014, 78).

The catalog of the exhibition ends with quotes by Norbert Kartmann, the president of the Parliament of Hesse, and by Peter Simon, former chairman of the Romanian branch of ABB, a multinational corporation specialized in automation technology. Both of them straightforwardly spell out the existence of a highly important economic dimension embedded within Romanian German identity. According to the former, the Romanian-German relationship has "an element that has to be seen in connection with economy: the more than 850 years old presence of Germans in this territory and hence also the cultural-spiritual dimension of a long phase of coexistence" (Demokratisches Forum der Deutschen in Rumänien, 2014, 154). For the latter,

> the German minority was, is and remains an important component, mainly of the economic development of Romania. The German minority constitutes the bridge to its most important trading partner – Germany, but also to the other German-speaking countries. With hard work, rigorousness, trust and discipline, the members of the German minority have built and continue to build successful long-term business relationships, especially at the level of small and medium-size businesses. This is reassuring for the future.
> (Demokratisches Forum der Deutschen in Rumänien, 2014, 154)

The representation of a connection between German identity in Romania, German-Romanian economic relations and the promise of a "German" and "European" future are also particularly relevant for understanding the reasons behind the breakthrough watershed moment for the German minority in Romania and for the Forum as its representative body, which took place in the summer of 2000. The unexpected winner of the mayoral elections in Sibiu, one of the traditional cultural and political centers of Transylvanian Saxons, was local physics teacher and school inspector Klaus Iohannis, a rather unknown candidate proposed by the Forum. His success was accompanied by the success of the Forum in the elections for the Sibiu Local Council. To get a sense regarding just how surprising the electoral results in Sibiu were, even for the representatives of the Forum themselves, one only needs to consider the fact that although the number of votes it received entitled the Forum to appoint seven local councilors, it lost two of the seats because it had not placed enough people on the ballot paper (Klein, 2010, 12). Iohannis's success can also partially be explained through the high level of disillusion present in Sibiu at the time, as a consequence of the extremely poor performance of the previous administrations.[24] Iohannis would subsequently be reelected as mayor of Sibiu in 2004, 2008 and 2012, each time with an overwhelming majority of the votes, with the Forum also winning the elections for the Local Council. Furthermore, in 2004 and 2008, his success was accompanied by the success of the Forum at the level of the entire Sibiu County, meaning that between 2004 and 2012, the president of the Sibiu County Council was Martin Bottesch. In the first decade of the 2000s, the candidates of the Forum were successful in other localities in Sibiu County, such as Mediaș (Mediasch in German, Medgyes in Hungarian), Cisnădie (Heltau in German, Disznód in Hungarian) and Avrig (Freck in German, Felek in Hungarian), a trend that has continued into the 2010s.

The symbolic and political capital of Iohannis in particular and of the Forum in general has very much been built on the existence of a so-called Saxon myth and on the positive image of Germans within Romanian society (Dragoman, 2005; Dragoman & Zamfira, 2008; Stroe, 2011a; Dragoman, 2013). In this context, the name of Iohannis came to be associated relatively quickly with a potential national political career, either as a candidate for the presidency of Romania or as a potential nominee for the position of prime minister.[25] Nonetheless, his first concrete attempt to enter national politics did not take place until 2009, when he was supported by an expedient parliamentary coalition to become the country's prime minister. The bid was unsuccessful, however, because then president Traian Băsescu obstinately refused to appoint him to the job. Subsequently, in 2013, Iohannis joined the National Liberal Party, and one year later he ran for the presidency of Romania. This time, the "Iohannis Project" proved successful: he defeated his opponent, Victor Ponta, who ran on behalf of the Social Democratic Party, and became the country's president.

In an interview granted to the Romanian weekly *Formula As*, shortly after his success at the Sibiu local elections in 2000, Iohannis was asked a question about his positive reception in Germany by German politicians, despite his allegedly not having "political support" and not receiving "directions from the centre". Iohannis answered: "It seems there are new dawns in Romanian political life. Technocrats, young and active people win terrain, to the detriment of professional politicians". Iohannis has cultivated from the very beginning of his career in local administration the image of an expert – his expertise being tightly linked with his

"A contribution to Romanian society" 89

ethnicity – and of someone not touched by the flaws of politics and "politicking". In the same interview, he also emphasized the links between Saxonness, (lost and retrieved) Europeanness and economic investments:

> We want to make out of Sibiu what it used to be. We want it to be a European city, an outpost of Romania's integration in the European Union. . . . We will be harsh, we will fine those who do not keep it clean, we will stimulate the return of Saxons so that they invest in the city.[26]

In a book published shortly before the presidential elections that he would eventually win, Iohannis (2014) reflects on his political career and his involvement in the German Forum. The tension between politics and apolitical technocracy underlies his account. He titles the relevant subchapter "Political apprenticeship", yet he feels the need to assert "from the very start that the Democratic Forum of Germans in Romania is not a political party: this is something that I suppose I will still have to emphasize a long time from now" (Iohannis, 2014, 33). He sees no mismatch between putatively lacking a political doctrine and getting involved in the local administration: "Local politics had less to do with the essence of politics and more with administration" (Iohannis, 2014, 34). This perspective is largely compatible with technocratic visions of apolitical elites and experts who should hold the reins of power in order to ensure economic development and economic stability. Yet throughout the book, Iohannis also asserts that he eventually joined the National Liberal Party because he is a right-wing politician. The mandates of Iohannis in Sibiu were marked by the economic development of the town based on foreign investments and also by the development of a touristic and cultural brand of Sibiu. The constantly increasing salience of Sibiu was then also connected to Sibiu being named European Capital of Culture in 2007 (Dragoman, 2005, 2013; Iancu, 2007; Stroe, 2007; Vasiliu & Dragoman, 2008; Stroe, 2011b; Iohannis, 2014, 44–133).

Dwelling on the reasons leading to Iohannis's election as Romania's president in 2014, political analyst Florin Poenaru (2017, 91) stated:

> The vote which made Klaus Iohannis president was not a political, but a cultural one. . . . It was an anti-political vote. . . . Klaus Iohannis was not voted in because of a particular program or because of a political idea, but because of the promise that he will not do politics, but administration, that he will be a 'good manager', as he was in Sibiu. . . . The perfect image of administrative technocracy.

In the same context, Poenaru (2017, 95–97) also remarked that Iohannis's election was very much connected to the self-Orientalizing and self-colonializing representations that are common in Romanian discourses. For Poenaru, Iohannis is the symbol of the Romanian middle class, which discursively rejects politics while actually doing politics and standing for particular (class) interests. This image, together with the class dimension of Romania's post-1989 European project, is related not only to the person of Iohannis but also on a more general level to both the self- and hetero-representations of the German minority in Romania. The emphasis on expertise, specialism and management, coming together with a rejection of politics in the name of technocratic know-how, has played an important role in the Romanian German identity discourses disseminated by the Democratic Forum of Germans. At the same time, this emphasis provides the Forum with the possibility to construct a present and envisage a future for itself as an organization and hence for the German minority in general. In an interview from 2015, the current president of the organization, Paul-Jürgen Porr (2015a, 39), argued that the Forum should focus more on attracting and involving young people, "who come from the economy and also understand a lot about management".

In his comments on the election of Iohannis as Romania's president, the same Porr (2015b, 15) contended that the election of the former "offers us a real chance to introduce and also to respect European norms in our national politics, the chance to begin top-down the clearance of the Dâmbovița mentality". The reference to Dâmbovița functions as an Orientalist and Balkanist discursive trope in the Romanian context. Dâmbovița is the river flowing through Bucharest and stands for everything Iohannis and Romanian German elites present themselves as being the opposite of: corruption, mismanagement of funds, politicking and politics. Furthermore, despite the claims of not making politics, particularly following the election of Iohannis as the president of Romania in 2014 and the sweeping electoral success of the Social Democrats – who are now Iohannis' staunch opponents – in the parliamentary elections of 2016, the Forum has been openly positioning itself against the latter.

In 2002, the Forum started publishing an almanac, *Deutsches Jahrbuch für Rumänien*. The yearly publication provides a useful source for whoever wants to analyze Romanian German identification discourses over the past two decades. It offers a mixture of articles and interviews directly addressing various issues related to the German minority in Romania. Readers can find contributions covering the politics of the Forum at the local and central level, articles about cultural heritage (most often Romanian German), touristic recommendations, pieces on Romanian German historical personalities, short literary texts by Romanian German authors and so on. At the same time, the almanac has also constantly displayed a particular interest in economic topics and the economic opportunities that Germanness can bring with it. Articles about economic projects, as well as interviews with investors, have been published in almost every issue. In the same vein, the aforementioned economic foundations associated with the Forum, founded in the early 1990s, whose role has been to promote (mainly German or German-speaking) entrepreneurship, are frequent objects of interest for the editors and authors of the almanac.

Such accounts and interviews, sometimes published under the rubric "in the service of the community" (*Im Dienst der Gemeinschaft*), reinforce the image of Romanian Germans as being on the frontline of Romania's transition toward the (European) development brought by capitalism and the market economy, understood as key components of the process of European integration. Nonetheless, the careful reader can also spot some tensions between (1) the support of foreign investments in Romania and of the economic model they propose, based on low costs of production and low salaries, and (2) the competition with countries where the cost of production and salaries are even cheaper, such as Ukraine or China (Müller, 2005, 153–155). Yet the general tenor of the articles dealing with economic investments is largely investor-friendly. In the first issue of the almanac, readers come across an article authored by the managing director of the Banatia Foundation on the occasion of the tenth anniversary of the existence of the foundation. Its subtitle emphasizes that the foundation sponsored more than 500 economic projects in this ten-year period. Retrospectively addressing the beginnings of the Banatia Foundation, Horst Martin argues that its emergence was related to the pressing need in the immediate aftermath of the fall of state socialism to sponsor private initiatives in the economy, a need acknowledged by the Democratic Forum of Germans in Banat and by different local branches of the Forum (Martin, 2002, 29).

Addressing the economic outcome of the activities of the Banatia Foundation, Martin emphasizes that "the generated profit stays in the country and under no circumstances does it flow abroad, as it happens in the case of foreign investors, and hence is fundamentally more efficient". Furthermore, he explicitly argues that support for setting up businesses in the homeland (*Heimat*) provides beneficiaries with an alternative to migration (Martin, 2002, 30). In this vein, speaking on behalf of the Forum, Martin states that "The Forum in Banat is convinced that a steady economic development can also create the material basis for the members of our community in order for them to see a future for the young generation in their ancestral homeland" (Martin, 2002, 32). The idea that providing entrepreneurial opportunities has contributed and can contribute to stemming the tide of German migration from Romania has also been expressed elsewhere, and it is constantly brought forth in accounts about the activities of the economic foundations (Martin, 2002; Minkiewicz, 2004, 130; Martin, 2009). The main criticism in Martin's article in *Deutsches Jahrbuch* was directed against the Romanian state and against the absence of investor-friendly policies. In this context, an emergency ordinance issued by the Romanian government for the cancellation of the debts of the foundation was seen as fully legitimate (Martin, 2002, 33). Furthermore, for Martin,

> The constantly growing ancillary wage costs (*Lohn-Nebenkosten*) additionally strain the entrepreneurs in their early stages. Whereas the big state enterprises and state banks sustain high losses, barely pay their debts but continue to live it up, the small have to work hard so that something gets paid into the state budget, out of which a generous welfare policy has been practiced for many years.
>
> (Martin, 2002, 33)

Thus, the emphasis on German or German-led economic expertise and specialism comes together with a neoliberal rejection of the involvement of the state in economic matters – except when it comes to erasing specific private debts – and with an attack on the welfare state, on state involvement in the economy and on workers' rights, all seen by Martin and by other entrepreneurs as hindering economic development. Last but undoubtedly not least, the director of the foundation, presented as the "project-executing body" (*Projektträger*) of the Forum, clearly asserts its role in the economic development of Romania:

> Today we can very well say it: almost nobody in Romania has so much experience in the field of promoting small and medium enterprises, in the technical, economic and juridical field, and we are surely capable of taking on similar applications in order to attract both national and foreign funding; we possess the necessary infrastructure.
>
> (Martin, 2002, 34)

The next issue of the almanac includes a similar article about the Saxonia Foundation in Braşov. The author of the article, the manager of the foundation, emphasized that the role of the Saxonia Foundation was "to facilitate the development by private entrepreneurs of German origin of their own start-ups". Thus, they could also "develop their own value (*Stellenwert*)" (Ehrmann, 2003). In the 2004 issue, an article about the economic foundation in Satu Mare stressed that

> the foundation supports enterprises residing in the localities where the German minority is also represented. The entrepreneurs themselves do not need to belong to the German minority. Nonetheless, statistics of the foundation shows that over 60% of the applicants are of German origin.
>
> (Müller, 2004, 39)

In the 2005 issue, the manager of the Transcarpatica Foundation published his own account of the organization's activities. In his review of the early years of the Foundation in the 1990s, he stated that it "facilitated a certain economic improvement of some able and entrepreneurial German families and people from their surroundings" (Minkiewicz, 2005, 48). This is one of the arguments often put forth by the Forum and by German state authorities: the economic support of the German minority is meant to have an impact beyond the German minority per se, helping the entire social environment. Summing up the impact of the Foundation and its prospects for the future, Leopold Minkiewicz (2005, 49) concluded that

> In the case of the Germans in the former Kingdom (*Altreich*) we are dealing with a relatively stable population, and with a growing dissemination of German language (especially in the business sphere). The Transcarpatica Foundation would like to continue to make its contribution to the development of this favourable climate.

Articles in *Deutsches Jahrbuch* also address German and Austrian investments in Romania. For example, a contribution published in the first issue of the almanac dealt with the Dräxlmaier factory in Satu Mare, supplier of cables for companies such as Audi, BMW, Bosch, Daimler-Chrysler, Rover and Volkswagen: "The factory opened at the end of 1999. . . . . it radiates an atmosphere only rarely to be found in Romania: that of the dedicated, concentrated, focused and simply orderly act of creation" (Kremm, 2002, 129). The author of the article, Werner Kremm, appears to have completely adopted the perspective of the managing director of Dräxlmaier Romania, Ulrich Lübeck, inasmuch he severely criticizes the position of the representative of the labor union. Although acknowledging – almost reluctantly – the fact that low salary costs are one of the reasons that drove Dräxlmaier to open its factory in Romania, Kremm argues that the representative of the labor union (who is never named and who is not given a voice in the article) attempted to "interfere with the business philosophy and with the business management", in an "incompetent" manner. This supposed interference gave Lübeck some cause for concern. Kremm reflects on the situation in a straightforwardly Orientalist manner, rhetorically asking in a parenthesis whether this development is not perhaps something typically Romanian. The negative result of interference by the representative of the labor union is the disruption of the working environment. It is not at all clear from the text what the reason for strife between the labor union and the leadership of Dräxlmaier was, yet for Kremm it is obvious that the latter is in the right: "At the clarifying round table discussion, to which the County Presidency and the County Council invited the leadership of the company and the labor union, the representative of the latter left the room when he ran out of arguments". Thus, Kremm (2002, 130) concludes that

> Union leaders who are members of the enterprise council, who think positively in the terms of the enterprise (and who also think of how important such a big investor is for the entire area and how many other people, next to the 2700 employees, live off the factory and due to the factory) and who at the same time recognize the interests of the employees, do not yet seem to exist in Satu Mare.

In a similar vein, articles across the various issues of the almanac seem to function as little more than veiled propaganda on behalf of German investments in Romania, extolling the successes of bigger and smaller investors and enterprises with a German connection (i.e. Germans from the Federal Republic or Romanian German returnees or Romanian Germans who did not leave Romania). The German employers who came to Romania in the early 1990s refer to the country in that period as resembling the American "Wild West" and are presented as "pioneers", who had "courage and believed in the economic future of the country" (Wermke, 2013).

Another rejection of the possibility that workers' demands might actually be legitimate can be found in an article published in 2006 about Pompilia Szellner, the Romanian German manager of Delignit (a plywood enterprise), who was also a member of the Forum and potential candidate in the local elections in Turnu Severin. The author of the text emphasizes in awe "how complex a manager has to think in the market economy". One concrete aspect of this complexity is the difficult relationship with employees, who have to understand that they are in effect expendable. In Szellner's own words, as quoted in the article: "Once, as the workers raised untenable demands and went on strike, I brought in workers from outside for two days and simply left the personnel to strike" (Thiel, 2006). An article titled "Thinking outside the box, initiative, courage: Swabian achieved early EU-standards" presents the call center company Netex, opened in Western Romania by an entrepreneur who identifies herself as Swabian, Andreea Kremm. At Netex, employees offer customer service in twenty-three languages. One of her greatest assets in her business negotiations with "the German-speaking abroad" is that of speaking correct German. What was the entrepreneur's worst nightmare? "Being controlled by the financial authorities". The article ends with a semi-ironic, semi-serious assertion: "I have a bad accountant, who allows the state to get too much money" (Thiel, 2008).

The laudatory articles about and interviews with German investors and businesspeople reinforce the representation of Germans – be they Romanian Germans or Germans from Germany who recognized the business opportunities in Romania – as hard-working Europeans/Westerners who embody the virtues of capitalism, knowing how capitalism works and attempting to bring it to Romania, no matter the obstacles. Here they can nonetheless also encounter some difficulties – that is, workers going on strike or labor union representatives who enter into conflict with the managers. Generally, legitimacy is given almost solely to the latter. At least, this is overwhelmingly the case in the contributions published in *Deutsches Jahrbuch*, which tend to provide only the unnuanced perspective of managers, investors and entrepreneurs: they are about the (German) winners and producers of market economy. The class dimension of the easternist discourses underlying particular representations of Germanness in the Romanian context is thus highly relevant here.

The economic dimension of post-1989 Romanian German identifications is tightly connected with German economic interests in Romania. In this context, a network of seven German-language business clubs in Romania, founded in the late 1990s and in the 2000s with the support of the German state, also plays an important role in Romanian German identity politics. The language of communication in these clubs is German. Nationality and ethnicity are not membership conditions, yet knowledge of German is. In the 2009 issue of the almanac, the already quoted Werner Kremm explicitly welcomed the support of the German-language Business Club in Timișoara for the then mayoral candidate, Gheorghe Ciuhandu, arguing for the more sustained political involvement of the German economic actors in the region:

Since [most members of the club] live during the entire working week in Romania, since they have to live out their successes and frictions in the social and political environment of the country, it is only just and equitable that they also express their political opinion in the given framework, especially their opinion as citizens consciously living and working in Romania. In the future perhaps they will do this with even greater resolve.

(Kremm, 2009, 52)

More recently, after the result of the 2016 elections, Paul-Jürgen Porr (2017, 21) explained the decision to support Wiegand Fleischer, one of the young members of the Forum, for the position of vice-president of the Sibiu County Council in the following terms:

> Fleischer studied economics, he studied towards his PhD in this field, he teaches at the Lucian Blaga University and he is manager of the German Business Club in Transylvania, he is also really at home in this portfolio. He is surely the best choice for the German Forum and also for the County of Sibiu.

Porr's argument acknowledges the entanglements between German investments in Romania and the politics of the German Forum. German investments in Romania are seen as being able to contribute to the preservation and development of something resembling a German-language public sphere. In the aforementioned article about the business club in Timișoara, Kremm (2009, 51) suggests that economy and civil society are practically equivalent. Thus, German economic investments can actually have a direct contribution to the preservation and further development of a German identity in Romania, language being perhaps the most important marker of this identity.

A 2003 interview with Klaus-Peter Marte, at the time the newly appointed consul of the Federal Republic of Germany in Timișoara, captures very well the economic dimension of Romanian-German relationships. The interview was published in another almanac: the Timișoara branch of the German Forum. When asked "what are the most important economic interests of Germans in Romania?" the consul replied:

> Romania has a big importance for Germany for three reasons:
> We have here particular interests because of our German minority, this is the first point; then, of course, the interest to bring Romania close to Europe – and we are in the European Union one of the leading member states – and then, of course, the economic interests, to manufacture, to make use of contract manufactures (*Lohnfertigungen*) somewhere where the salaries are lower and cheaper, in order to also preserve the headquarters in Germany.
> This is precisely a mixed form, to outsource a part and to save the rest, that otherwise would probably not function anymore. You see, German investments are by far the largest here and I think they will remain so in the future.
> (Marte, 2003, 29)

The interview then continues with Marte commenting on the foundation of the German-language Business Club in Timișoara and mentioning how economic actors such as Siemens were contributing to the refurbishing of lecture theaters in the University of Timișoara. When he was asked about the advantages of the region for German investors, Marte referred to the presence of a "qualified workforce" and German-language schooling that trains German native speakers

(*Muttersprachler*) (Marte, 2003, 29). Incidentally, Marte was in effect the one who set up the German-language Business Club in Timișoara during his tenure in Romania (Kremm, 2009, 53).

The interconnections between the business world and Romanian German identity find a particular expression in discourses about upholding the network of German-language schools in Romania. In 2017/2018, the number of children enrolled in kindergartens, primary schools and secondary schools where teaching takes place in German was 23,950, whereas the number of self-declared Germans at the census in 2012 was 36,042.[27] In 2004, Martin Bottesch (2004, 105) estimated that about 90% of the pupils enrolled in German-language schools do not come from families identifying as German. Recently, in a welcoming speech on the occasion of the twenty-fifth anniversary of the signing of the German-Romanian Treaty, ambassador Cord Meier-Klodt quoted the president of the Forum, Paul-Jürgen Porr: "We have no problem with the numbers of pupils in German schools, we have a problem with the number of teachers!" (*Wir haben kein Schülerproblem Deutsch, wir haben ein Lehrerproblem Deutsch*).[28]

The philo-Germanism without Germans in Romania has an impact far beyond the discursive level. Even during communism, German-language schools were particularly popular among the Romanian population, since speaking German and being able to assume a German identity could entail, to a certain extent, the possibility to migrate out of the country. However, on the whole, the state-funded German-language educational network has significant problems. Providing high-quality German-language education is difficult, in particular due to the lack of teachers who speak German as their mother tongue and who are able to either teach German or teach in German (Bottesch, 2015, 26–27). Acknowledging that the future of German-language schools in Romania is not directly connected with the future of the minority as such, the Forum is also aware that the interest in German-language education is linked with the fact that speaking German is "an important advantage when looking for a workplace offered by German-language investors in their operations in Romania" (Demokratisches Forum der Deutschen in Rumänien, 2014, 100; Bottesch, 2004). German-language education is seen as being able to provide a "reservoir for the labor market", particularly for the needs of "German-language entrepreneurs", as the representative of the Forum in the Romanian Parliament, Ovidiu Ganț (2013), rather explicitly put it.

Thus, an educational policy meant in principle to contribute to the preservation of the identity of the German minority in Romania is increasingly being understood as a modality through which children coming from non-German families can learn German and thus can gain access to jobs provided by German investors in Romania (Ganț, 2013). At the same time, this situation enables entrepreneurs and investors coming from Germanophone countries to Romania to find a Germanophone workforce in the country. Some of the difficulties that arise from this state of affairs involve the educational policy being in principle tailored to the needs of the minority and thus presupposing that German is the mother tongue of the pupils (Bottesch, 2004, 108). For the Forum, "the maintenance (*Erhalt*) and the furtherance (*Förderung*) of the educational system in German language, as well as that of the existing cultural institutions of Germans in Romania" are "paramount concerns (*vorrangige Anliegen*)", considering its self-imposed task of assuring "the conditions for the preservation (*Fortbestehen*) and further development of the identity of the German minority" (Demokratisches Forum der Deutschen in Rumänien, 2014, 48).

Both directly and indirectly, German-language education in Romania can thus contribute to the reproduction of a German identity in Romania, and plays a role in the ongoing relevance of the Forum as a minority organization. According to its Statute, membership in the Forum requires knowing the German language. Moreover, the Forum also has a special category of "supporter" members, in principle open to citizens of countries other than Romania and to Romanian citizens of other ethnicities.[29] Thus, the German-language educational network in Romania can in effect bring new full members or new "supporter" members to the Forum. At the same time, another element that the representatives of the Forum have often envisaged as potentially strengthening the German minority and German identity in Romania is that of a German remigration and migration to Romania, particularly in the context of the economic opportunities brought forth by the process of European integration (Philippi, [2001] 2006, 279, 284; Bottesch, 2004, 110, 2015, 35). The preservation of a German-language educational network can only be an advantage in this respect.

Yet another aspect of the educational system that is connected to German economic interests is that of the work-based vocational education (*duale Berufsausbildung*). As noted in the catalog of the 2014 exhibition on the German minority, German business clubs in Romania and particularly the German Business Club in Braşov have played a crucial role in the (re)establishment of the work-based vocational education in Romania:

> The commitment of the clubs with respect to the work-based vocational education according to a German model has to be emphasized. The German Business Club Kronstadt, flanked by some of its member-enterprises, took the lead in the establishment of a new state vocational school with a practice-oriented profile. The German vocational school Kronstadt functions as a vocational school with a dual training system – a novelty in the Romanian educational system, that did away with its vocational schools after the political change (*Umbruch*) and picked up again the topic of vocational education only in 2012. . . . The sustainable efforts of German economy regarding dual vocational education in Romania benefit both trainees and enterprises, who will be able to cover a part of their staff requirement with qualified workforce.
> (Demokratisches Forum der Deutschen in Rumänien, 2014, 81–82)

The language of instruction is Romanian, yet the Forum is one of the main supporters of the vocational education system on the political level, in direct connection with its supporters from the economic field – that is, German business clubs and the German-Romanian Chamber of Industry and Commerce (Ganţ, 2013).

The first vocational educational school functioning on the basis of this system opened in Brașov and is officially called Școala Profesională Germană Kronstadt (The Vocational School Kronstadt).[30] The system, presented and advertised as the "German" system – the reference functioning as an acknowledgment of quality – plays a key role in contemporary Romanian-German economic relationships. By openly supporting it, despite the fact that it is only indirectly connected (if at all) with the preservation of German identity in Romania, the Forum effectively puts into practice its role of mediator in economic affairs between Germany and Romania. German diplomats in Romania have also constantly emphasized the role of enterprises from the German-speaking space in the introduction of work-linked vocational education in Romania and lobbied consistently for its expansion. On the occasion of the twenty-fifth anniversary of the signing of the Romanian-German Treaty for Friendly Cooperation and Partnership in Europe, German ambassador to Bucharest, Cord Meier-Klodt, referred to the way Romanian parents aspire to have their children enroll in German-language educational programs, calling for the development of the German-language education network to be made a priority by "us" (most likely referring to the German Embassy and to the Forum, who acted as the organizer of the event in Timișoara), together with "Romanian partners and supporters from the economy". Meier-Klodt also argued that this should happen because of the growing demand coming "from the side of the 'booming' economy, particularly German". Moreover, he went on to emphasize at great length the relevance of vocational education, openly pleading for its expansion, in order to provide the qualified workforce needed by investors.[31] Meier-Klodt's argument brings the vocational education system to the fore in relation to the existence of a German economic model that Romania can supposedly emulate in order for its economy to continue to grow.

Journalist Ruxandra Hurezean presents in one of her recent books on Romanian Germans the story of Hans Prömm, a Romanian German who left Romania with his family when he was seventeen years old, only to come back later as an entrepreneur to Romania. One of the founders of the German Business Club in Brașov, Prömm is also depicted as one of those whose efforts – together with the efforts of his associate, Werner Braun – led to the introduction of the vocational educational system. Despite opposition from the Romanian government, the entrepreneur Prömm, who feels at home in both Romania and Germany, manages "to begin to change reality, step by step" (Hurezean, 2017, 208). German efforts are represented as enabling the success of real entrepreneurship in Romania.

The emphasis on entrepreneurship, expertise and economic development as a key element of German and Romanian German identity legitimizes the ongoing relevance of a German presence in Romania and allows discourses about Romanian Germans to be oriented not only toward the past but also toward the future. By highlighting the links between the needs of German entrepreneurs and investors and the direction that the educational system in Romania ought to take, as well as by making concrete efforts in this respect, Germans appear as agents of change, directly enabling the economic growth of Romania. German economic investments in Romania have thus become a crucial self-legitimizing element of contemporary German identification in the Romanian context. They can provide a way forward for the future, something that is much needed from an internal point of view, given the constant shrinking of the Romanian German population. For the representatives of the Forum, the prospects for the future existence of a German minority in Romania are also connected with outside migration:

> It seems as though the German minority in Romania cannot have a long-lasting existence without settlement from outside. If a migration of German speakers takes place to a sufficient extent, then most of the questions regarding the future identity of this minority remain *a fortiori* open.
>
> (Bottesch, 2015, 35)

In this context, granting the economic dimension an important role in the production and reproduction of Romanian German identity and attempting to create the necessary conditions for a German-driven economic life in Romania, can provide important impulses for such a migration and for the potential imagination of a German identity in Romania in the future.

Notes

1 "Comunicatul către țară al Frontului Salvării Naționale," in *Monitorul Oficial al României. Comunicate, decrete-lege, decrete, hotărâri ale Guvernului și alte acte*, 22 December 1989.
2 "Declarația Frontului Salvării Naționale cu privire la drepturile minorităților din România," *Adevărul*, 6 January 1990.
3 For an interpretation of the Declaration of 1 December arguing that it did not in effect refer to collective rights as autonomy and hence that it was actually implemented in spirit, see Pop 2018, 45–47.
4 Cristian Cercel, "1 decembrie, promisiunea neîndeplinită," *Observator Cultural* 452, 4 December 2008.
5 Bogdan Aurescu, "Drepturi individuale versus drepturi colective. Drepturi exercitate individual și drepturi exercitate împreună cu alții," *Observator Cultural* 434, 31 July 2008.
6 "Wir wollen selbst bestimmen können. Demokratisches Forum der Deutschen in Rumänien zur Verbesserung unserer Lage," *Hermannstädter Zeitung*, 5 January 1990.
7 "Wir wollen selbst bestimmen."
8 For official German numbers on German migration from Eastern Europe to Germany, from the 1950s to 2000, divided by country, see Levy, 2002, 33–34, tables 1.3. and 1.4.
9 "Sesiunea Consiliului Provizoriu de Uniune Națională din zilele de 9, 10, 13 și 14 martie 1990," in *Monitorul Oficial al României. Ședințele Consiliului Provizoriu de Uniune Națională*, 16 March 1990.
10 "Ansprache des Aussenministers," *Hermannstädter Zeitung*, 19 January 1990.
11 "Erklärung des Demokratischen Forums der Deutschen in Rumänien 9. Juli 1990," *Zugänge* 14 (1993), 46.
12 "Lege nr. 95 din 16 septembrie 1992 pentru ratificarea Tratatului dintre România și Republica Federală Germania privind cooperarea prietenească și parteneriatul în Europa, încheiat la București la 21 aprilie 1992. Textul actului publicat în M. Of. Nr. 237/24 September 1992," https://lege5.ro/Gratuit/gy2tenrs/tratatul-intre-romania-si-republica-federala-germania-privind-cooperarea-prieteneasca-si-parteneriatul-in-europa-din-21041992 (accessed 27 August 2017).

13 The signing of the German-Romanian Treaty came after the signing of the Polish-German Treaty, which also included provisions for the promotion of the minority rights of the German minority in Poland (but also of the Germans of Polish origin, who are nonetheless not designated as "Polish minority"), although it was clearly of a more comprehensive nature than the Romanian-German case. Nonetheless, some of the articles in the Romanian-German Treaty copied the provisos in the Polish-German Treaty. See Jacobsen & Tomala, 1992, 552–564.

14 "Document of the Copenhagen Meeting of the Conference on the Human Dimension of the CSCE," www.osce.org/odihr/elections/14304?download=true (accessed 18 May 2018).

15 Traian Chebeleu, "Statutul minorităţilor nu poate fi obiect de negociere," interview by Rodica Chelaru, *Meridian*, 7 December 1992. For the Hungarian-Russian Statement, see "Declaration on the principles guiding the co-operation between the Republic of Hungary and the Russian Federation regarding the guarantee of the rights of national minorities (November 11, 1992)," www.forost.ungarisches-institut.de/pdf/19921111-2.pdf (accessed 21 June 2018).

16 "Lege nr. 74 din 17 iulie 1992 pentru ratificarea Tratatului de prietenie, colaborare şi bună vecinătate dintre România şi Republica Bulgaria. Textul actului publicat în M.Of. nr. 174/23 iul. 1992," www.monitoruljuridic.ro/act/tratat-din-27-ianuarie-1992-de-prietenie-colaborare-si-buna-vecinatate-intre-romania-si-republica-bulgaria-emitent-parlamentul-publicat-n-31002.html (accessed 20 May 2018).

17 "Lege nr. 129/1997 pentru ratificarea Tratatului cu privire la relaţiile de bună vecinătate şi cooperare dintre România şi Ucraina, semnat la Constanţa la 2 iunie 1997," www.dri.gov.ro/lege-nr-1291997-pentru-ratificarea-tratatului-cu-privire-la-relatiile-de-buna-vecinatate-si-cooperare-dintre-romania-si-ucraina-semnat-la-constanta-la-2-iunie-1997/ (accessed 20 May 2018); "Tratatul de bază. Tratat de înţelegere, cooperare şi buna vecinătate între România şi Republica Ungaria," www.monitoruljuridic.ro/act/tratat-din-16-septembrie-1996-de-intelegere-cooperare-si-buna-vecinatate-intre-romania-si-republica-ungara-emitent-parlamentul-publicat-n-39628.html (accessed 20 May 2018).

18 "Lege nr. 79 din 22 septembrie 1994 pentru ratificarea Tratatului privind relaţiile de prietenie şi colaborare dintre România şi Republica Croaţia, încheiat la Bucureşti la 16 februarie 1994. Textul actului publicat în M.Of. nr. 273/27 sep. 1994," www.cdep.ro/pls/legis/legis_pck.htp_act_text?idt=14545 (accessed 20 May 2018); "Lege nr. 28 din 24 mai 1993 pentru ratificarea Tratatului cu privire la relaţiile prieteneşti şi la cooperarea dintre România şi Republica Polonă, încheiat la Bucureşti la 25 ianuarie 1993. Textul actului publicat în M.Of. nr. 112/31 mai 1993," www.cdep.ro/pls/legis/legis_pck.htp_act_text?idt=13734 (accessed 20 May 2018); "Lege nr. 112/1996 pentru ratificarea Tratatului cu privire la relaţiile de prietenie, bună vecinătate şi cooperare dintre România şi Republica Federală Iugoslavia, semnat la Belgrad la 16 mai 1996," www.dri.gov.ro/lege-nr-1121996-pentru-ratificarea-tratatului-cu-privire-la-relatiile-de-prietenie-buna-vecinatate-si-cooperare-dintre-romania-si-republica-federala-iugoslavia-semnat-la-belgrad-la-16-mai-1996/ (accessed 20 May 2018); "Lege nr. 10 din 7 martie 1994 pentru ratificarea Tratatului privind relaţiile de prietenie şi colaborare dintre România şi Republica Slovacă, încheiat la Bratislava la 24 septembrie 1993. Textul actului publicat în M.Of. nr. 64/11 mar. 1994," www.cdep.ro/pls/legis/legis_pck.htp_act_text?idt=14266 (accessed 20 May 2018).

19 Ingmar Brandsch and Hugo Schneider, "'Avem' nemţi, dar nu ştim să-i păstrăm," *Adevărul*, 23 April 1992.

20 "Programm des Demokratischen Forums der Rumäniendeutschen," *Hermannstädter Zeitung*, 19 January 1990.

21 Brandsch and Schneider, "Avem nemţi"; Wolfgang Wittstock, "Guvernul României a încălcat spiritul şi litera Tratatului dintre România şi Germania, privind cooperarea

prietenească și parteneriatul în Europa," interview by Ion Longin Popescu, *Formula As*, 6 August 2001. That the issue of property restitution continues to be of relevance is also illustrated by the fact that it has been constantly addressed by Romanian politicians participating in the 2000s and 2010s at the Transylvanian Saxon *Heimattage* (Days of the Homeland) organized every year in the Bavarian town of Dinkelsbühl. See, for example, Gheorghe Flutur's speech in 2005 (Flutur was then minister of Agriculture), "Rumänien will Folgen des Kommunismus beseitigen," MP3 file, 2:41, www.siebenbuerger.de/reden/heimattag2005/dkb2005flutur.mp3 (accessed 18 June 2018); Vasile Blaga's speech in 2011 (Blaga was then minister of Interior Affairs), "Festrede von Vasile Blaga," MP3 file, 18:56, www.siebenbuerger.de/reden/heimattag2010/Festrede_Vasile-Blaga.mp3 (accessed 18 June 2018) or Dacian Cioloș' address in 2016 (Cioloș was at the time prime minister of Romania), "Ansprache – Dinkelsbühl 2016 – Heimattag der Siebenbürger Sachsen," www.youtube.com/watch?v=Xhu_7_lzBLY&feature=youtu.be (accessed 18 June 2018).
22 See also *Zugänge* 14 (1993), where some of these posters were reproduced.
23 Forumul Democrat al Germanilor din România, "Organizația FDGR la nivel național," www.fdgr.ro/ro/statutul/111 (accessed 7 June 2018).
24 This is also the explanation advanced by Paul-Jürgen Porr, the current president of the Forum, in Florin Iepan's documentary about Klaus Iohannis, *2 pentru România. Klaus Iohannis*, www.dailymotion.com/video/x2a6e8o (accessed 16 June 2018).
25 R. C., "Călin Popescu Tăriceanu despre primarul Sibiului: 'Mi-ar face mare plăcere să avem oameni de calitatea sa în PNL'," *Adevărul*, 6 October 2004.
26 Klaus Iohannis, "Vrem să facem din Sibiu ceea ce-a fost cândva. Un oraș european, un avanpost al integrării în Uniunea Europeană," interview by Ion Longin Popescu, *Formula As* 431, 18 September 2000.
27 Figures taken from the website of the Democratic Forum of Germans in Romania. See www.fdgr.ro/ro/statistici/536, www.fdgr.ro/ro/statistici/535, www.fdgr.ro/ro/statistici/534 (accessed 19 June 2018). In this context, it is nonetheless also worth emphasizing that census questions in Romania do not allow choosing more than one ethnic identity.
28 Cord Meier-Klodt, "25 Jahre Deutsch-Rumänischer Freundschaftsvertrag – mitund füreinander für ein gemeinsames Europa," www.rumaenien.diplo.de/contentblob/5057686/Daten/7571581/ddatei_rede_bo_cmk_tms2017.pdf (accessed 18 May 2018).
29 "Calitatea de membru," www.fdgr.ro/ro/statutul/107 (accessed 8 June 2018).
30 www.sgk.ro/ro/ (accessed 21 June 2018).
31 Meier-Klodt, "25 Jahre Deutsch-Rumänischer Freundschaftsvertrag."

6 "They who have no Germans, should buy some"

6.1. Romanian Germans as victims: Remembering the deportation to the Soviet Union

Directly involved in the politics of the Democratic Forum of Germans in Romania as member of Parliament (1992–1996 and 1997–2004) and also as its president between 1998 and 2002, Wolfgang Wittstock (2004, 34) saw the core areas of his activity as a representative of the German community in the Romanian Parliament as having to do with minority protection, reparations for the arbitrary measures taken during the communist dictatorship and the restitution of nationalized properties. In a similar vein, when asked about the reasons behind the fact that Romanian German migration to the Federal Republic did not stop after the dissolution of the socialist regime but rather continued and actually reached its acme in the early 1990s, literary critic Stefan Sienerth alluded to a counterfactual history scenario while, however, admitting that it was a "thought impossible to verify": "if the land restitution had taken place at the beginning of the 1990s and if the official apologies of the Romanian state had come earlier, the history of the Germans in Romania might have looked different".[1]

According to the utterances of both Wittstock and Sienerth, twentieth-century German history in Romania – particularly after the Second World War – is largely interpreted as a history of victimhood. In this context, the fall of state socialism is seen as having offered the possibility to redress past wrongs against the German population, a possibility that was, however, neither fully nor speedily taken up by the relevant Romanian authorities. The importance granted to historical processes that took place in the recent past and to the need to address these processes by means of restorative and compensating measures indicates the particular relevance of memory-related issues in the unfolding of the entangled post-1989 Romanian-German relationships, although such issues were clearly less important as compared to cases such as the German-Polish or the German-Czech ones (De Trégomain, 2007; Cercel, 2009).

In narratives emphasizing Romanian German victimhood, one of the most important anti-German measures, purportedly showing the totalitarian character of Soviet-imposed rule in Romania, is the deportation of civilians for forced labor in the Soviet Union. This took place in January 1995 and was officially framed at the time as a measure "for the reconstruction" of the Soviet Union (Weber et al., 1995; Baier, 1994, 2003). The first land reform in the immediate aftermath of the Second World War, which meant in effect a large-scale expropriation of Romanian Germans, and their subsequent migration to the Federal Republic – presented mainly as "human trafficking", "selling of people" or "ransom" – are the other two phenomena most brought up when construing post-1945 Romanian German history as a history of victimhood. At times, the paradigm of victimhood is even extended to the period of the Second World War, by presenting Romanian Germans as victims of Hitler and Nazi Germany too.

In this context, following the dissolution of the socialist regime in December 1989, the January 1945 deportation to the Soviet Union has rapidly turned into a key Romanian German *lieu de mémoire*, acknowledged as such not only by Romanian Germans themselves but also by external observers. The former deportees rapidly founded an association to represent their interests. A profusion of memorialistic texts and oral history projects followed (Rehner, 1993; Weniger, 1994; Berner & Radosav, 1996; Ulrich, 2005; Betea et al., 2012). In the second book he authored, Romanian President Klaus Iohannis (2015, 56) referred to the deportation as a traumatic event for the Romanian German community, describing it as a "true catastrophe". A documentary about Iohannis, screened on the television right before the second round of the 2014 presidential elections, also addressed the issue of the deportation.[2] Among the interviewees questioned about the event in the documentary are historian Paul Philippi, president of the Democratic Forum of Germans in Romania between 1992 and 1998 and honorary president of the organization from 1998 up to his death in 2018, and Gerhild Rudolf, director of the Cultural Centre "Friedrich Teutsch" in Sibiu. Both of them, as well as Iohannis himself, emphasize the unjust character of the action and situate it within a broader narrative highlighting the anti-German measures that took place in Romania toward the end of the Second World War.[3] Rudolf suggests that the Romanian authorities were those who decided to deport the German population exclusively, although historiography broadly agrees that the Soviets specifically asked that Germans be sent to Ukraine for "reconstruction" (Weber et al., 1995). The documentary – which addresses the deportation soon almost as its first topic – makes no mention whatsoever of what preceded the deportation, namely of Nazism or of the mass enlistment of Transylvanian Saxons and Banat Swabians in the SS.

On the legal level, addressing the plight of former deportees in the immediate aftermath of the fall of Ceaușescu's regime was not a straightforward process. When the post-1989 Romanian authorities drafted the first laws aimed at the reparation of wrongdoings perpetrated during socialist rule, their initial temporal milestone was 6 March 1945 – that is, the date when a Moscow-backed government, led by Petru Groza, was installed. This meant, however, that the Germans deported to the Soviet Union in January 1945 were not at first included in the text of the law granting particular rights to those politically persecuted "by the dictatorship installed starting with 6 March 1945".[4] Only in December 1990 were the provisions of the law extended to include those who were "deported abroad after

23 August 1944".[5] Since July 2013, the provisions of the law are also applicable to those Romanian Germans who were deported and yet no longer hold Romanian citizenship.[6]

In January 1995, on the occasion of the fiftieth anniversary of the deportation, a series of events were organized in Brașov in order to commemorate the event, under the title "In memoriam deportationis 1945–1995". The main organizer was the Democratic Forum of Germans. Both president Ion Iliescu and prime minister Nicolae Văcăroiu sent their official messages to the survivors of the deportation and to all those convened in Brașov.

At the time, the leadership of the Forum was actually hoping that Iliescu would officially apologize for the deportations, but this did not happen as such.[7] The message Iliescu sent was milder in tone than the Forum would have wanted. The then Romanian president situated the "drama of the German minority" in the wider context of the final stages of the Second World War and its aftermath, an era marked by "geostrategic upheavals and political mutations". Furthermore, he placed German suffering on par with the suffering of "numerous Romanian citizens, from all social, ethnic, and religious categories", who were the victims of unjust behavior and abuses and blamed the Soviet-dominated Allied Control Commission for the deportation. Iliescu also referred to the mass migration of Romanian Germans "due to the specific conditions of the years of communist dictatorship", although he also argued that in effect the "overwhelming majority of the Romanian population" had to suffer "resettlements and abusive expropriations, privations and human rights abuses". Last but not least, he reinforced the typical philo-German tropes by emphasizing the "sympathy and affection of the Romanian people" for the "cultural traditions" of the German minority, as well as for its "contribution to the general development of Romanian society".[8]

Văcăroiu's letter addressed to the participants in the commemoration directly blamed the "explicit order of Moscow", which forced the Romanian government of the time to deport its adult German citizens to the Soviet Union for the reconstruction of the latter country. Furthermore, for Văcăroiu "all this happened with the absurd imputation that they were of German origin, although they were Romanian citizens!" He called this a "collective incrimination" for an "imaginary guilt". Thus, Văcăroiu implied that the "German origin" incrimination was made absurd by the Romanian citizenship, since the latter should have had preeminence over the former. The Romanian prime minister also emphasized the opposition of the Romanian government to the deportation. He finished his message by reiterating a series of positive stereotypes with which Germans are associated in Romania: "their seriousness, their giftedness, their industriousness".[9]

The two messages are not fully compatible with Romanian German victimhood-centered narratives that emphasize the particularity of Romanian German suffering and that turn Germans into the victims par excellence of twentieth-century Romanian history. However, they showed nonetheless that the integration of German suffering within Romanian memory discourses is possible and that this integration can be construed as very much compatible with anti-communist and especially anti-Soviet discourses. It was the first time that central Romanian authorities acknowledged German suffering, although in doing this, they – especially Iliescu – also partially attempted to tone down the particular German character of this suffering and to place it within a broader context. Nonetheless, it must be noted that the messages of Iliescu and Văcăroiu, on the occasion of the fiftieth anniversary of the deportation, were issued in a period in which Ion Antonescu, the Romanian fascist leader during the Second World War, was effectively being rehabilitated in Romanian society and in which there was no acknowledgment whatsoever of Romanian participation in and responsibility for the Holocaust, a particularly contentious and contested topic.

On the same occasion, Paul Philippi, at the time president of the Forum, also delivered a message, issued in the name of the Forum, and formally addressed to President Iliescu. Philippi went so far as to state that "the deportation of Saxons and Swabians in January 1945 was – as far as we know – the only collective discrimination centrally steered by state bodies in Romania, which was exclusively underlain by an ethnic criterion" (Philippi, [1995] 2006, 97, 98). He repeated the assertion two times during his speech, although the insertion of the clause "as far as we know" did leave space for potential future adjustments to the claim. Philippi presented the deportation as being just the first step in a wider series of anti-German discriminations, also referring to the deprivation of civic rights – that is, the right to vote – in 1946, the deportation of Banat Swabians to the Bărăgan Plain in the 1950s and the eviction of Saxons from Transylvanian industrial towns (Philippi, [1995] 2006, 98].

In Philippi's 1995 address, Romanian Germans come up as *the* fundamental ethnic victims of twentieth-century Romanian history. This meant writing off both the eliminatory persecution of Jews and the Roma before and during the Second World War, as well as the prehistory of the deportations, which would have been bound to entail engaging with the influence of Nazism among the Romanian German communities. Although displaying notable differences in tone and emphasis, the statements issued by Iliescu, Văcăroiu and Philippi in 1995 indicated the existence of potential meeting points between two processes of whitewashing or downplaying of the pre-1945 fascist past – one of them Romanian, the other one Romanian German – which spell out victimhood while effacing perpetration and culpability. In this vein, it is also worth noting that Philippi addressed his claims for the official recognition of Romanian German victimhood not only to the Romanian government but also to the German authorities. Writing in January 1996 to the then president of Germany, Roman Herzog, after the latter declared 27 January The Day of Remembrance for the Victims of National Socialism, Philippi suggested that the Romanian Germans who served in the SS and those who were deported to the Soviet Union should also be regarded as "victims of National Socialism" (Philippi, [1996] 2006, 150–151).[10]

November 1996 marked a governmental change in Romania that at the time was optimistically hailed as fundamentally modifying the face of Romanian politics. A motley conservative-neoliberal coalition of anti-communist Europeanists came to power. One of the main objectives of the new authorities was to speed up the negotiations in order for Romania to enter both NATO and the European Union.

Membership in the two organizations was largely perceived as a joint enterprise. Moreover, framing NATO and EU integration as a national objective also corresponded to the strong assertion of a true "European" political (and cultural) identity. On the discursive level, the emphasis on Europe, represented as a project of cultural, political and economic belonging, was used to establish a clear marker of differentiation from what the former government was supposed to stand for.

It was against this background, in April 1997, on the occasion of an official visit of the German minister of Foreign Affairs, Klaus Kinkel, in Romania, that the Romanian government, through the voice of Kinkel's counterpart, Adrian Severin, expressed the government's deepest regret and apologized for the wrongdoings perpetrated against the German minority during socialist rule. The declaration explicitly referred to the 1945 deportation of Germans to the former Soviet Union, the deportations to Bărăgan that took place during the Stalin-Tito conflict in the 1950s and the so-called selling of Germans by the Ceaușescu regime.[11]

Several observations ought to be made of this moment. The first one is of a conceptual nature and refers to a distinction operationalized by political scientist Melissa Nobles. Nobles distinguishes between two types of apologies: apologies made by governments and apologies made by heads of state. The former apologies are usually "highly scripted affairs"– that is, the result of debates and "deliberative processes" and often bringing forth monetary compensations. In contrast, the latter are "verbal utterances" or gestures from government officials of a more spontaneous nature, which rarely entail financial requitals. German Chancellor Willy Brandt kneeling in 1970 in Warsaw, in front of the monument of the Ghetto Uprising, is one of the best-known examples of gestures that can be regarded as falling under this latter category (Nobles, 2008, 5–6). Severin's declaration belongs to the same category, as his own post-factum statements suggest.

The other observations to be made with respect to this statement regard its contents and the subsequent explanations provided by Severin on what pushed him to utter it. First, the declaration straightforwardly acknowledged the contribution of Romanian authorities to the deportation to the Soviet Union, "under the pressure of foreign occupation", a nuanced change from the statements of Iliescu and Văcăroiu barely two years earlier, which placed the blame exclusively on the Soviets. Văcăroiu went so far as to stress the opposition of the Romanian government of the time. Second, Severin's declaration also referred to the resettlement of Swabians from border localities in Banat to the Bărăgan Plain in Southeastern Romania. These measures, which took place during the Stalin-Tito conflict in the early 1950s, affected not only Swabians but other inhabitants of the border villages as well: ethnic Serbs, Romanians, Bulgarians, Hungarians, Roma etc. Adrian Severin disavowed these events in a context of exculpatory attention granted to the German minority in Romania. Thus, he indirectly established a hierarchy of victimhood. Among the deportees, Swabians – since they were Germans, one could add – were the most important and worthiest of receiving apologies. Last but not least, Severin also apologized for the so-called selling of Germans. It is worth emphasizing that no Romanian high-ranked official has ever done the same with respect to the Jewish population, whose history under Romania's communist regime is very similar to that of the German minority.[12]

After the end of his governmental tenure, Severin offered some insights from his activity as minister of Foreign Affairs, including background information regarding his encounters with Klaus Kinkel. Referring to their first meeting, which took place in February 1997, in a semi-official setting, Severin delineated the arguments he set out for his counterpart, in order to support Romania's plea for NATO accession.[13] For him, joining NATO was part of the process of European unification, and it was therefore closely related to the endeavor of asserting a European and Western Romanian identity. He remembered calling Romania in front of Kinkel "a country from the most Oriental part of Central Europe", thus being "the furthest zone of extension of German culture towards East" (Severin & Andreescu, 2000, 91). The attempt to situate Romania on the border of "Central Europe" is essentially a reproduction of an "Orientalist" discourse, a case of "nesting Orientalisms", as Bakić-Hayden (1995) would call it. It is indicative of an attempt to de-Easternize Romanian identity, implicitly referring to the discourses about Central Europe as a "kidnapped Occident".[14] Speaking about Romania as a Central European country signaled the desire to assert such an identification and, on the basis of it, to join NATO in the first round of enlargement, together with Poland, Hungary, the Czech Republic and Slovakia, paradigmatic "Central European" countries (Janowski, Iordachi & Trencsényi, 2005). Bakić-Hayden (1995) shows, in her article focusing on the Yugoslav case, the complexity of the East-West relationships and the way the "Orient", perceived as the Other, underlies identity discourses not only in Western Europe but in Eastern Europe as well. In other words, the "Orient" as the Other is used as a legitimization tool in identity discourses promoted by elites in Eastern European countries to get rid of easternist ascriptions and to affirm their belonging to "European" culture. This is often done by means of discursively "Orientalizing" whatever lies further to the east of the respective countries. Placing Romania at the border of "Central Europe" is an attempt to de-"Orientalize" it, a process that implicitly leads to the ascription of an "Oriental" identity to everything lying east and south of Romania. There were thus two implicit differentiations entailed by Severin's symbolic geographies: a differentiation from the Balkans and the former Yugoslavia and a differentiation from the former Soviet Union.

Continuing in the same vein, Severin directly referred to the Romanian-German cultural relationships, arguing that "Romania has developed a great part of its culture under the influence of and intimately connected with German culture" (Severin & Andreescu, 2000, 91). The statement implicitly stands for a breach with the traditional common knowledge narratives and discourses emphasizing the Francophile character of modern Romanian culture. Of course, Severin was acting as a diplomat wanting to win Kinkel's support and goodwill. A Germanophile discourse is not surprising in this context. However, his choice of arguments and his emphases are not arbitrary. Other discourses could have been imagined; other approaches could have been concocted. Nevertheless, Severin opted for an identity- and memory-oriented discourse that defined Romania's European identity as largely due to German culture and influence. He explicitly built his argument around the German minority in Romania, trying to instrumentalize the status of Germany as its kin state:

> I told him: we have a German minority and, no matter how small, it definitely asks itself what will its country – of the same cultural origin – do so that it does not remain outside an enlarged Europe or outside a Europe secured through the enlargement of the Northern Atlantic Alliance.
> (Severin & Andreescu, 2000, 91)

In this context, it is worth noting that the Forum was in effect pleading with German state authorities for the same things. In a 1997 letter addressed to Helmut Kohl regarding Romania's NATO accession, leading representatives of the Forum argued on behalf of the accession because "our ability to exist as Germans in Romania is crucially dependent on the integration of our country into European structures" (Philippi, [1997] 2006, 189).

Severin's statements to Kinkel represent a prime example of the discursive attempt to legitimize Romania's aspirations to NATO accession on the basis of a (Central, and therefore not Eastern; Central, hence rather Western) European cultural belonging. To successfully assert this cultural belonging, Severin discursively inscribed German influence as a key element of Romanian identity. His premise was that Germanness is par excellence a European identity: he aimed to transfer this Europeanness onto Romanian identity. Identity and memory discourses are very much related to power and legitimacy and to political aspirations. The short identity narrative that Severin remembered offsetting out to Kinkel aptly illustrates this.

This first meeting laid the foundation for Kinkel's subsequent visit to Bucharest, which took place in April 1997. It was on this occasion that Severin expressed his apologies for the treatment of the German minority in Romania during state socialism. He subsequently argued that the apologies were meant to dissipate the distrust in Romanian-German relationships, which was allegedly caused by this discriminatory treatment of the German minority. Furthermore, Severin claims to have presented his stance as being in line with the German process of coming to terms with the past:

> Since Germany makes such a critical self-analysis and tries to solve the problems of the present only after having critically understood its past, it means that she will evaluate the capacity to make alliances with one or the other on the basis of the experiences that she had in the past in its contacts with those countries or nations.
> (Severin & Andreescu, 2000, 95)

According to probably the most self-stylized recollections of the former Romanian minister of Foreign Affairs, the declaration stirred emotions and surprise in the German delegation, with Klaus Kinkel on the verge of crying and remembering the Banat Swabian nanny he grew up with (Severin & Andreescu, 2000, 97–98). Severin's account of the reaction of the German delegation acquires an even treaclier tone when he details Kinkel's supposed recollection of his role in the process of Romanian German migration to West Germany, which took place during communism.[15] Kinkel allegedly

> [. . .] remembered . . . the way in which social welfare was curtailed in every annual budget, the Christmas presents for German orphans were cut, and other similar savings were made, in order to make available the sums of money necessary for the piecemeal ransom of the Romanian Germans that Ceauşescu's regime was selling.
> (Severin & Andreescu, 2000, 98)

Thus, the communist regime in Romania ended up being painted as responsible not only for the rather dubious and morally questionable practice of allowing Germans to migrate from Romania to West Germany only in exchange for financial reimbursements but also for the present-free Christmas of orphans in Germany. Severin contended that through his apologies he made important steps toward Romania's NATO accession. They indicate the perception that discourses about Germanness in Romania can be instrumentalized to assert a European identity and to attain concrete political objectives. Moreover, according to his account of the various projects that he subsequently proposed to Chancellor Helmut Kohl, such as the construction of a highway between Bucharest and Budapest or the redrawing of the Pan-European Transport Corridor IV, Severin claimed to have emphasized how these projects were meant to be beneficial to the Saxon and Swabian populations in Transylvania and Banat (Severin & Andreescu, 2000, 103).

Severin also pointed out that the decision to apologize was his own and that he did not discuss the contents of the statement with President Emil Constantinescu. Furthermore, he commented on the negative reception of his gesture in the Romanian press, also underlining the opposition he encountered after the event within his own coalition, for example from Ion Caramitru, the minister of Culture at the time.[16] Nonetheless, the reality is that Severin's gesture was the first gesture made by a high representative of the Romanian state that recognized Romanian responsibility for and the direct participation of Romanian authorities in the enactment of discriminatory measures against an ethnic group. It was a much stronger acknowledgment than the one found in the discourses of Iliescu and Văcăroiu two years before. That such a recognition concerned phenomena that took place under state socialism and that Severin framed it in effect as a coming to terms with the past according to the German model betokens an implicit equation of Nazism and communism. An ambiguous official acknowledgment of Romanian participation in the Holocaust, through the voice of President Emil Constantinescu, would take place for the first time in September of the same year, only to be afterwards soon forgotten.[17] Furthermore, Constantinescu's message was not devoid of equivoques, emphasizing that the "planners of the genocide" were not Romanians and that, during the war, Romanian authorities not only "organized deportations, set up camps and promoted racial legislation" but also "tried more than once to oppose Nazi requests to liquidate the Jewish population, organized the emigration to Palestine of some Jewish groups and even straightforwardly protected figures from the Jewish community in Romania".[18] President Iliescu's subsequent re-acknowledgment, which took place in 2004, would be much more straightforward, perhaps because it was also accompanied by the founding of an International Commission for the Study of the Holocaust in Romania, led by Elie Wiesel (International Commission on the Holocaust in Romania, 2004). Regarding Romanian state persecution against the Roma, an integral part of the Holocaust in Romania, not until October 2007 did President Traian Băsescu officially apologize to the Roma community, in a rather low-key context.[19]

In one of the first post-1989 works of history published in Romania and critically dealing with Romanian communism, economist and former political detainee Gheorghe Boldur-Lățescu (1992, 21) referred to the "first tragedy of the population of German origin from Romania", namely the deportation to the Soviet Union. He did not go into details, arguing that the facts are "pretty well known". Subsequently, in the third volume of his work, he also provided the figure of around 150,000 ethnic Germans deported to the Soviet Union (Boldur-Lățescu, 1998, 8). This is a considerable overestimation when compared to the figures advanced by researchers who looked extensively into the topic, who advance a figure of between 70,000 and 80,000 deportees (Weber et al., 1995). The Final Report of the Presidential Commission for the Analysis of the Communist Dictatorship in Romania acknowledged the deportation of Romanian Germans to the Soviet Union as underlying the criminal nature of the communist regime. The phenomenon is first referred to in the second chapter of the Report, as being one of the preparatory steps of the "communist genocide", undertaken at the behest of Moscow and with the presumed complicity of the Communist leaders in the country. The chapter seems to have been written by means of a copy-and-paste method, as it borrows heavily from the abovementioned work by Boldur-Lățescu. The Report starts by advancing the same figure of 150,000 ethnic Germans deported to the Soviet Union in 1945 (Comisia Prezidențială, 2006, 158–160). Nonetheless, some thirty-eight pages later, the figure is halved, and the number of those deported becomes 75,000 (Comisia Prezidențială, 2006, 198). The short special section within the Report dedicated to the German minority between 1944 and 1990 presents the history of the German minority after Romania's change of sides in August 1944 by emphasizing repression – that is, deportation for the reconstruction of the Soviet Union, land reform and the "selling of Germans" (Comisia Prezidențială, 2006, 541–548). The Report does include a reference to the 1943 Romanian-German state agreement that led to the mass enrollment of Romanian Germans in the SS (Comisia Prezidențială, 2006, 541).

The relevance of the deportation for the victimhood-centered identity discourses and practices of Transylvanian Saxons, Banat Swabians and Satu Mare Swabians is highlighted by the commemorative events that take place every January in both Romania and Germany, by the numerous articles that appear in Romanian German (or even in Romanian) publications every year in the same period of time and by the many commemorative plaques in localities in Transylvania and Banat. Such plaques and other memorializing initiatives often merge together the soldiers who fought in the Second World War and those who died during the deportation. In 1995, a monument dedicated only the deportees was erected in Reşiţa, in Western Romania. The international success of Nobel Prize laureate Herta Müller's most recent (2009) novel, *Atemschaukel* (translated into English as *The Hunger Angel*), has contributed to the increasing centrality of the memory of Romanian-German deportation to the Soviet Union, a phenomenon that can be easily integrated into broader memory discourses on "Germans as victims" (Niven, 2006).

Such memory discourses are also interwoven with the general focalization on victimhood and on the Holocaust, which is a key element of contemporary hegemonic cosmopolitan memory discourses at the European level (Cento Bull & Hansen, 2016). A relatively recent (2014) initiative concerning the erection of a memorial to Transylvanian Saxon deportees to the Soviet Union draws explicit parallels between the memorialization of the Holocaust and the need to memorialize the deportation. The instigator of the initiative, Peter Jacobi, is a Transylvanian Saxon sculptor living in Germany, who, incidentally, was also the creator of the memorial to victims of the Holocaust in Bucharest, inaugurated in 2009. In his plea, Jacobi referred explicitly to the Holocaust memorial project, which was also supported at the time by the "Elly [*sic*] Wiesel Commission". Jacobi evidently saw a parallel between this project and his own idea, calling for Herta Müller's participation, on account of what he called her "exceptional work . . . based to a large extent on the literary adaptation of the deportation of Germans in the Soviet Union", just as the work of "Elly Wiesel" was, he said, based "on research and the fight against a repetition of the Holocaust".[20] The reference to Herta Müller's work, and specifically to her novel, *The Hunger Angel*, suggests that the memorial would be, in essence, one dedicated to all Romanian Germans, not only to the Transylvanian Saxon ones, although Jacobi also refers to the fact that such a monument already exists in Reşiţa (Reschitz in German, Resicabánya in Hungarian).[21]

Discourses about the history of Romanian Germans in the twentieth century and particularly about the deportation to the Soviet Union tend to eschew any critical discussion regarding the strong appeal of Nazism within Romanian German communities and their subsequent participation in the Holocaust and the Second World War. The focus on German victimhood is, in effect, made possible by this obliteration. Thus, the central place of deportation within both self- and hetero-representations of Romanian Germans ties in well with the larger liberal-conservative anti-communist paradigm that has informed post-1989 discourses and evolutions at both the Romanian and the European level and that at the same time seems to actually lead toward a whitewashing and trivialization of fascism. The largely decontextualized emphasis on victimhood writes off the broader context leading to the deportation and the political and social conflicts, the social and economic processes that created the conditions that made it possible.

In a recent book about the Transylvanian village Criţ (Deutsch-Kreuz in German, Szászkeresztúr in Hungarian), authored by Ruxandra Hurezean, one of the country's most appreciated journalists,[22] and prefaced by Emil Hurezeanu, former journalist for *Radio Free Europe* in the 1980s and Romania's current ambassador to Berlin, one can read:

> From the small village between the hills almost all men went to fight in the First World War. Then in the Second World War. After the first war, 12 of them did not come back, and after the Second World War, 28 of them did not come back. Others died in the work camps in Russia.
> (Hurezean, 2017, 139)

Two and a half pages about the deportation follow, which include a list of all the deportees from Criț, but no elaboration on the service of local soldiers in Hitler's armies. In the preface of another book by the same author (Hurezean, 2016), historian Anneli Ute Gabanyi presents Romanian Germans as victims of both Hitler and Stalin: the former made them enlist in the Wehrmacht and in the Waffen-SS, whereas the second deported to Ukraine those who were able to work (Gabanyi, 2016, 11). The tensions embedded within the oversimplifying perpetrator-victim dichotomy are resolved by another act of simplification: there are no more perpetrators anymore, only victims. Ruxandra Hurezean even argues for the pure innocence of Transylvanian Saxons, by referring to their putative Flemish origin, an argument uncritically borrowed from the aged respondent Sofia Folberth, who is the central character of Hurezean's book: "[These were] people who did agriculture, women who had never left the village, had barely heard about Hitler, but they paid for a general guilt. They were Flemish, but Hitler was not Flemish" (Hurezean, 2017, 41).

Undoubtedly, it would be short-sighted not to acknowledge the important role played by authorities in Berlin in the history of Romanian Germans in the interwar period and during the Second World War. Romanian German history at the time did indeed unfold "between Hitler, Stalin and Antonescu" as the title of a book by Paul Milata (2009) says. But presenting Romanian German history in the twentieth century as a history of victimhood whose starting point is the January 1945 deportation silences the developments that took place within Romanian German communities in the interwar period. The display of a selective memory about the role of Nazi or Nazi-oriented ideology within Romanian German twentieth-century history and the interpretation of communism as the root of all evil while emphasizing the tight links between Romanian German identity, Europeanness and European civilization suggest that the implicit paradigm at work here is one eerily close to radical conservatism. November 1940 (the granting of autonomy to the German Ethnic Group in Romania), April/May 1943 (Romanian-German enrollment in the SS) and January 1945 (the deportation of civilians to the Soviet Union for forced labor) ought to be linked as part of one and the same narrative, a narrative that critically engages with the adherence to Nazism and to a Nazi-conservative idea of Europe of a significant part of the Romanian German communities. Yet doing this would, critically, also entail that the history of Romanian Germans is not a history of pure Romanian German victimhood but rather a history in which the embrace of Nazism that took place within Romanian German communities, the mass enlistment in the SS and the 1945 deportation to the Soviet

Union are in effect tightly interwoven. In essence, the deportees *were* victims forced to pay for the guilt of those who actively took part in a war of extermination and annihilation unleashed by Nazi Germany (the gender imbalance among the deportees is also telling in this respect). Remembering and speaking solely about the former and their suffering is nothing more than a way to avoid addressing thorny issues in Romanian German and Romanian history. Underlining the fact that before some Romanian Germans were deported putatively *only because* they were German, (some other) Romanian Germans embraced Nazism precisely because they saw in it an expression of Germanness worth adhering to, acted as concentration camp guards in Auschwitz and Treblinka, went to war and fought in the SS in the name of Nazi Germany and *because* they believed that their Germanness bestowed an inherent superiority on them would shed a different light on the deportation.[23] This would not diminish the personal drama of the deportees but rather would place the "collective German drama" in Romania in a different context and would lead to much more caution when it comes to the uncritical embrace of victimhood discourses.

6.2. Human trade

Severin's apologies expressed in front of his German counterpart, Klaus Kinkel, concerned not only the deportation to the Soviet Union but also the "selling" of Germans during the communist regime. On 18 December 2006, the then president of Romania Traian Băsescu officially condemned the communist regime on the basis of the already mentioned report, hastily drafted by the Presidential Commission for the Study of Communist Dictatorship in Romania, a body that he had set up just eight months beforehand. In the condemnation speech, delivered in front of the combined chambers of the Romanian Parliament and in the presence of well-known anti-communist figures such as Lech Wałęsa from Poland, Zhelyu Zhelev from Bulgaria and former Romanian king Mihai I, Băsescu enumerated the "main criminal actions mentioned in the Report", which served as argument for symbolic condemnation. "The persecution of ethnic, religious, cultural or sexual minorities" and the "deportations aiming for extermination, the ethnic repressions, the chasing away and 'selling' of Jews and Germans" were among the twenty criminal actions that Băsescu distinctly referred to in his speech.[24]

The Cold War migration of Romanian Germans to the Federal Republic of Germany – presented within both popular and historical narratives as "trafficking in human beings" (*Menschenhandel*), "ransom", "human trade" and other similar expressions – is a key element put forward in order to emphasize the victimhood that is constitutive of discourses about Romanian Germans. Most often, a rudimentary form of anti-communism underlies such discourses and representations. The representations oscillate between the depiction of Germans as being fundamentally passive objects of the arbitrariness of communist despotism – "sold like in the market", "sold like cattle", "goods for export" – and the depiction of Germans as agents looking for the freedom that they could not enjoy in communist Romania yet could enjoy in capitalist West Germany.[25] The deeper political, cultural, social and economic processes associated with the migration – which could be categorized as a "migration of ethnic unmixing", to use an expression coined by Rogers Brubaker (1998) and placed within the broader context of East-West migrations – are relegated to the background or are pseudo-explicated by an oversimplifying discursive reference to the totalitarian character of communist rule. Furthermore, addressing the migration and its effects is often associated with the assertion of the typical self-Orientalized philo-German tropes:

> Thus, in the postwar period, Romania lost its population of German origin, after a period of eight centuries in which German colonists lived and imposed a model of civilisation and culture on these lands. Values typical to the German environment, such as seriousness, unfailing diligence, order, correctness, zealousness and discipline gradually disappeared from Romania after the ethnic Germans left, leaving behind a society that lost the habit of organizing itself and of bringing prosperity to its citizens.
>
> (Gheorghiu, 2015, 7)

The consequence of German migration, namely German absence from Romania, is equated to a "void left by Communism in our history" (Hurezean, 2017, 12–13). For Adrian Cioroianu, historian and former minister of Foreign Affairs, the migration of Romanian Germans led to "one of Romania's greatest losses in the twentieth century" since the German minority was an ethnic group "that had definitely brought more benefits than problems" (Cioroianu, 2007, 172). It is easy to infer from such an assertion that for Cioroianu there are also ethnic groups who bring forth more problems than benefits.

Following a pattern already used in the case of Jewish migration from Romania to Israel, the migration of Romanian Germans from Romania to the Federal Republic of Germany was economically conditioned (Ioanid, 2005). Concretely, according to secret agreements between the two states and through secret channels involving the securitate and West German lawyers, the Federal Republic of Germany paid an amount of money for every German that was granted permission to leave Romania (Dobre et al., 2011; Hüsch, Baier & Meinhardt, 2013; Hüsch, Leber & Baier, 2016). Some of the documents related to the issue indicate that from the perspective of the Romanian state, the sums that the West German government had to pay depended on the qualifications of the migrants (Dobre et al., 2011). They were framed as a compensation for the financial efforts undertaken by the Romanian state for the education of Romanian Germans and for the economic losses and damage that the Romanian state would suffer as a consequence of the migration of its workforce. The fact that the Romanian authorities were compensated by the West German state for Romanian citizens of German origin who received legal permission to leave the country also reinforces the idea of a relationship between Romanian Germans and economic gains, which continues to play an important role in self- and hetero-representations of Romanian Germans.

This process of migration also had a role to play in the development and stabilization of particular positive images about West Germany, since Germans who migrated would often come back to visit their relatives and friends after they got hold of West German citizenship. This contact contributed to a general Romanian fascination with West Germany. Material goods brought from West Germany by Saxons and Swabians on their trips to Romania symbolized capitalist luxury (Petrescu, 2008, 215–217; see also Koranyi, 2008; Mcarthur, 1981).

A well-received documentary film from 2014, directed by the late Răzvan Georgescu, largely illustrates the main paradigm informing the understanding of Romanian German migration to West Germany in the twentieth century. The Romanian title of the documentary is *Pașaport de Germania* (Passport for Germany). The German translation is faithful to the original (*Ein Reisepass für Deutschland*), whereas the official title in English is *Trading Germans*. Interviewing several Romanian Germans who migrated to the Federal Republic – either legally, meaning after receiving permission to leave and hence being officially "bought" by the West German state, or illegally – as well as some of the actors directly involved in the process of negotiation between the two sides, the film embraces rather uncritically the West German side of the narrative. The picture it paints is one of Germans looking for freedom and of a Romanian state arbitrarily setting a price for that freedom. At a certain point, the documentary stages an encounter between Heinz-Günther Hüsch, the German lawyer who negotiated on behalf of the German government, and Stelian Octavian Andronic, one of the Romanian Securitate officers who was responsible for the process and directly negotiated with Hüsch. The latter takes the opportunity to affirm that what the West Germans did was in the name of human rights, whereas for the Romanian side, it was only a lucrative business. Capitalist West Germany acted on the basis of humanitarianism; communist Romania acted solely on financial grounds. The former was morally legitimate; the latter was immoral. Romanian Germans were bought by the West German state in order to be set free. Hüsch's narrative, that the West German policy of (financially) supporting the migration of ethnic Germans to the Federal Republic, was a humanitarian policy, is to a large extent the narrative that the film appropriates and presents.

Nonetheless, a closer look at the phenomenon reveals the paradoxes, tensions and frictions embedded within this narrative. These paradoxes and tensions can be discerned in the film, yet only if reading between the lines, as is the case in many of the typical accounts of the "human trade" connecting Romania and the Federal Republic of Germany during the Cold War. First and foremost, as one of the Romanian German respondents in Georgescu's film indeed argues, migration to West Germany was also closely connected with the mass enrollment in the Wehrmacht and in the SS, which took place as a consequence of the Hitler–Stalin Pact in 1943. This was one of the main reasons accounting for a consistent and organized Romanian German presence in West Germany after the Second World War, albeit not the only one. The interviewee, writer Johann Lippet, suggests that the enlistment in the Wehrmacht and the SS was neither properly voluntary nor entirely compulsory. The film does not go on to engage in any more depth with the influence of Nazism on the Romanian German communities.

Many of those who settled in West Germany and became leading ethnopolitical entrepreneurs in the Romanian German homeland associations had, in effect, a Hitlerite past. At the same time, these homeland associations were also the ones pushing for migration, both in the name of human rights and humanitarianism and in the name of identity discourses heavily indebted to older Nazi and *völkisch* concepts. This is but one paradox of Romanian German history after the Second World War. Another one is connected to the fact that the Romanian state to a large extent created the conditions in which key markers of German identity could be maintained, by providing, for example, education in German language, which then allowed Germans from Romania to integrate more easily in the Federal Republic. Yet another paradox is that members of a group supposedly discriminated against because of their ethnicity (particularly during Ceaușescu's nationalism) could actually envisage migrating legally to the West, something that was largely out of the question for Romanian citizens who were not of German ethnicity. The possibility to emigrate can also be regarded as a privilege in the given context. However, ethnopolitical entrepreneurs in West Germany constructed the image of the German minority in Romania as an endangered community that could be saved only if it were allowed to leave Romania. This led to rather dubious discourses, best symbolized probably by the expression "expelled, yet kept in the expelling country", used by a Transylvanian Saxon activist in West Germany in the 1980s in order to describe the situation of the community in Romania (Hartl, 1985).

The narrative according to which the West German process of "buying" Germans was nothing other than a humanitarian policy pursued in the name of human rights also requires significant nuancing. In Georgescu's documentary, the German negotiator states that West Germans did not want to pay for non-Germans migrating to the Federal Republic, which indicates that the scope of the policy had its limits, being ethnically circumscribed and hence essentially based on a form of German nationalism rather than pure humanitarianism. There are even documents indicating that Hüsch suggested to Romanian authorities at the time that they ought to be harsher when granting exit visas for tourism, since some of those who received such visas then absconded or claimed asylum after reaching West Germany. This in turn impacted the numbers included in the yearly agreements regarding German migration from Romania. Furthermore, documents also indicate that the compensations paid to the Romanian state took, for example, the form of wire-tapping technology (Dobre et al., 2011).

In effect, qualifying and nuancing the victimhood discourse related to Romanian German migration during state socialism, and moving beyond the Germans-looking-for-freedom narrative would actually entail bringing to the fore the dire economic situation in Romania as a main rationale for migration. From the point of view of the Romanian state, desperately in need of foreign currency, the economic situation was one of the main reasons for accepting migration, although this was a phenomenon not devoid of contradictions, given that the loss of qualified labor force could also have negative effects on the economy. Yet if too much emphasis is placed on this material dimension, it would mean that Romanian Germans end up being presented as economic migrants. The legitimacy that can be derived from narratives of victimhood would be forfeited. Such an emphasis would also question the place of Romanian Germans within broader German society. At least on the institutional level, Romanian German identity in the Federal Republic is based on a sense of victimhood shared with the other "expellee" groups, gathered under the umbrella organization of the Federation of Expellees. At the same time, presenting Cold War Romanian German migration in an interpretive framework emphasizing anti-communism and humanitarianism also justifies interpreting this migration as part of the broader process of Romania's decoupling and veering away from Europe, notionally set in motion by communism. This then entails that a potential remigration of Germans following the fall of communism is apt to contribute to a (renewed) symbolic and concrete rapprochement to Europe.

6.3. Germans leaving, Germans staying, Germans returning

In the immediate aftermath of the revolution of 1989, on 8 January 1990, an interview with the new de facto Romanian head of state, Ion Iliescu, was published in *Die Welt*.[26] The title reproduced Iliescu's plea against a German migration from Romania: "I ask the Germans: stay with us, in Romania!" Iliescu referred to his own good contacts with members of the German minority, from the period when he used to work in Timişoara (Temeschwar in German, Temesvár in Hungarian, Temišvar in Serbian), the most important city in Banat, an economic, educational and cultural hub for Banat Swabians. Furthermore, not only did he plead with Germans not to leave Romania – thus aware of the migration process that was in motion – but he also expressed his wish that some of the Germans who had left the country would now return.

After a visit to Sibiu in 1992, another of the three candidates at the 1990 elections, Ion Raţiu (2001, 119), wrote the following in his diary:

> I want to serve Romania, not only the Romanian nation I come from. . . . I want to make all its citizens proud that they belong to this country. This is, probably, the influence of the many years I spent partially, yet regularly and frequently, in Switzerland. This is how we have to be. This is how many of our Saxons and Swabians will return to the country. To help us have a better local and central administration, more just, fuller of love for the neighbour.

Raţiu, a prominent member of the Romanian diaspora during the Cold War, seemed to be nurturing the same type of wishful thinking regarding a German remigration to Romania as his main counter-candidate, Ion Iliescu. Looking for European models to emulate, Raţiu placed his views on Saxons and Swabians into an "Europeanizing" framework, choosing Switzerland as the model to be emulated, with a Saxon and Swabian return imagined as both a consequence of and a direct contribution to attaining the desired status.

In September 1990, Petre Sălcudeanu, a well-known writer turned into a pundit in the new political context, published an op-ed in *Adevărul*, one of the most popular Romanian newspapers at the time, describing a putative dream of his. In this dream, Sălcudeanu entered a dialogue with Helmut Kohl, discussing with the

German Chancellor a potential remigration of Germans from the Federal Republic of Germany to Romania, because they "have been an element of stability and civility for Romanians". Wishing to revert the migration process for which the last fifty years were to blame (that is, the period of state socialism), Sălcudeanu suggested that the returnees should receive 8,000 Deutsche Marks, the same amount of money that had been allegedly paid by the West German state for each Romanian German who migrated before 1989. Furthermore, to convince the Germans to return, the article authored by Sălcudeanu also envisaged a complete process of property restitution, enhanced by some additional facilities:

> If you [Chancellor Kohl] agree, we would give this sum of money to anyone wishing to return, but also to those wishing to stay. In addition, they will get their houses back, their lands, their old lands or new ones, they can establish whole settlements of their own if they want to, although, amongst all nationalities, with them we had the best relationship.

In Sălcudeanu's view, particularly the German work ethics would have made such a return very useful for Romania, since Germans "come to work fifteen minutes ahead of time". Furthermore, the potential German return would have set in motion a process of Romanian reconnection with the pre-1945 entrepreneurial traditions, symbolized in the text by Sălcudeanu's nostalgia for the (German-run) Czell beer factory from the Brașov of his childhood.[27]

Some months later, in February 1991, Sălcudeanu would revisit the topic. Once again, he made use of the same stylistic artifice, writing about a "dream". The reverie included anew "my friend Mr. Helmut"– that is, Helmut Kohl – imagined as pleading in front of a crowd of Saxons that they return to Romania, where they would be able to "found small enterprises" and "spread manure on the ground" the same way they "have been doing it for centuries". As in other accounts too, Saxons stand for the entirety of Romanian Germans.[28] Kohl's speech, as imagined by Sălcudeanu, appealed to the representation of a Romanian-German compatibility and of a tradition of historical cooperation against outside threats, stereotypically racialized as Asian: "together with Romanians you have defended the borders from the invasions of those with almond-shaped eyes". Sălcudeanu's imagination went further. In his dream, Germans positively respond to Kohl's plea and then queue to enter Romania, an orderly country most eager to have them back, with "no autochthonous or coloured racketeer" to be seen at the border. In villages and towns, local councils offer Germans their title deeds, loans and some additional reparations money, in order for them "to forget the difficulties you went through". Upon entering the villages where they used to live, Romanians "dressed in Saxon and Swabian attire" wait for Saxons and Swabians. In effect, this representation would prove to be a fateful prediction: Transylvanian Saxon and Banat Swabian traditional celebrations in localities with a formerly strong Saxon or Swabian presence are currently performed mostly by ethnic Romanians, just like the pupils attending both public and private German-language schools come more often from the majority population (and presumably also from the other minority groups) than from the 30,000 Romanian Germans (Botea, 2008; Câmpeanu, 2012). Visions of Romanian performances of Germanness have also been addressed in fiction, in an ironic and ludic manner: Ioan T. Morar (2006) wrote a novel in which he imagines the story of a nostalgic Romanian German turned billionaire who returns to visit the village in Banat where he was born. There, Romanian actors of the German-language section of a local theater bring back the "German" village to life on the occasion of the billionaire's visit.

Following his introduction, Sălcudeanu made a discursive leap, from the dream of German remigration to Romania to the concrete reality, symbolized by the decision made by Nicu Vlad, a highly Romanian heavyweight lifter, to leave the country. The writer turned pundit clearly regretted this decision, seeing in Vlad a symbol of Romania:

> I have only seen him on television and the kindness on his face resembling a purely Romanian icon, without anything Byzantine in it, the serenity on his face and the probity in his eyes drew him nigh to me to such an extent, that for me he is one and the same with the country.

Thus, Sălcudeanu overtly drew a parallel between two departures from Romania: Nicu Vlad, an athlete and champion standing in effect for one of the best and most successful representatives of the Romanian nation, and Saxons and Swabians, who thus were also imagined as symbolically belonging to Romania's elite. Germanness was represented as a value in itself. For Sălcudeanu, both departures – of Nicu Vlad and of Romanian Germans – were telling of Romania's tragic situation. The final lines of the article reinforced this conclusion: "Why, folks, why? What have we done so bad that the best of the best are leaving us, i.e. the Country? Folks, why is the Country leaving, what have we done to it?"[29]

Nonetheless, after the fall of state socialism, the trope of Romanian German migration from Romania could also be accompanied by a new opposite, namely the idea of a Romanian German return migration, sometimes imagined as a potential harbinger of change. We have already seen this in Iliescu's statement quoted at the beginning of this section. In the early 1990s, the twin ideas of migration and return migration were addressed in the Romanian press through the voices of those directly involved in it: the representatives of the Democratic Forum of Germans in Romania. An interview with Thomas Nägler, who was president of the organization at the time, was published on 23 May 1990 under the title "Etnici germani care pleacă sau revin în țară" (Ethnic Germans who leave or return to the country).[30] Despite the fact that the title seemed to place the two categories on the same level, the contents of the article offered the true image of the two phenomena: dozens of thousands wanted to leave, while only dozens were coming back. The interviewer named the former "a real loss for Romania", also endowing Germanness with a positive value.[31]

In another example of an article written in the aftermath of the regime change in 1989, this time published in *România liberă*, different voices from within the Saxon community in Țara Bârsei, the region around Brașov, were presented. The article, whose author was one Dumitru Bujdoiu, wanted to answer the question, "why are the Saxons still leaving?" The interrogation subtly addressed one of the paradoxes implied by the general narrative regarding Romanian German migration to the Federal Republic of Germany: if socialist rule is to blame for the resettlement taking place during the Cold War, why didn't the migration stop instead of largely increasing, once state socialism fell? The respondents in Bujdoiu's contribution emphasized on the one hand the economic rationale behind the decision to migrate and on the other hand the dissolution of the social and cultural structures enabling a "German" life in Romania. One of the several interviewees quoted in the article framed her decision as a clear-cut embrace of "Europe", impossible in the Romanian context, despite the emotional links with the country: "We know that our meaning is here, but if the entire country does not make efforts to enter Europe, why would we, Saxons, be stopped from doing this?".[32] The decision to migrate to Germany was thus framed as enabling Romanian Germans to assert their own Europeanness, an assertion perceived as increasingly difficult in the Romanian context.

Perhaps the most important torchbearer of the Romanian philo-Germanism without Germans has been, since the early 1990s, the weekly newspaper *Formula As*. *Formula As* is a popular magazine addressing topics of general interest: celebrities, recipes, social and political life, ecology, culture, reportages and so on. Its publication began in 1991, and the magazine soon acquired a numerous readership. The articles published by *Formula As* and the numerous letters received from its readers mostly revolve around an expression of "Romanianness"; "Romanianness" and Romanian "cultural memory", construed in various forms and guises, constitute by and large the crux of the themes recurrently addressed in its pages (Burnett & Nocasian, 2008). At the same time, *Formula As* has also been regularly addressing issues related to the German population in Romania, particularly in Transylvania and Banat.

For example, in 1992, the writer and literary critic Voicu Bugariu wrote in the pages of *Formula As* about the "saddening exodus" of the Germans from Romania. In this context, he clearly asserted the Europeanizing value of the Germans in Romania: "It seems that all there is to do is to regret these correct people, living together with us until yesterday, as true emissaries of a Europe to which we only tend". The sadness related to German out-migration is, for Bugariu, the sadness of losing the contact with the "Europe" nearby, the tangible Europe represented by the German population. German schools shut down, and hence Romanians lose the possibility to get acquainted with the "old and prestigious" German culture. Germans migrate, hence the personal relations between Romanians attracted by German culture and Germans dwindle.[33]

Nonetheless, attempting to provide a counterweight to such sobbing accounts, *Formula As* has also constantly granted particular attention to those ethnic Germans who decided to stay. On the same page with the piece authored by Bugariu, an interview with Rohtraut Wittstock was published. Wittstock was at the time (1992) cultural editor of *Neuer Weg*, the daily newspaper catering for the German-speaking community in Romania, since 1993 renamed into *Allgemeine Deutsche*

Zeitung. At the time of writing – May 2018 – she is the editor in chief of the newspaper. The interview published in *Formula As* touched on two main issues: on the one hand, the fate of the newspaper under the difficult new auspices of the postcommunist convulsions and, on the other hand, the German migration from Romania and the possibilities of the stabilization of the German communities. The narrative spelled out by Wittstock emphasized the existence of a permanent historical rapport between the German communities in Transylvania and Banat and German and European culture (in Wittstock's words, "the great German culture"). She regarded communism as an attempt to "annihilate" the community.

However, Wittstock was one of the Romanian Germans who decided to stay in Romania. She used the self-identification "German from Romania" and underlined the existence of "strong sentimental bonds with some of the things here". Furthermore, she emphasized the high importance granted by the Germans in Romania to belonging to a community, seen as an explanation for the survival of the ethnic group: "For the Germans in Romania, this feeling is important and the interests of the individual have been always subordinated to those of the community".[34]

Throughout the years, readers of *Formula As* could also come across interviews with or articles about German personalities who decided to stay in Romania rather than to migrate to the Federal Republic, such as historian Adolf Armbruster,[35] musician Hanno Höfer,[36] writer and Lutheran pastor Eginald Schlattner[37] and, after 2000, mayor Klaus Iohannis.[38] Moreover, overtly displaying a distinct appreciation of things German, *Formula As* transformed a well-known Romanian proverb that emphasizes that one should always appreciate old people into a saying underlining the value of Germans, with "Germans" replacing old people. Thus, *Cine n-are bătrâni, să și-i cumpere* (They who have no elderly, should buy some) becomes in its philo-German version *Cine n-are nemți, să și-i cumpere* (They who have no Germans, should buy some). A subtle irony can be detected given the common discourses about Germans having been "sold" by the Romanian state during the Cold War. Hence, in *Formula As*, one can discern a particular attempt to construct Romanian memory and identity as a locus in which German prestige is invested. Transylvanian Saxons and Banat Swabians thus seem to act like an added value to Romanian identity, witnessing and at the same time making possible or enhancing the European character of Romanian culture, understood concurrently as a potentiality and a reality. This also leads to the discursive construction, in the name of a conservative and traditional Europe in touch with its past, of a particular German-Romanian compatibility.

The overt references to Europe are particularly visible, for example, in interviews with the writer Eginald Schlattner and with politician Klaus Iohannis. Schlattner appears to be an ardent supporter of the European value of Romanian culture. A Lutheran pastor and author of several novels dealing with Transylvania's past, he is fascinated by the religiosity of Romanians, expressing his belief that "God cannot forget such a world". At the same time, in his public statements, Schlattner has been disseminating a nostalgic discourse about life in Romania before the Second World War, using this as an argument in favor of Romania's European integration.[39] In one of the interviews published in *Formula As*, he argued that "the Romanians of today are the nephews of those who in the 1930s were travelling through Europe and paying everything in gold lei". An even more definitive argument for Romania's Europeanness can be found in an interview with the same Schlattner, taken by Ion Longin Popescu in 2005. The introduction referred to Schlattner's putative words in front of Otto Schilly, minister of Internal Affairs in Germany, on the occasion of the latter's visit to the fortified church in the village of Roşia, Schlattner's parish. The passage deserves to be quoted in its entirety:

> When, in the forests and in the swamps, where nowadays lies Berlin, the twitch was growing, here, in Transylvania, German was sung and Latin prayers were said. This is Saxon oldness! And if nowadays I can greet you in our common language, German, I am thankful for this to my homeland, Romania, which never banned our mother tongue, not even in those nine months, when the Romanian kingdom was at war with the German Reich, from 23 August 1944 to 9 May 1945.[40]

These utterances are perfectly contiguous with the conservative and nationalistic views largely disseminated in *Formula As*. By argumentatively harking back to the old age of Transylvanian Saxon churches and insisting on their anteriority compared to Berlin, they also cater to Romanian identity-related issues. Transylvania acts almost as a synecdoche for Romania – while also standing for the better part of Romania – whereas Berlin acts as a synecdoche for Germany. Had Schlattner referred to Trier, for example, his demonstration would have been significantly hindered by the fact that Trier (or other places in Germany) does have an older history than Berlin. Nonetheless, his aim was to prove the essential Germanness of Transylvanian Saxons, in what is an almost implicit reference to the *germanissimi germanorum* discourses and, strongly linked to that, to prove their Europeanness and that of Romania as a whole. Transylvanian Saxons are presented as representatives of a German culture whose credentials are older than German culture in Germany itself.[41] The putative discourse in front of Schilly took place in 2005 – that is, before Romania's accession to the European Union. Furthermore, Schlattner strongly argued on behalf of Romania's "European" treatment of national minorities in history. His answer to the first question posed by the interviewer was the following: "I wanted to prove that Romanians are Europeans by vocation and by mindset, that this country comes from history having appropriated the *acquis communautaire*, even surpassing it as regards minorities".[42]

If Schlattner acts as the Transylvanian Saxon intellectual acquiescing in the representation of Romania as a minority-friendly country in general, extremely sympathetic toward its German minority in particular and hence European par excellence, a slightly different perspective, more focused on politics and local administration, is found in the discourses promoted by and with respect to Klaus Iohannis, the mayor of Sibiu between 2000 and 2014 and one of the favorite political personalities of *Formula As*. Shortly after being first elected as a mayor,

Iohannis openly spoke of the objective of bringing Saxons back to Sibiu, "as a symbol". In the first interview that he granted to *Formula As*, soon after the electoral success in 2000, Iohannis emphasized that he speaks Romanian with no accent and that he is married to a Romanian, thus showing his strong links with Romanian culture. At the same time, he also referred to his attempt of transforming Sibiu into an outpost of Romanian integration into the European Union.[43] In effect, under Iohannis's administration, Sibiu successfully applied to be European Capital of Culture in 2007. In 2006, the Saxon mayor could already state that "the old Saxons who left Sibiu would be proud of our work", envisaging that Sibiu "would never again be the provincial town that we had all known until now".[44]

Formula As has been striving not only to emphasize the added value brought by German cultural and political personalities who stayed in Romania but also to bring to the fore the positive impact of lesser-known Germans, farmers, owners of small businesses, tourism entrepreneurs and so on. Moreover, in the same context, the readers of the magazine have also constantly had the chance to come across articles about Germans from the Federal Republic of Germany who decided to settle in Romania, most often in rural Transylvania, drawing on the region's "German" links. Such articles stress the traditional and natural character of life in Romanian villages, and hence are indicative of the conservative, traditionalist understanding of European, German and Romanian identity that *Formula As* disseminates. The underlying representation is that of Romania as a country where Germans have preserved and continue to preserve their traditional identity and at the same time have contributed and continue to contribute to its development. An interview published in April 1997 presented "the wonderful story of a German falling in love with Romania". The title of the piece captured the interconnections of the two migration processes: "The Saxons are leaving, the Germans are coming". The interviewee was Gerlinde Gabler-Braun, director of the Sibiu "Carl Wolff" hospital and retirement home, meant to cater to the distinct needs of the aged Transylvanian Saxon population and generously funded by the German Ministry of Interior Affairs.[45] Another article presented the cases of both Saxon returnees ("our Saxons") and Germans originating from the Federal Republic who decided to settle in Romania. German presence in Transylvania is depicted under the aegis of hope, the article being titled "Footprints of hope in Transylvania".[46]

The Saxons and Swabians who remained in the country stand almost perforce for the entire community, their value being practically enhanced by their having remained in Romania. The extended byline of an article signed by Beatrice Ungar, on Michael Lienerth, the Saxon mayor of the village Vurpăr (Burgberg in German, Vurpód in Hungarian), is exemplary in this respect: "Not all Saxons left Romania. And of those who stayed, one equals seven".[47] Thus, lastness and scarcity end up being two added values of Saxonness and Germanness. By "lastness", I refer to Germans who did not leave Romania being endowed with positive traits precisely on the basis of the fact that they are still there and that they are considered to be the last Germans to be there. Germans still in Romania have to be appreciated because there are so few of them. Several other examples of articles can be adduced: a Satu Mare Swabian, Francisc Moser, the head of an agricultural cooperative in the village of Petrești (Petrifeld in German, Mezőpetri in Hungarian), is shown to contribute, on a local scale, to the post-1989 agricultural development of Romania. The text builds on the commonplace that Romania once used to be "the granary of Europe", deploring the current state of Romanian agriculture, where few initiatives such as the one in Petrești take place. Moser emphasized his connection with Romania, made salient also by his decision to stay in the country when he could have migrated, also suggesting that even those who left cannot get rid of the strong emotional and physical bonds with their Satu Mare homeland. At the same time, he underlined the existence of a German work ethic. When asked about what Romanian agriculture could borrow from the German model, he answered, "Work. . . . I saw the seriousness with which they work there, from morning until the evening. It's the same in my case".[48]

In the introduction of a 2002 interview with Hermann Spack, Saxon returnee and owner of a touristic boarding house in Cristian (Großau in German, Keresztényisziget in Hungarian), a village close to Sibiu, the interviewer, Ion Longin Popescu, referred to Saxons and Swabians as a population acting as a "standard" to be emulated in the process of development and European integration. Popescu deplored the migration of the German population in Romania, calling Romanian Germans a "'bridgehead' on Romanian soil of one of the most developed European civilizations", "strategic outpost of eastern Germanness". The interviewee Spack emphasized his deep emotional connections in Romania, which also made him move back to the country. By opening a business in Cristian, he wanted "to show that even in Romania one can make business and strictly respect the legislation". At the same time, he affirmed that although he and his wife always spoke Saxon at home, they always felt Romanian.[49]

In the already quoted interview with Iohannis from September 2000, the interviewer asked the newly elected mayor of Sibiu whether he had in mind "a program for Saxons to return to their hearths".[50] Eight years later, the same journalist published an account about what he perceived to be a "true miracle": Saxons returning to Romania, to help the economic progress of the country. The one-page-long account referred to two Saxon returnees, Erich Schell and Dietrich Schuster, investing on the real estate market in Romania, more precisely in Tălmaciu (Talmesch in German, Talmács in Hungarian), a village in the immediate proximity of Sibiu. According to Ion Longin Popescu, a Saxon return to Romania would be "the great luck of our country":

> Rather than looking for Asian immigrants, who are also necessary, but with a mentality foreign to the European space, Romanian employers should better call up young Saxons, to encourage them to step on their ancestors' footsteps, who came here 800 years ago.

Popescu's argument continues: "If some thousands of Saxons (and Swabians) would return, this would be mirrored in the positive evolution of business". Hence, the Romanian government should bring forth a "smart project of renaissance, on new grounds, of the Germanic civilization in the Carpathians". The way the entrepreneurship of the two returnees is presented in *Formula As* provides a glimpse into the imaginary associated with German return and with German investments in Romania: "We build everything from scratch, the German way, out of respect for the customers and for things which are well done", says one of the two investors.[51] Either as a cause for or as a consequence of, Romanian Germans are represented in connection with progress and economic growth. Ever since 1991, articles in *Formula As* have been constructing a particular Romanian-German affinity, emphasizing its potential (and at the same time desired) outcome: a German-Romanian mix, an appropriation of typical "German" values such as order and discipline, all peppered with a nationalist conservative dedication for things Romanian and for spirituality and with visions of soulful capitalist development building on tradition and traditionalism.

German prestige in Romania is enhanced by the scarcity of the German population in the country and calls forth nostalgic undertones and overtones. The "lastness" of Romanian Germans, albeit at times also softened by reports about Saxon and Swabian remigration, is a key component of this nostalgia. Wistfulness imbues articles, accounts and interviews dealing with the German minority. The commonplace "our Germans left", in its multiple variants, elicits melancholic, wailful considerations, which are part and parcel of representations of the German minority in Romania, constantly reiterated. Precisely this reiteration enables their integration into Romanian memory discourses. Such discourses also refer to the current state of dereliction in which former Saxon and Swabian houses, monuments and localities stand, in a constant opposition to the good old times in the past, which is always the precommunist past. Nostalgia needs to construct a bleak present to be able to praise the perceived virtues of the past (Boym, 2001).

Sobbing accounts about Transylvanian villages lacking a future because of the German out-migration were prevalent in the 1990s. The situation in Transylvanian localities formerly inhabited by Saxons was commonly depicted in rather bleak terms: they were referred to as "fortified towns that die standing" despite the acknowledgment of the efforts made, for example, by an activist such as Caroline Fernolend in Viscri (Deutsch-Weißkirch in German, Szászfehéregyháza in Hungarian).[52] An article published in *Adevărul*, in 1997, touched on the fate of Hărman (Honigberg in German, Szászhermány in Hungarian), a village with a fortified church in the vicinity of Brașov. The locality is presented as desolate, under siege by carelessness and decay. The same decrepit image is found in an article published in *România liberă*, connecting the degradation of the locality with German migration: "Founded by the Teutonic Knights, inhabited for hundreds of years by Saxons, the locality degraded once they definitively left for Germany". If Hărman had succeeded in coping with attacks and sieges in the past, it did not seem to cope with the Romanian transition, such articles argued while acknowledging Hărman's belonging to Romanian national heritage.[53] Decay and poverty were also represented as getting hold of Brateiu (Bratei in German, Baráthely in Hungarian), a village at the periphery of Mediaș (Mediasch in German, Medgyes in Hungarian), or of a number of villages around Sighișoara (Schäßburg in German, Segesvár in Hungarian).[54] In the 1990s, articles about Sibiu, nowadays the Transylvanian Saxon *caput mundi*, presented the town on the verge of ruin, very much unlike the current, more glamorous image of the town, which very much emphasizes its "Europeanness".[55]

Two articles in the same *Formula As* deserve to be granted particular attention in order to illustrate the nostalgia associated with German past in Romania, one signed by Sânziana Pop, the other by Sorin Preda.[56] The article by Pop, editor in chief of *Formula As*, painted a representation in which the glorious German past was contraposed to both communist and postcommunist realities. The nostalgia enacted in Pop's article is, according to a categorization proposed by Svetlana Boym (2001, 41), a reflective one, lingering "on ruins, the patina of time and history". Nonetheless, it also seems to be elicited by two different aspects of memory discourses: on the one hand, Pop displayed a fully constructed nostalgia for times immemorial, when Saxon colonists arrived in Transylvania and started to build up civilization; on the other hand, a nostalgia for the lived past can also be discerned in her text, for a past in which the author experienced the cohabitation with the Saxons in the Sighișoara of her adolescence. The whole text is lachrymose. The reader is immersed into a world magnificently transformed by settlers, who, coming "from Germany to Transylvania", brought with them "their models of civilization": "Saxon vicinity propelled the Romanian population in the area with about a thousand years in advance on the civilizational ladder". In Pop's account, the historical past is transformed according to the needs of the present. Thus, she referred to settlers coming from "Germany", a modern political reality that did not exist in the twelfth century. Furthermore, studies on Saxon settlement in Transylvania emphasized that the medieval settlers actually came from a variety of regions, which would not qualify for being categorized as "Germany" according to today's geographies. Luxembourg and Flanders, among the places of origin of twelfth-century settlers, have never been "Germany", with the exception of particularly short-lived twentieth-century German military expansion in Europe. Nonetheless, by referring to "Germany", Pop "Germanized" post factum the Saxons in an echo of older understandings of a Pan-German nation, tragically instrumentalized by radically conservative and far-right ideologies.

Her text continued, referring to the looks of the Romanian population, who were watching the Germans building up civilization, which suggested they were bewildered: "Under the (probably) astonished eyes of the Romanian inhabitants, they [Germans] started to raise citadels, gigantic churches, public squares". Pop's account proposes a translucent hierarchization of ethnic groups: Germans, coming from the West, allegedly embarked right away on concretizing their civilizing mission, while Romanians are represented as not able to overcome their status of passive on-lookers, waiting to be "civilized". Furthermore, beyond the visible nostalgia, the way Pop framed her memory discourse on German feats in Transylvania is also telling of a putative Transylvanian superiority toward other regions in Romania:

> Without the cursed red deluge, without the dramatic exodus of Saxons back to Germany, Transylvania would have been today a standard of European civilization. But even so, despite the misery and the discomfit, the civilizational

advance of Transylvania with respect to all the other geographical areas in Romania stayed and is visible as soon as you cross the rocky border of the Carpathians. A gift made to Romanians by German colonists that not only marked the material life and the moral behaviour (the respect of law and of the given word, discipline, punctuality, rigor), but also stimulated their dignity and national pride, through the constant reference to a model close to them, a . . . European one.

Pop's narrative is a fine example of what Bakić-Hayden (1995) called "nesting Orientalisms". It emphasizes a "Western" identification of Transylvania while also transparently suggesting that the other regions in the country are less civilized, more backward. But the most important aspect of Pop's discourse given the argument this book advances is that the presumed superiority of Transylvania over the other regions is strongly linked with the influence of Germans on the social and cultural development of the region. Having been inhabited by Germans, Transylvania became more civilized, Pop argued, deriving out of that an entire hierarchy of states, ethnic groups, cultural affiliations, political ideologies and geographical regions.

She also noted that Transylvanians display a feeling of nostalgia for the pre-1918 institutions of German extraction. Positive representations of Transylvanian Saxons interweave with and lead to the commonplace image of Transylvania as a more civilized region in Romania and with remnants of a melancholic intellectual discourse on the Habsburg Empire, reminiscent of the "Central Europe" versus "Eastern Europe" division arising out of the related debate in the 1980s (Okey, 1992). Thus, Saxon past and Saxon memory are embedded within a regional Transylvanian identity discourse. But regionalist discourses and the discursive creation of regional identities cannot be decoupled from the quest for legitimacy. Fundamentally, regional identity discourses are about symbolic and political power and legitimacy, just like any other type of identity or memory discourses (Bourdieu, 1991).

One finds a similar tone in the article signed by Sorin Preda, who wrote about the Saxon community of Roşia (Rothberg in German, Veresmart in Hungarian), one that aims to exemplify the tragic character of the German exodus. The reference to German "civilizing patterns" is once again to be found. In order for his message to be more effective, Preda spoke of "one thousand years of historical loyalty" when referring to the German presence in Transylvania (albeit that the date of Saxon settlement in the region is historically considered to be 1141). The first sentences of the article are telling:

> For years, our heart has beaten with the hope that the Saxons in Transylvania will stay home, in the villages they built, and where they were happy for one thousand years. . . . A millennium of Saxon history in Transylvania ends dramatically, in total indifference, erasing its civilizing patterns to which Transylvanian Romanians owe a lot. . . . Their departure is, first of all, a Romanian defeat. . . . Now, what separates us from them is the word with which one

crosses the Styx: farewell. We thank you for one thousand years of historical loyalty.

The image of a millennium of bliss and historical loyalty is one that cannot do anything other than elicit nostalgia, and this is the tone in which the entire two-pages-long material is written, including two interviews, one with Eginald Schlattner and the other with Julius Roth, who was one of the last Saxons to live in Roşia.

Preda's article emphasized the lastness of Transylvanian Saxons, adding to it overt religious undertones. Thus, a moral feature of Saxons is also created, visible from the title, which states that the Saxons in Roşia prepare for Heaven. On the one hand, the expression suggests that Saxons are actually on the verge of extinction, while on the other hand, it authorily endows German ethnicity with morally positive traits, on the basis of which ethnic Germans would presumably enjoy an afterlife in Heaven. Religious connotations often underlie the positive and nostalgic representations of Romanian Germans. Schlattner emphasizes that he remained in Romania because here God knows him "by name".[57] Furthermore, the readers find out from the text that Schlattner is the hundredth Lutheran priest of Roşia and likes to add to his letters the signature "the last Evangelical priest in Roşia". An article about Swabians coming back to Romania during the summer is titled "Our Daily Swabians", where the Romanian expression used for "daily" is the same with the one used in the religious prayer "Our Father" and in effect not used in common parlance (*cei de toate zilele*).[58] The motto of an article about Viscri, taken from an inscription above a gate in the village, is this: "I think of You, God, every morning I wake up and every evening when I go to sleep I pray that You also think of me".[59] Nostalgia has a strong "spiritual" component (Boym, 2001, 8). The nostalgia for the Romanian German past acquires straightforward religious dimensions.

The Saxons still living in Roşia, the village that Preda wrote about, are fewer than twenty, all of them old. Feelings of nostalgia for a livelier past and images of derelict emptiness are intensified by the portraits of those who are still there, who do not want to leave. Through Preda's account, and other accounts of the sort, Saxons are presented as an extinct species, whose last members are an object of interest for the wide public and who are important precisely because of their lastness. This approach and this representation of Saxonness and Swabianness are visible in a multitude of other articles and texts, some already cited, such as the text about Michael Lienerth that I have referred to previously. Moreover, there are also many other examples of articles and reportages on localities where nowadays there are either no or very few, Saxons and Swabians, often highlighting their state of abandonment or at least the sadness implied by the aging and gradual disappearance of the German-speaking population. In other cases, readers can come across the other side of the coin, namely the success stories of the last Saxons or Swabians who manage to transform them into touristic attractions while also preserving traditions and customs. The particular emphasis placed on the case of Viscri is relevant in this respect, mostly because of it becoming a tourist attraction under the efforts of Caroline Fernolend, one of the few Saxons who decided not to leave

Romania,[60] but also for some more unusual reasons, such as the selling, under German guidance, of woolen hand-braided socks made by the women of Viscri to customers in Germany.[61] An even more peculiar story was that of Thomas Herbert, a Saxon from Sibiu who made a business out of opening a reindeer farm in the Transylvanian town.[62] For Beatrice Ungar, Hărman provided a "small paradise",[63] while Prejmer (Tartlau in German, Prázsmár in Hungarian), itself in the vicinity of Hărman, was seen by another author as a village refusing to die, the keeper of the keys to the church thanking God each evening that she was born there.[64] The German villages in Banat also have their own success stories, such as Gărâna (Wolfsberg), a village that, the author notices, thrived after it was deserted by most of the autochthonous inhabitants – the Bohemian Germans. They did come back eventually, transformed their houses into vacation cottages, and now Gărâna lives off tourism, or at least this is how an article from 2005 was presenting it.[65]

The migration of the Germans is generally presented as a sad, even tragic, phenomenon, a rupture in the life of the community and at the same time a partial decoupling of Romania from Europeanness, from the Occident. In this context, a particular interest has been granted to those who did not go with the wave, to those who stayed in the country or to those who returned, thus showing that it is still possible to marry German (hence European) culture and German (hence European) values and Romanian mentality. The articles dedicated to such individuals emphasize the existence of specific positive traits associated with Germanness. Germans are successful, enterprising and a model to be emulated; they love Romania, bringing a so-called oasis of successful "normality" in the daily life of various local communities. Through them, it's Europe speaking, that Europe to which Romanians want to belong, brought closer by Germans, as such narratives imply. In 1998, *România liberă* journalist Virgil Lazăr wrote about the wish to return of ethnic Germans who had left Romania during communism. Reminiscing about his own personal experience of living alongside Transylvanian Saxons, Lazăr made eulogizing observations about their lasting households and about the performances of their agriculture. He was quite convinced that if the Saxons returned to the region, they would set up farms "as only they knew to initiate", thus representing a model to be emulated by the Romanian population.[66] In his introductory text to an issue of *Dilema* dedicated to Romanian Germans, Adrian Cioroianu referred to the migration of Germans from Romania as caused by economic reasons, wishfully adding that Germans might come back once the economic situation of Romania would improve.[67] Thus, Cioroianu presented the German return as a potential consequence of Romanian economic development, hence a supplementary reason for Romanians to make efforts in this direction.

Addressing the issue of German migration and of German remigration to Romania, philosopher Vasile Morar (2011, 289–297) suggested the existence of a distinct Saxon ethic, informed by the sense of duty, transferred in part also on the neighbouring Romanian population, and by the rejection of disorder, abnormality and void. Morar argued that the meaning of a hypothetical Saxon return is to make us dream and imagine how many events would have looked if "they" had not left: "how would our daily life have looked if these carriers of values had been present and not absent?" (Morar, 2011, 296).[68] The answer has to do with Europe and with the European Union:

> Simplifying, the historical and rational equation is this one: there is a strong relationship of determination between the return of Romanians to Europe and the 'return' of Saxons to Romania, and this is related to the possible overlap between the *institutions of the open society* and the substance shaping itself of the *open moral* of the European communities that were till yesterday rather closed.
>
> (Morar, 2011, 297)

Morar's elaborations have a different scope than those we can find in the articles in *Formula As* and in the mass media in general, yet they do have in common the representation of Saxons in relationship to Europe, of Saxons potentially bringing Europe closer to Romanians. At the same time, as many of the examples that I adduced show, this Europe is often understood as a conservative traditionalist project with religious-cum-spiritual dimensions, adjoined by visions of development and advancement that a German work ethic can bring about. Romanian Germans turn into the (nostalgic) embodiment of such a capitalist-conservative representation of Europe.

Notes

1 Stefan Sienerth, "Dacă Herta Müller ia mâine Premiul Nobel, literatura română o va accepta subit," interview by Cristian Cercel, *Observator Cultural* 391, 27 September 2007.
2 Florin Iepan, *2 pentru România. Klaus Iohannis*, 2014, www.dailymotion.com/video/x2a6e8o (accessed 16 June 2018).
3 The voice-over narrating the documentary says that Iohannis's grandparents were deported after the end of the war. However, the deportation took place mainly in January 1945, while the war was still ongoing. It is not clear whether Iohannis's grandparents were actually deported later than most Romanian Germans or whether this was a factual error in the documentary.
4 "Decret-lege privind acordarea unor drepturi persoanelor persecutate de dictatura instaurată cu începere de la 6 martie 1945," in *Monitorul Oficial al României*, 9 April 1990.
5 "Lege privind extinderea prevederilor Decretului-lege nr. 118/1990 şi la persoanele deportate în străinătate după 23 august 1944," in *Monitorul Oficial al României*, 13 December 1990.
6 "Lege nr. 211 din 27 iunie 2013 privind acordarea unor drepturi persoanelor care nu mai au cetăţenia română, dar care au fost persecutate din motive politice de dictatura instaurată cu începere de la 6 martie 1945, precum şi cele deportate în străinătate ori constituite în prizonieri," *Monitorul Oficial al României*, 2 July 2013, available at www.banaterschwaben.org/fileadmin/redakteur_uploads/dokumente/pdf/lege_nr_211-2013.pdf (accessed 25 May 2018).
7 Wolfgang Wittstock, interview by author, 7 January 2011, Braşov.
8 "Mesajul domnului Ion Iliescu, Preşedintele României, adresat participanţilor la manifestările comemorative prilejuite de împlinirea a 50 de ani de la deportarea în URSS a unor grupuri de etnici germani din România – Braşov, 14 ianuarie 1995 -," http://old.presidency.ro/pdf/date_arhiva/482_ro.pdf (accessed 25 May 2018).

9 The text of Văcăroiu's message, in German: "Eine schreckliche Vergeltung. Brief des Premiers Văcăroiu an die Teilnehmer der Veranstaltung," *Allgemeine Deutsche Zeitung für Rumänien*, 21 January 1995.
10 Two years before the 1995 commemoration of the deportations, Philippi actually wrote an article in *Allgemeine Deutsche Zeitung für Rumänien*, about the SS enrollment of Romanian Germans. The article was also published in the Romanian press. Therein, he did plead for a "reflection" on the phenomenon – albeit speaking as well of "idealism" and of the Romanian German members of SS as "victims of National-Socialism" – also linking it with the subsequent deportation, an impulse that he had apparently left aside some two years later. See Philippi, [1993] 2006, 41–43, as well as Paul Philippi, "În urmă cu 50 de ani, etnici germani din România s-au înrolat în 'Waffen-SS'," trans. Annemarie Weber, *România liberă*, 25 May 1993. In this context, it is also worth noting that Philippi himself was one of those who enrolled in 1943 in the SS (he was 19 years old at the time). See Milata, 2009, 340. See also Paul Philippi, "Von der Schulbank 1943 in den Zweiten Weltkrieg," lecture, 3 November 2015, Democratic Forum of Germans in Sibiu, www.siebenbuerger.de/ortschaften/hermannstadt/multimedia/sonstiges/46655-vortrag-des-zeitzeugen-prof-dr-paul.html (accessed 16 June 2018). Furthermore, Philippi's address on the occasion of the sixtieth anniversary of the deportation, in the context of the commemorative events organized in 2005 in Reşiţa (Reschitz in German, Resicabánya in Hungarian), had a partially different tenor, being more open toward the acknowledgment of embracing Nazism among Romanian German communities: "Didn't we allow to be engrossed by the enthusiasm for the 'Third Reich'? Didn't we give in to those amongst us who wanted to educate us towards full identification with this 'Third Reich', that is didn't we give them the reins for the leadership of our community? Didn't we sing along with them?" (Philippi, [2005] 2006, 395)
11 "Guvernul Ciorbea dezavuează total deportarea şi vânzarea etnicilor germani din România în perioada comunismului. Declaraţia d-lui ministru Adrian Severin," *România liberă*, 3 May 1997.
12 Radu Ioanid, "Ceauşescu şi Dej au vândut 250.000 de evrei," interview by Andrei Bădin, *Adevărul*, 12 October 2006, www.adevarul.ro/life/sanatate/Ceausescu-Dej-vandut-evrei_0_47395574.html (accessed 13 August 2017). See also Ioanid, 2005.
13 It is impossible to ascertain to what extent Severin's recollections correspond to reality, and Severin's statements seem on more than one occasion to be part and parcel of an exaggerated self-PR (self-promoting) exercise. At the same time, I see no reason to question that the spirit of Severin's discourse in front of the German minister of Foreign Affairs was the one he presented some three years later in his book of dialogues with Gabriel Andreescu. The text is anyway telling of Severin's representations of the German minority in Romania and of Romanian-German relations.
14 Milan Kundera, "The Tragedy of Central Europe," trans. Edmund White, *New York Review of Books*, 26 April 1984.
15 Severin states that Kinkel was secretary of state in the Ministry of Interior Affairs at the time, which is wrong because Kinkel was secretary of state in the Ministry of Justice between 1982 and 1990.
16 For a stance that was during this time critical of Severin's apologies, see Bogdan Chirieac, "Germania – un refuz călduros," *Adevărul*, 3 May 1997. In Chirieac's words, "If Romania apologized for something like this, then Germany should have also apologized for the Ribbentrop-Molotov Pact, for the Vienna Diktat, or for the bombing of Bucharest after 23 August 1944."
17 Apparently, in June 1997, on the occasion of an official visit to Israel, Severin also expressed his regret for Romania's role in the Holocaust, although this was allegedly not reported in the Romanian press (Severin & Andreescu, 2000, 135).
18 Emil Constantinescu, "Jertfa evreilor de pe pământul României e o povară în inima noastră," *Adevărul*, 10–11 May 1997.

19 "Comunicat de presă (22 octombrie 2007). REF: Ceremonie de decorare a etnicilor romi supraviețuitori ai Holocaustului," www.old.presidency.ro/pdf/date_arhiva/9708_ro.pdf (accessed 13 August 2017).
20 Peter Jacobi, "Öffentlicher Aufruf. Konzept für die Errichtung eines Denkmals für die Deportierten Siebenbürger Sachen [sic!], 1945–50 in die Sowjetunion," www.siebenbuerger.de/forum/integration/2471-denkmal-fuer-die-deportierten/#forumid132072 (accessed 25 May 2018).
21 Ibid.
22 Brîndușa Armanca, "Jurnaliști de elită: Ruxandra Hurezean," *Revista 22*, 16 May 2017, https://revista22.ro/70262737/jurnaliti-de-elit-ruxandra-hurezean.html (accessed 25 May 2018).
23 As it is often the case, literary works seem more willing (more capable?) to address in a more complex manner these sensitive issues than are other type of public discourses. See, for example, Schlattner, 1998; Schlesak, 2011; and Ackrill, 2015.
24 "Discursul președintelui României Traian Băsescu, prilejuit de prezentarea Raportului Comisiei Prezidențiale pentru Analiza Dictaturii Comuniste din România (București, 18 decembrie 2006)," www.lapunkt.ro/2014/12/18/18-decembrie-2006-condamnarea-comunismului-in-parlamentul-romaniei/ (accessed 25 May 2018). For a collection of critical positions about the Report see Ernu et al., 2008.
25 Stefan Both, "'Pașaport pentru Germania', cum a vândut Ceaușescu ca la piață un sfert de milion de cetățeni ai României," *Adevărul*, 15 February 2014, http://adevarul.ro/locale/timisoara/title-1_52ff3b56c7b855ff565c3eae/index.html (accessed 25 May 2018); Stefan Both, "Cum au ajuns evreii și germanii 'marfă' de export în România comunistă. Sute de milioane de dolari, profitul regimului," *Adevărul*, 12 July 2016, http://adevarul.ro/locale/timisoara/cum-ajuns-evreii-germanii-marfaf-export-romania-comunista-sute-milioane-dolari-profitul-regimului-1_5783d6455ab6550cb8c38a3e/index.html (accessed 25 May 2018); Alex Nedea, "Români vânduți ca pe vite," *Jurnalul*, 15 March 2016, http://adevarul.ro/locale/timisoara/cum-ajuns-evreii-germanii-marfaf-export-romania-comunista-sute-milioane-dolari-profitul-regimului-1_5783d6455ab6550cb8c38a3e/index.html (accessed 25 May 2018).
26 Ion Iliescu, "Ich bitte die Deutschen: Bleibt bei uns in Rumänien," interview by Walter H. Rueb, *Die Welt*, 8 January 1990.
27 Petre Sălcudeanu, "Fir-ar să fie . . . de vis," *Adevărul*, 9 September 1990. Sălcudeanu would also be appointed minister of Culture, occupying the position for a short period of time in 1993.
28 See for example the recent book by Ruxandra Hurezean (2016), whose title translates as "The History of Saxons from Transylvania. As Told by Themselves". Nonetheless, two out of the twelve chapters focus on Banat Swabians.
29 Petre Sălcudeanu, "Migranții din Carpații Bavarezi," *Adevărul*, 1 February 1991.
30 Thomas Nägler, "Etnici germani care pleacă sau revin în țară," interview by Ion Marin, *Adevărul*, 23 May 1990.
31 Ibid.
32 Dumitru Bujdoiu, "De ce mai pleacă sașii?" *România liberă*, 5 December 1990.
33 Voicu Bugariu, "Întristătorul exod," *Formula As* 28(16), May 1992.
34 Rohtraut Wittstock, "Rădăcinile mele spirituale sînt în acest spațiu," interview by Dieter Werner, *Formula As* 28, May 1992.
35 Adolf Armbruster, "Sașii nu se mai întorc niciodată deși au vrut din tot sufletul să facă treabă aici," interview by Claudiu Ionescu, *Formula As* 235, 28 October 1996.
36 Iulian Ignat, "Avem și noi nemții noștri: Hanno Höfer," *Formula As* 296, 26 January 1998; Iulian Ignat, "Cine îl oprește pe Hanno Hofer?" *Formula As* 347, 1 February 1999; Hanno Höfer, "Mi-ar părea rău dacă ar trebui să plec acum în Germania," interview by Corina Pavel, *Formula As* 398, 31 January 2000; Hanno Höfer, "Nu am nici un regret că am rămas aici. Fac ceea ce-mi place și trăiesc din asta," interview by

"They who have no Germans, should buy some" 133

Iulian Ignat, *Formula As*, 9 December 2002; Corina Pavel, "Neamțul care a uitat să mai plece. Hanno Höfer," *Formula As* 829, 19 July 2008.
37 Eginald Schlattner, "În 1200, când la Berlin orăcăiau broaștele, biserica din Roșia avea cor în limba latină," interview by Sorin Preda, *Formula As* 375, 16 August 1999; Eginald Schlattner, "Țin la această țară și știu că Dumnezeu mă vrea aici. Aici mă cunoaște Dumnezeu după nume," interview by Ion Longin Popescu, *Formula As* 668, 23 May 2005; Eginald Schlattner, "Românilor le lipsește mândria de-a fi români," interview by Sorin Preda, *Formula As* 470, 25 June 2001.
38 Klaus Iohannis, "Vrem să facem din Sibiu ceea ce-a fost cândva. Un oraș european, un avanpost al integrării în Uniunea Europeană," interview by Ion Longin Popescu, *Formula As* 431, 18 September 2000; Klaus Iohannis, "Prea mulți politicieni români sunt simpli figuranți. Ei excelează prin a povesti problemele, nu prin a le rezolva," interview by Ion Longin Popescu, *Formula As* 641, 8 November 2004; Klaus Iohannis, "La o Țară Europeană se cuvine și o Capitală Europeană," interview by Ion Longin Popescu, *Formula As* 749, 25 December 2006.
39 Schlattner, "Românilor le lipsește mândria".
40 Schlattner, "Țin la această țară."
41 In the already mentioned documentary about Klaus Iohannis, *2 pentru România*, Emil Hurezeanu – then journalist, currently Romanian ambassador to Berlin – emphasizes the anteriority of Sibiu with respect to Berlin.
42 Schlattner, "Țin la această țară."
43 Iohannis, "Vrem să facem din Sibiu."
44 Klaus Iohannis, "La o Țară Europeană."
45 Gerlinde Gabler-Braun, "Sașii pleacă, nemții vin," interview by Beatrice Ungar, *Formula As* 257, 7 April 1997.
46 Beatrice Ungar, "Pași ai speranței în Transilvania," *Formula As* 300, 1 June 1998.
47 Michael Lienerth, "Un om credincios nu părăsește țara în care l-a așezat Dumnezeu," interview by Beatrice Ungar, *Formula As* 261, 12 May 1997.
48 Bogdan Lupescu, "Extemporal cu grâu în câmpia Sătmarului," *Formula As* 471, 2 July 2001.
49 Hermann Spack, "În copilărie, la Sibiu mi se zicea 'hitleristul'; mai târziu, în Germania, toată lumea îmi zicea 'românul'," interview by Ion Longin Popescu, *Formula As* 505, 4 March 2002.
50 Iohannis, "Vrem să facem din Sibiu."
51 Ion Longin Popescu, "România e țara noastră," *Formula As* 808, 25 February 2008.
52 Mihai Creangă, "La Amnaș, cele mai tinere sunt suspinele," *România liberă*, 18 September 1991; Ciprian Chirvasiu and Dumitru Manolache, "Cetăți care mor în picioare," *România liberă*, 1 September 1993.
53 Carmen Chihaia, "Cetatea Hărman este asediată azi de nepăsare și ruină," *Adevărul*, 15 February 1997; Vasile Șelaru, "O localitate săsească fără sași," *România liberă*, 5 March 1997.
54 Adrian Cercelescu, "Sărăcia se întinde ca o epidemie," *Adevărul*, 21 June 1999.
55 For Sibiu as a city threatened by ruin, see Adriana Vela, "1500 de imobile stau să cadă în capul locatarilor," *Adevărul*, 16 May 1996; Carmen Chihaia, "În Cetatea Sibiului, casele se prăbușesc peste oameni," *Adevărul*, 12 June 1997; Adriana Vela, "195 de clădiri monument istoric din Sibiu – în pericol de prăbușire," *Adevărul*, 6 April 1998; Camelia Popa, "Cetatea Sibiului stă gata să se surpe," *România liberă*, 20 March 1997; for the representation of Sibiu as a success story, see, for example, the articles in *Dilema Veche* 205, 20 January 2008, and also Silvia Kerim, "Astă vară la Sibiu," *Formula As* 684, 19 September 2005. Kerim's article calls Sibiu "The Occident from the gates of the Orient".
56 Sânziana Pop, "Sașii din Ardeal," *Formula As* 388, 15 November 1999; Sorin Preda, "Sașii din Roșia se pregătesc pentru Rai," *Formula As* 374, 9 August 1999.

57 Schlattner, "În 1200".
58 Sorin Preda, "Șvabii noștri cei de toate zilele," *Formula As* 685, 26 September 2005.
59 Dan Tapalagă, "Satul cu blazon," *Formula As* 738, 9 October 2006.
60 Caroline Fernolend, "Prințul Charles a spus că satul nostru e cel mai frumos din lume și nu înțelege de ce ne trebuie 'Dracula Park'," interview by Ion Longin Popescu, *Formula As* 519, 10 June 2002; Tapalagă, "Satul cu blazon".
61 Adrian Popescu, "Viscri – satul care s-a scos din foame cu 'ora de șosete'," *Adevărul*, 5 October 2004.
62 Loredana Voiculescu, "Un sas și-a făcut fermă de reni în Sibiu," *Gândul*, 28 April 2006.
63 Beatrice Ungar, "Micul paradis de la Hărman," *Formula As* 521, 24 June 2002.
64 Valentin Iacob, "Cetatea care nu vrea să moară," *Formula As* 633, 13 September 2004.
65 Caterina Nicolae, "Al doilea descălecat al pemilor," *Gândul*, 12 October 2005.
66 Virgil Lazăr, "Se reîntorc germanii?" *Satul. Supliment săptămânal de agricultură al ziarului România liberă*, 26 May 1998.
67 A. C. (Adrian Cioroianu), "Argument," *Dilema* 334, 2 July 1999.
68 Morar's text is about Saxons and about Saxon-Romanian interactions, yet the "they" in the question also refers to Jews and Greeks. Nonetheless, his answer focuses on Saxons.

7 "The rich villages around Sibiu and Braşov have been invaded by the Gypsy migration"

7.1. Romanian German heritage as European heritage

To what exactly can the "valuable and unmistakable contribution" of Romanian Germans onto Romanian society be attributed? A recent short text on "the influence of German and Germanophone models on Romanians", written by historian Ioan-Aurel Pop (2016), rector of the Babeș-Bolyai University in Cluj-Napoca since 2012 and president of the Romanian Academy since 2018, captures the main positive features associated with German influence on Romanian society. The text illustrates the interpretation of the history of German-Romanian entanglements in Transylvania and Banat (and beyond) as a history of unmistakably Europeanizing and Occidentalizing (hence positive) contributions brought by Germans to Romanians. It starts with the indication that, geographically, Romanians "lie at equal distance to the extreme eastern and western points of the Continent", which means that they combine in their natures "western and eastern aspects alike" (Pop, 2016, 151). This suggests a rejection of an essentially Eastern European Romanian identity. The claim Pop makes instead is that both Western and Eastern influences play a role in Romanian identity, but mainly the former rather than the latter needs to be nurtured and supported. The liminality identified by Todorova in her work on the imagination of the Balkans is unmistakably at work in Pop's argument.

Specifically, the Western influences are traceable to the Saxons, whose name Pop erroneously regards as showing "one of their places of origin, Saxony" (Pop, 2016, 153).[1] As a consequence of Saxon colonization, "Romanians, just like the other inhabitants of Transylvania" learned the meaning of urban civilization, advanced agricultural methods, how to build houses and sewage systems and how to clean streets and homes (Pop, 2016, 153). Moreover, Saxon settlement in Transylvania was but the first "impulse coming from the German world", to be followed first by the modernization of Transylvania during the Renaissance and the Reformation, whose bearers were yet again, in part at least, Germans, and second by the imposition of Habsburg rule on Transylvania. The latter brought with it the Union with Rome of a part of the Orthodox Church and the colonization of Swabians, who were also "carriers of values belonging to Western civilization" (Pop, 2016, 153–155). Pop's short account aims to emphasize Transylvania's and Romania's "European vocation", a vocation made possible due to German influence (Pop, 2016, 159). Like almost any discourse about the past, its stakes are rather in the here and now. Subsequently, this European vocation of Romania is further emphasized in the last chapter of the book dedicated to Transylvania, in which Pop makes a plea for Romania to follow the "magisterial path of the Occident" (Pop, 2016, 298). He stresses once again that Romanians are not Eastern Europeans or not only Eastern Europeans, since they are situated in between East and West. At the same time, his narrative establishing a direct correlation between the German historical presence in the western regions of contemporary Romania and Romania's European vocation comes together with the discursive representation of a symbolically hierarchical relationship between German colonists and the other ethnicities in Transylvania, as well as in the other regions where the effects of German colonization are similarly construed.

Thus, the fundamental German contribution in Transylvania and, by extension, in Romania is that of having brought European and Occidental civilization to Romanians. It is directly related to the creation of potential for the assertion of a Romanian European identity. Against this background, German cultural heritage in Transylvania (but also in Banat and elsewhere) plays the role of the physical, stone-carved trace of this Western-oriented European identity. Consider, for example, an article published in 2009 in the cultural weekly *Dilema veche*, on the Transylvanian Saxon fortified churches that are officially recognized as United Nations Educational, Scientific and Cultural Organization (UNESCO) world heritage sites. Its author is Emil Hurezeanu, Romanian ambassador to Berlin since 2015. Hurezeanu draws symbolic parallels between the *Burgkirchen* in Transylvania and Moorish palaces in places such as Granada, Seville or Cordoba. Just as the latter allegedly represent the "indelible mark" of the Orient on the Occident, the Saxon fortified churches in Transylvania, according to Hurezeanu, stand for Western influence in the East. Their presence acts as a marker of the Europeanness of the territory in which they were erected. In his article, Hurezeanu also quotes a supposed statement by French poet Paul Valéry, namely that Europe ends where one finds the last (i.e. the most Eastern) Gothic churches:

> The last Gothic churches were built by Saxons, between Sibiu and Brașov, in Southern Transylvania, at the beginning of the Middle Ages. If you come from Hamburg and Vienna, Sibiu and Brașov mark the end of Europe. If you come from the warm seas and still wear on your cloak the dust of the Silk Road, the Gothic naves of the Transylvanian Saxons are the first true blazon of the old Europe.[2]

The equation of Europeanness with Gothic architecture and the reference to "the old Europe" make evident the interpretative horizon and the representational apparatus in which the emphasis on the Europeanness of Saxon identity is situated. Saxon cultural heritage is seen as bestowing a European identity on Transylvania. However, connecting the spread of Christian Gothic architecture with the delineation of symbolic and physical boundaries of Europeanness is rather more reminiscent of conservative German understandings of the Occident and of the West than of Valéry's cultural references. In this context, it is also worth mentioning that out of the seven Romanian sites inscribed in the UNESCO Cultural World Heritage database, two are considered "Transylvanian Saxon" ones, namely a complex of seven Lutheran fortified churches (Biertan/Birthälm/Berethalom, Câlnic/Kelling/Kelnek, Prejmer/Tartlau/Prázsmár, Viscri/Deutschweißkirch/Szászfehéregyháza, Dârjiu/Ders/Székelyderzs, Saschiz/Keisd/Szászkézd, Valea Viilor/Wurmloch/Nagybaromlak) and the medieval city center of Sighișoara (Schäßburg/Segesvár). The fact that the fortified church of Dârjiu is actually a Unitarian, Szekler church is rarely mentioned.

Cultural heritage discourses are tightly linked to the assertion of identities. Connecting the German cultural heritage in Romania with the postulation of a European identity makes clear that what is at stake is the issue of cultural and political belonging. The policies of Ceaușescu's nationalistic regime partly aimed toward the "razing of Romania's past", although this phenomenon was paradoxically accompanied by an increasing emphasis on an imagined glorious past, in line with Ceaușescu's nationalist orientation (Giurescu, 1990). At the same time, Saxon heritage in Transylvania in particular was apt to be instrumentalized because it could provide relatively easy access to a symbolic European premodern identity. There are not too many material traces from the period that can be ascribed to ethnic Romanians (Bergel, 1976). Such instrumentalizations attempted to appropriate German cultural heritage while writing off its German character. In this context, the fact that a fiercely nationalist politician such as Corneliu Vadim Tudor chose to place on the back cover of one of his books an illustration of what can easily be taken to be a Transylvanian Saxon fortified church indicates the symbolic value of "German" cultural heritage in Western Romania (particularly Saxon heritage in Transylvania). The book in question is titled *Jurnal de vacanță* (Holiday Diary). Therein, Tudor rhetorically asks who "gave" the Black Church in Brașov to the Saxons, arguing that beyond its religious cult characteristics, "the Black Church is a component of Romanian National Patrimony, an important point of reference for Romania" (Tudor, 1996, 135–136).

At the same time, another relevant line of argumentation particularly emphasizes the German and hence European character of cultural heritage in Transylvania and Banat. The state of this cultural heritage is then used to make a case on behalf of Europeanness, either as something that is increasingly lost or as something that can and should be maintained, preserved or saved. Skimming through post-1989 Romanian press, one comes across news articles and opinion pieces addressing German cultural heritage in Transylvania and Banat, often placing it in direct relationship with a European identity. For example, an article published in *România liberă* on 3 October 1990 – the day of German reunification – and signed by theater director Sorana Coroamă Stanca argued for the preservation of German monuments and houses in Romania, directly linking the value of such efforts to the buildings' Europeanness and to their spiritual dimension: "We live in the year 1990. In Europe. We can let neither our towns, nor our monuments, our villages or our souls go to waste".[3] The use of the possessive determiner "our" suggests a Romanian appropriation of things German, but this appropriation is different in both degree and kind to the one by Corneliu Vadim Tudor, referred to above. It is a symbolic appropriation based on the wishful imagination of a Romanian-German compatibility, whereas Tudor's assertion – following in the footsteps of Ceauşescu's brand of nationalism – was rather an attempt to erase the Germanness and Romanianize (assimilate) Saxon heritage. Coroamă Stanca's article deplores the depopulation of German localities due to the migration of Germans from Romania. In the aftermath of the fall of state socialism, the desolate condition of German monuments in Romania's western regions was interpreted as evidence of the decoupling from Europe that state socialism had allegedly represented and achieved. The German legacy thus becomes something bequeathed to Romanians, something that Romanians ought to take care of because this Germanness is also a marker of Europeanness.

Other articles from the early 1990s that address issues related to cultural heritage in Transylvania try to reconcile the emphasis on supposed Romanian anteriority and the indication that medieval heritage is particularly a Saxon one. What is nonetheless clear in such accounts is the lamentable condition of the heritage and the fact that it was in need of being salvaged.[4] Impassioned pieces pleading for the salvation of this heritage could easily be framed in an Orientalizing logic: "It has become a cliché to say that Romania has, through God's blessing, ten Switzerlands. It is however true that, since December 1989, we have had here ten Beiruts".[5]

Starting roughly at the second half of the 1990s, a significant growth in the interest for Romanian German (first and foremost, Transylvanian Saxon) cultural heritage has become visible. The actors involved in associated processes of preservation have been both from within the community, namely the German Forum in Romania, Transylvanian Saxons living in Germany and the Transylvanian Saxon Foundation, and from outside of it, namely the Romanian authorities, the German state through GTZ – Deutsche Gesellschaft für Technische Zusammenarbeit (German Society for Technical Cooperation) – and the Mihai Eminescu Trust, based in the United Kingdom and whose patron is the Prince of Wales. The high profile acquired by issues related to Transylvanian Saxon heritage has been visible, for example, in the debates surrounding the potential construction of a Dracula-themed park in the close vicinity of Sighişoara or in the cultural processes related to Sibiu's selection as European Capital of Culture in 2007 (Câmpeanu, 2008; Grama, 2010; Oanca, 2010; Stroe, 2011b). In both situations, the Germanness of the cultural heritage of the locality played a key role in debates and in the respective cultural politics despite the small percentage of ethnic Germans now living in both Sighişoara and Sibiu.

In the early 2000s, the plan of Tourism minister Dan Matei Agathon to build a huge amusement park – Dracula Park – close to Sighişoara, elicited a stubborn opposition that unfolded mainly in the pages of the daily newspaper *România liberă*.[6] The Prince of Wales himself also joined the plethora of national and international protests against the creation of the park and for the preservation of Sighişoara's medieval heritage. He personally intervened and apparently managed to contribute to halting the project, his argumentation relying mainly on visions of sustainable tourism and on an emphasis on the significance of Saxon cultural heritage for the region. The interventions of the Prince of Wales, together with the involvement of other European institutions and authorities – from Germany and Luxembourg, for example – show the symbolic Europeanization of the issue of Transylvanian Saxon heritage, a topic much embraced by the Romanian press. Prince Charles has also become patron of Mihai Eminescu Trust, one of the main foundations lobbying and acting for the preservation of Transylvanian cultural heritage, Saxon included. His representation of a Europe deeply in touch with its rural, traditional roots, found a perfect object of interest in Transylvanian Saxon culture and heritage. His lobbying on behalf of the region surrounding Sibiu was based on the fact that this is an "unaltered corner of Europe", an expression also taken up in Romanian mass media.[7] The author of an article in *Formula As* even expressed hopes that Charles's advocacy for the preservation of Transylvanian Saxon villages would entail a return of Transylvanian Saxons to their former homeland.[8]

Looking in depth at the case of Sighișoara, anthropologist Claudia Câmpeanu (2008, 8) noticed the "hopeful fixation on German heritage" that underlay the debates on the project. In 2001, the medieval town of Sighișoara was the site of strife and contestation as central authorities in Bucharest, supported by local authorities, endorsed the construction of the Dracula-themed park, which would have fundamentally changed the landscape of the area. German cultural and architectural heritage were at risk of being blemished by the long-term consequences of the potential investment, and this led to overt conflicts between the German community in Romania, the Lutheran Church and Transylvanian Saxons in Germany on the one hand and the Romanian authorities on the other hand. However, it is also worth noting that the "German card" was played in various ways, not only by the opponents of the project but initially also by its staunchest supporters, as Câmpeanu showed. Her observations on this phenomenon deserve to be quoted in extenso:

> The German mentions were in part preemptive, if misguided, gestures of goodwill toward the local and diasporic German communities, signaling to them that they had been included in the project and that the project was designed with *them* in mind. But, what this German innuendo was mainly doing, I would argue, was sketching and accessing an imaginary – let's call it modern or developmental – where Romanian hopes for a Western future and a Western prosperity have been settling for decades. Agathon's [minister of Tourism at the time] rendering of the project – and it wasn't just his personal vision – was brushing against German tips of this landscape of desire and hope: the German work ethic, seriousness and success, German prosperity and its promise of sharing and spilling over into our needy pockets. The German referent was probably one of the most credible and well contoured of the many invoked by this imaginary, thanks to the lingering memory of all the émigrés and the streams of packages flowing back into the country before 1989. Germany had been a concrete, real sign of the West, a credible proof of its existence and success, but a sign nevertheless, and a sign of remote reality,

at that. Agathon made the mistake of trying to do more than to reference it; he tried to make it material, to promise its perfect replication through a hyperbolic project that would bring to Sighișoara – he declared – a million tourists a year, would eventually create 6000 local jobs, and would total 18 million Euros worth of direct investments and 20 million Euros in indirect investments. A project made for Germans and by Germans, after a German model, would not fail. This was what we all had been waiting for.

(Câmpeanu, 2008, 65–66)

Thus, the imaginary underlying the debates regarding the future of Sighișoara largely revolved around the discursive construction of the town in multiple and contradictory ways, by both opponents and supporters of the project, "as a German one" (Câmpeanu, 2008, 97). Eventually, the winners of the conflict were the opponents of the project.

The transformative trajectory proving the high profile acquired by German cultural heritage in Transylvania is extremely relevant, because it shows that the case of Sibiu, whose post-2000 (re-)branding has also emphasized its German (Saxon) character is not necessarily one sui generis, although one should not hasten toward making overly sweeping generalizations. Almost two decades ago, geographers Joseph J. Gallagher and Philip N. J. Tucker (2000, 309) looked at the case of Brașov, concluding that despite the absence of the German minority, its traces "in the cultural landscape show every sign of lasting far longer than the community itself". The preservation and consolidation of more than one Transylvanian village emphasize their former Saxonness, thus sometimes clashing with the present needs of the inhabitants of those villages, usually Romanians and Roma (Hughes, Hughes & Koranyi, 2010; Hughes, 2011). In Viscri, the village where the Mihai Eminescu Trust is particularly active, the focus is on "Saxons' culture as heritage", since it is "considered the most authentic, worthy of preservation and attractive for tourists". Hence, "although Saxons are numerically scarce nowadays, their culture still shapes the tourist image of the village", a process that "overshadows the heritage belonging to Romanians and Roma" (Corsale & Iorio, 2014, 22–23).

Sibiu definitely constitutes a peak of German cultural branding in Transylvania, as its post-2000 development and identity-building have played the "Saxon heritage card" to a huge extent. The cultural policies preceding the title of European Capital of Culture, acquired in 2007 (together with Luxembourg), and the ECC events themselves indicate the symbolic re-Germanization of the town. The European Capital of Culture program is largely about identity and about the self-representation of cities before a national, as well as a broader, European audience. The story of Sibiu unexpectedly and rather suddenly becoming European Capital of Culture has already been told, and emphasis has been placed on the almost fortuitous character of this rise to cultural preeminence by means of the ECC program. Luxembourg was supposed to be the only European cultural capital in 2007 until the Luxembourgeois authorities decided to co-opt the town of Sibiu, resorting in their bid to the presumed "myth of common origins", according to which the ancestors of Saxons came to Transylvania from what is nowadays Luxembourg (Oanca, 2010; Vasiliu & Dragoman, 2008). In Romania, the result was particularly welcomed because it took place at the same time as Romania's accession to the EU. Romania was politically and symbolically rejoining the European family. Emblematically, the German lineage of the town was spelled out. Sibiu – ECC 2007 stood under the aegis of a rediscovered Saxonness, which also established a symbolic hierarchy within the urban fabric, as the great winners of the disputes surrounding what to represent and how to represent it were mostly Saxon institutions, for example the Brukenthal Museum or the Lutheran Church. At the other end of an imaginary scale stood institutions such as the Romanian Astra Museum, dedicated to Romanian rural life. Despite an apparent discursive emphasis on multiculturalism understood as a European value, Sibiu – ECC 2007 made visible first and foremost Saxon traditions and Saxon heritage (Iancu, 2007, 80; Stroe, 2011b).

In the buildup for Sibiu – ECC 2007, through the already mentioned GTZ, the German state partially supported the restoration of buildings in the city center; this was done by means of a "heritage-as-practice" approach, as historian Emanuela Grama called it, which also aimed at teaching the residents of the city center, mostly Romanians and Roma, to "be" Saxons – that is, to appropriate a set of behaviors and practices deemed to appertain to the Saxon community (Grama, 2010, 315–326). The Sibiu case is not the only one in which Germanness ends up being preserved and performed by non-Germans. In Viscri, the Romanians and the Roma "are expected to become the custodians of Saxons' heritage" and to act in such a way as "to preserve and exploit this valuable heritage in the best way" (Corsale & Iorio, 2014, 27). At the same time, this process "is being produced by and for literate people of the West" (Klimaszewski et al., 2010, 99). Anthropologist Bianca Botea (2008, 231) analyzed the case of Jimbolia (Hatzfeld in German, Zsombolya in Hungarian, Žombolj in Serbo-Croatian) in Banat and noted that on the occasion of the *Kirchweih* festivities, a traditional Swabian yearly celebration, the children performing the various dances are actually Romanian.[9]

The relevance of such phenomena can be better understood if they are combined with sociologist Paul Connerton's theoretical observations on memory and its place in social life. Connerton (1989) noted the relationship between memory, legitimacy and hierarchies of power, showing how social memory is formed and disseminated through social practices and behaviors. The emphasis on German heritage and on German social practices, typical for Sibiu and for other localities formerly inhabited by Transylvanian Saxons or Banat Swabians, is indeed telling not only of the high prestige of Germanness these disseminate but also of the integration, in many cases, of the German past into Romanian social memory. Furthermore, reproducing Germanness and integrating Germanness in social memory practices, in a context in which vanishingly few Germans still actually live, therefore acts as a useful symbolic Europeanizing resource in the Romanian political and cultural environment (see also Batt, 2002; Koranyi, 2011). This also implies that the German past, in an idealized form, gains precedence over the current needs of the (mostly non-German) population, whose potential economic development is conditioned by embracing particular heritage discourses, which effectively reproduce various ethnic and social hierarchies.

The concrete process of the heritagization of Transylvanian villages by emphasizing the Saxon past to the detriment of the largely non-Saxon present in order to attract tourists is accompanied by a "narrative colonization process", which transforms Saxon villages into a "bucolic medieval landscape", something similar to a "pre-industrial Saxon Arcadia" (Stroe, 2017, 24; see also Corsale & Iorio, 2014, 28; Koranyi, 2011). Hence, the reconstruction of a German past in Transylvania is to a certain extent part of a process of reinvention of rural Europe, whose particular expression is that of the nostalgia for an idyllic past meeting contemporary discourses and practices of environmentally friendly, sustainable development. "The last refuge of rural Europe" (Corsale & Iorio, 2014, 29) is then offered to the world under the guise of authentic Saxonnness, which is actually reinvented for the sake of a specific touristic market.

7.2. Antagonistic representations of Germans and the Roma

As it has already transpired on different occasions throughout this book, discourses about Germans in Romania both implicitly and explicitly refer to some of the other ethnic and national minorities living in Romania. Counterposing the representations of Romanian Germans in post-1989 Romania with those regarding other ethnicities can be particularly useful in unraveling the deeper meanings of these discourses. In this context, particularly a closer look at the positive representations of Germanness in opposition to the representations of the Roma population in Romania can allow for a better understanding of the meaning of the former, of what they stand for and of the ideational horizon in which they are situated.

România liberă dedicated, in its issue published on 3 October 1990, a *fotoreportaj* (photo-reportage, in effect a one-page-long article accompanied by several photos) to the Germans in Romania, called in a poignant and rather novel manner "Românii-germani" (the German Romanians).[10] The emphasis in the title is placed on *românii*, the articled noun, a rather rarely used way of discursively appropriating/Romanianizing the Germans in Romania, of discursively making evident the representation of an idealized German-Romanian compatibility. The text signed by Sorana Coroamă Stanca, to whom I have already referred to in the previous section, is heavily informed by a nostalgia for the German past in Transylvania, presented in opposition to a much bleaker present. It illustrates the various identity and representational issues concerning Romanians and their relationship with Germans, Germany and Europe while also indicating the link between these issues and the relationship of Romanians with the Roma. The article was elicited by German reunification. Publishing on this occasion a reportage on the Germans in Romania indicates not only the acknowledgment of the "Germanness" of Transylvanian Saxons, Banat Swabians and so on but also the recognition of the role of the Federal Republic of Germany as a kin state with respect to these ethnic groups. In effect, the vision of a Pan-German nation informs the tone of the article. At the very beginning of the text, Coroamă Stanca, a reputed theater director, referred in a highly commending manner to the "Saxons, Swabians, Austrians and other Germanic communities". Several German-related ethnic referents are discursively coalesced. For Coroamă Stanca, Saxons, Swabians, Austrians, Germans and "other Germanic communities" share a Germanness whose characteristics are "national genius, untiring work, the spirit of order and administration, the exemplary cohabitation with Romanians, whose language they know and they speak perfectly, with no foreign accent". The reference to the flawless knowledge and use of Romanian – that one sometimes comes across in discourses on Romanian Germans – reinforces the representation of a particular German-Romanian compatibility. It can also function as an implicit allusion to other ethnic groups in Romania, particularly Hungarians. Discourses about the latter that emphasize that they do not speak proper Romanian and that they do not want to integrate in Romanian society are common.

Deploring the fact that the only ethnic Germans who remain in the country are elderly people, author Sorina Coroamă Stanca regretted both the economic and the spiritual losses linked to the migration of Germans from Romania. Furthermore, she expressed a particular distress with respect to the demographic changes occurring as a consequence of this migration, writing about an "unwanted population exchange" that was taking place. The picture she described has the features of an anarchic apocalypse: in the "long alleys of the beautiful villages of yore", there are now "gadders-about" who "devastate, destroy, steal gates, windows, doors, walls even". Alas, some of them, "dirty and filthy" even took refuge there. Coroamă Stanca made no explicit reference to the ethnic identity of these unwanted newcomers. However, one of the photos accompanying her text showed a woman dressed in traditional Roma clothing. The photo was rhetorically titled "The future ethnics of Hărman?", providing thus an easy visual interpretative key for the readers of *România liberă*. The other photos accompanying the text were visual illustrations of the desolate and dilapidated state of villages left by their inhabitants, showing old people, abandoned houses and cemeteries, all standing as proof of the secular history of the village.

In her article, Coroamă Stanca also touched on another aspect that would become a recurrent theme within the representation of Romania's relationship with Western Europe: Romanian migration. She argued that Romanian Germans should act as mediators between Romania and Germany in order to build a common and honest future, opposing this to the putative invasion of Germany by "swindlers and beggars" from Romania. Following the fall of communism, representations of a Romanian migration to Western Europe consisting of thieves, crooks, beggars, prostitutes, petty criminals and mafia groups have been widespread, both in Romania and abroad. The imposition in the 1990s of a visa regime for Romanian citizens by Western European countries was presented and understood as a direct consequence of this phenomenon. Furthermore, within Romania, this has been frequently represented as a Roma migration, thus allowing for the expression of racist views about the Roma population. Such discourses implicitly and explicitly excluded the Roma from the Romanian nation, transforming them into the scapegoats for Romania being symbolically and politically rejected by

Europe. Opposing the "swindlers and beggars" allegedly invading Germany to the Romanian Germans who could act as our "easiest way towards Germany" anticipates the tensions and frictions contained within contradictory representations of Romanian migration to Western Europe: the representation of a migration of the scum and of the wretched, creating a negative image of Romania in the eyes of the West, versus the representation of a Romanian diaspora culturally and politically connected to Europe and to the West, having the proper European mentality and that could hence act as a bridge between Romania and Europe, as agent of change and of development. Representations of Romanian Germans and of Romanian German migration to the Federal Republic of Germany tie in well with this latter image, whose classist features are transparent.

Coroamă Stanca stated the following toward the end of her text: "Let's greet the arising of the new Germany, peaceful, democratic, factor of equilibrium, balance between East and West".[11] She then finished: "And, may it be that Romania, placed by History at the gates of this East, remains the much beloved country, heavily defended, belonging to all its populations".[12] The careful reader of Coroamă Stanca's article would have difficulties understanding whether in the author's view Romania belongs to the East or to the West. If Germany is to act as a balance between East and West, it can be inferred that Romania is placed on the Eastern side of this balance, but if Romania lies at the gates of the East, the question regarding the boundaries of East and West becomes rather fuzzy. This fuzziness is reminiscent of what Maria Todorova ([1997] 2009) called "liminality", the being in-between that is specific of identification discourses prevailing in countries in Eastern Europe. Nonetheless, one thing is clear: Germany's Europeanness is not debatable, whereas Romania's belonging to Europe is something to be questioned, the presence of the Roma (albeit never actually named!) being linked with such questions of belonging. The last sentence in the article, according to which Romania lies "at the gates of this East" and hence should be "heavily defended", suggests that Romania's Europeanness has not been assured and is not a given but rather is something that must be fought for in order to be attained. The presence of "our Germans" could have actively contributed to pushing away the doubts about Romania's Europeanness, hence the sadness associated with their leaving the country, since this is bound to lead to interrogating this much-desired Europeanness.

The last sentences in Coromă Stanca's article are telling of the underlying tension regarding Romania's cultural and political belonging between East and West and of the Europeanizing aspirations that can be fulfilled by means of a better relationship with Germany. This relationship can be mediated by "our Germans". The subtle references about the Roma replacing the Germans also indicate the distance that is considered to separate Germans and Roma. Such references have been and continue to be extremely common in Romania. Imagining Romania as symbolically situated between East and West, between Orient and Occident, ties in with the representation of Romanians being caught between Roma and Germans. The departure of the latter makes way for the former, a process in effect construed as bringing Romanians themselves closer to the uncivilized and backward Orient. The all-encompassing final line might suggest more openness toward the Roma population, as one among several of Romania's "populations". Nonetheless, the image of the "heavily defended" country invites the reader to draw connections with the history of the Saxon presence in Transylvania, because one of the goals of Saxon medieval settlement was actually a defensive one. Connecting this with the considerations about the "unwanted population exchange" taking place in Germany, with those about the "swindlers and beggars" invading Germany and with the rhetorical question accompanying the future presence of Roma in Transylvanian villages indicates in effect how Coroamă Stanca was on the one hand ready to see Germans as compatible with Romania and with Romanian identity (or with a wishful representation of Romanian identity) and on the other hand also very much disposed to reject the Roma.

Largely similar representations of the Roma population, emphasizing the Roma-German opposition structured by means of a variety of Orientalist dichotomies, have also been disseminated in Romanian German publications. For example, at the end of 1990 and beginning of 1991, furious letters of Romanian Germans were published in *Hermannstädter Zeitung*, a Sibiu daily newspaper published in German, in connection with the screening on German state television (ARD) of a documentary about the Roma in Romania. The documentary also interviewed two Transylvanian Saxons: Annemarie Weber, a journalist, and Horst Weber, president of the German Democratic Forum in Transylvania. The positions of the two, who, by their own account, aimed to speak "prejudice-free" about "Gypsies", were met with stupor and rejection by the readers of *Hermannstädter Zeitung*.[13] Weber and Weber argued, for example, that the black market trade in which Roma were involved during socialist rule allowed people living in Romania to have a taste of "freedom" and of the "society of consumption" in the form of "jeans, sneakers, video recorders, cosmetics, books and newspapers".[14] Thus, according to them, the Roma had furnished to a certain extent the same type of products that relatives of Romanian Germans in West Germany had also been providing in the same period. Furthermore, the two emphasized that in the economic situation during austerity-ridden communist Romania, Romanian Germans had also been doing illegalities and had been involved in the black market. Against this background, the two Transylvanian Saxon intellectuals criticized the transformation of the Roma into the scapegoat for all evils in Romanian society. Moreover, in addressing the issue of stealing and theft, Weber and Weber drew a comparison that was bound to be extremely negatively received by the Romanian German audience of the documentary:

> What did our parents do in Russia? Whenever possible, they trawled around the farmsteads and, next to the egg they begged for, they immediately also hid the hen under their coats. Misery knows no morality! Whoever lives in the lager or in the ghetto, whoever is excluded by society – and Gypsies are excluded by society – flouts its rules.[15]

Such opinions (also further qualified in the context of the debate that then unfolded in the pages of *Hermannstädter Zeitung*) aroused emotional and outraged answers from readers who felt the need to take a stance. In one such letter, one offended author, purporting to speak "on behalf of a group of Romanian Germans", asked about the Roma: "Didn't you have often enough the chance to realize that they are a furtive, disinclined to work, dishonest people, and that they engage in shady business?"[16] Another, much lengthier retort was published in the following issue, the author also stating that her opinion was "shared by others".[17] Grete Tischler was much disturbed by the attempt to establish similarities between German deportees in 1945 and the Roma in communist Romania. A former deportee herself, she extensively described her life during the deportation in order to emphasize the trivialization implied by the comparison drawn by Weber and Weber. She then explicitly commented on this comparison:

> I have nothing against Gypsies. They are also humans like us, but they should work. Some indeed do. But why did so many of them go to Germany? Did they simply want to be supported there by the state, i.e. by the people who work? It is understandable that Germans are outraged about this. . . . I was in Germany to visit and I know that one has to work hard and honest for a salary there. Our people have received nothing for free there. They started from scratch, just like we did after our return from Russia.[18]

The representation of Romanian Germans who migrated to Germany, where they started everything from scratch and then simply worked hard in order to successfully build a new life, totally eschews how Romanian Germans could resort to an entire network of administrative support provided by the Federal Republic, which was meant to enable their integration into Germany. In addition, Tischler also referred to the reform of 1945, which brought Roma in the houses of Saxons: "Gypsies came to our houses, they tore open and burned the floor".[19] In a similar vein, the author of another (shorter) letter titled "1990 is not 1945" stated: "Here, Gypsies have tormented us enough, particularly in the years 1945–1948. Should they continue to do this in Germany? Now they 'inherited' the Saxon villages. We will see how these villages will look like in five or ten years".[20]

Counterposing Germans and Roma is strongly linked with the representation of a population exchange, with the houses deserted by Saxons and Swabians being taken over by Roma. The way in which this phenomenon is almost always described in public discourses is heavily infused by anti-Gypsism. The common representation of the civilized and civilizing Germans who left, replaced by the anarchic Roma who quickly manage to undo centuries of civilization, informs representations of the two groups. Rarely, if ever, does one come across any attempt whatsoever to address the underlying social conflicts and antagonisms informing the German-Roma entanglements in Transylvania or Banat in the twentieth and twenty-first century. The culturalization and essentialization of the cleavage between the two groups enables the construction of insurmountable ethnic hierarchies, which also have an important social dimension. Wolfgang Rehner, at the time a young Lutheran pastor in Sibiu, spoke in 1990 about two different mentalities, two mutually incompatible ways of living, and asked rhetorically whether the interviewer saw how a Saxon house looked before and after it was occupied by

Gypsies.[21] Mainstream and hegemonic Romanian and Romanian German representations of Roma otherness seem to overlap. The compatibility that this shared anti-Gypsism suggests should invite toward greater caution with respect to the uncritical embrace of philo-Germanism in Romania.

Philo-German representations paired with anti-Roma representations are constantly reproduced. In post-1989 Romanian media, one finds numerous press accounts reproducing this kind of dichotomy between Germans and Saxons on the one hand and Roma on the other hand. The emphasis on the prosperous Saxon past is opposed to "Gypsy" poverty, whose causes are described as "laziness" or "lack of appetite for work".[22] Before the current hype about Sibiu's rediscovery of its Europeanness, under the guidance of a Transylvanian Saxon mayor, the town was also presented as threatened by a Gypsy takeover. An article published in *România liberă*, in 1996, by Bogdan Burileanu, referred to Sibiu as a potential "transnational capital of Gypsies". It started with a description of the history of Sibiu, acknowledging the Transylvanian Saxon influence on it. Saxons have inhabited and have molded the town, from socioeconomic and cultural points of view. Bewailing the deportations and the communist policies toward Saxons, the author identified the two categories having benefited most from the departure of the latter, namely party activists and Gypsies:

> The houses left by Saxons were immediately occupied, either by the former or by the latter. Slowly, the latter have ended up representing the main ethnic minority, quickly proliferating through the profuse natural growth. Nowadays, there are only some hundreds of Saxons in the whole county, whilst the Gypsies (self-titled Roma) are 17% of the population of the county and 4% of the population of the town.[23]

This was just the beginning of an extremely critical article about various illegalities of Gypsy leaders, who have become the real masters of the town, Burileanu suggested. On other occasions, Timișoara was presented as a "Little Vienna" on its way to becoming "the Gaza Strip", due to the proliferation of Gypsy and Arab buildings in a town known for its Central European architectural style.[24] Roma identity and Occidental identity are seen as incompatible: in an article on Viscri, journalist Adrian Bucurescu noted that "despite the Gypsy demographic pressure, some Occidental Europeans bought or built homes here".[25] He was probably alluding to the two German entrepreneurs who settled down in Viscri and set up a business by means of which the Roma in the locality sold their hand-woven woolen socks in Germany. According to press accounts, this eventually successful story had to overcome the initial distrust of the Roma who replaced the Saxons who had migrated.[26]

Another article published in 1996 in *România liberă* presented a plan to repopulate some Saxon villages. The author started by explaining their current situation in the following terms:

> Until 1989, these villages were inhabited in a proportion of over 60% by Saxons. Immediately after the Revolution, a great part of them left for Germany.

148 *"The rich villages . . . have been invaded by the Gypsy migration"*

> The Saxons who stayed in Transylvania can be counted on the fingers of one hand. The households of those who left have been abandoned. Gypsies stole everything there was to be stolen.[27]

More recently, Ruxandra Hurezean described the transformations taking place in Viscri following the fall of state socialism in similar terms, yet in a subtler tenor:

> In Viscri, after the '90s only the family of Sara the Saxon remained. Then, one by one, new people started to come. Most of them Rroma. They filled the courtyards and settled in the houses of Saxons. Far from the maddening world emerging after the fall of Communism, an entire new world constructed hundreds of years ago, by the first free people of the Empire, was being replaced with another one.
>
> (Hurezean, 2016, 77)

The chaos that the image of the Roma (called *rromi* rather than *romi*, which also draws a symbolic boundary between them and Romanians) filling courtyards and living in Saxon houses conveys is then further reinforced by emphasizing the shame it brings with it, the kind of shame that should be hidden away from the eyes of a European royal such as the future king of England: "In the year when Prince Charles decided he wants to come to Romania, Ion Caramitru, the Romanian minister of Culture, did not let him enter Viscri. Because there were too many Gypsies, he brought him only to Moşna" (Hurezean, 2016, 77). In 2009, in *Deutsches Jahrbuch für Rumänien*, Gheorghe Ciuhandu (2009, 42), at the time mayor of Timişoara, was bluntly asked by the two interviewers: "Is there a risk that the center of Timişoara becomes a Roma quarter?" His answer was just as blunt: "This should not happen, if state authorities do their duty. The mayor's office has been dealing with this since 2000, has started many lawsuits and has informed the relevant authorities about the situation. . . . The mayor's office should be more efficiently supported".

Formula As, the abovementioned rostrum for the dissemination of an extremely positive and nostalgic image of the German communities in Romania, also provides excellent material for illustrating how Germans and Roma are juxtaposed and how anti-Gypsism is often a key component of Romanian philo-Germanism and of Romanian attempts to assert a European identity. In a text emblematic of the apologetic and eulogizing view of Saxonness and Swabianness in Romania, Sânziana Pop, editor in chief of the magazine, wrote:

> In the spirit of socialist equity, the immovable German property was transgressed, and, by state order, the rich villages around Braşov and Sibiu have been invaded by the Gypsy migration that also imposed its models of civilization, lighting the fires under their cauldrons directly with the oaken floors of the centuries-old houses.[28]

Pop counterposed a presumed splendid, German-related past of Transylvania to the post-1945 events, when, in her view, the German civilization model in

Transylvania got destroyed by the communist authorities, which soon led to the mass migration of Germans to the Federal Republic of Germany. The antonymic representation of two ways of life – on the one hand, the steadfast civilization symbolized by centuries-old houses and, on the other hand, the cauldrons used by nomads to prepare their food – is blatant. The order and the discipline embodied by Saxons were replaced by the chaos and the mediocrity brought in by the Gypsies, all in the name of "socialist equity". Thus, an ethnic hierarchization is constructed, with Germans faring best, whereas Roma are quintessentially the last on the civilizational ladder and at the same time capable of physically undoing the acquisitions of German civilization. Ideas of social equality are thrown away to the dustbin of history. For Pop, such ideas contributed to the decay of civilization, since they allowed "German property" to be transgressed by the uncivilized Roma. There is also a particular cynicism and irony in imagining the Roma population, targeted by a project of physical annihilation by both the Romanian and German governments during the Second World War, as being responsible for the physical disappearance of German heritage in Transylvania.

Discursively constructing Roma as illegitimate "migrants" coming to "replace" the Saxons indicates how the processes of exclusion aim to delegitimize their presence in Transylvania (and in Romania in general) despite this presence being also centuries old. In exchange, German migration to Romania is presented in very different terms: it is a migration that putatively took place in the name of freedom, and hence is seen as legitimate. The nostalgia for a past in which Germans were living in the centers of Transylvanian villages and the bemoaning of a present in which Roma have taken their places are nothing but the yearning for the Europe of conservative hierarchies, for the segregation and the invisibility of the Roma and of the poor. In her description of post-1945 realities, Pop limned a derelict picture of suffering, weeds, skeletons, oblivion and stupidity. Nonetheless, Pop's text ended with grounds for optimism, fundamentally connected with the preservation and restoration of cultural heritage: "Go and see Sighișoara! The cheerful, pastel, varnished, sky-blue, rosy colours have been yet again refreshed over the mould and the dampness of the walled city".[29]

Framing representations of Germanness and representations associated with Roma in Romanian society as parallel and antonymic leads to relevant conclusions on more general issues pertaining to contemporary identity discourses in Romania. If Germans are seen as colonizing agents of Europeanization, the references to Roma (who also migrated to the contemporary territory of Romania but seemingly three centuries after the first waves of Saxon migration and without being granted any privileges by the then rulers of Transylvania) have often brought forth the putative "Roma problem" as an obstacle in front of the European integration. The Roma stand for the danger that Romania and the Romanian nation moves away from Europe and close to the Orient (Mihăilescu, 2014). The nomadic Roma, perceived as representative of a totally different way of life, are therefore counterposed to the stability associated with the German fortified churches and with the perceived German rootedness in Romania. The Roma-German dichotomy and the Romanian positionings with respect to the two ethnic groups are best understood against the backdrop of the tensions and frictions related to the assertion of a Romanian identity between the Occident and the Orient and to the social antagonisms and conflicts embedded within these tensions and frictions.

The migration of Saxons and Swabians to West Germany is presented as having left behind a loss. Dreams and yearnings of a German return to Transylvania and Banat illustrate the same body of thought. In exchange, Roma migration to Western Europe and the Roma return to Romania are presented as reasons to be ashamed. Germans allegedly Europeanize and Occidentalize Romania; Roma de-Europeanize and Orientalize it. Particularly after 1989, the Romanian assertion of a European identity has been constructed by means of a rejection of the "Țigan Other" (Woodcock, 2007). Consider only the criticism of the fact that the denomination "Roma" has come to replace the denomination "Gypsy", thus producing potential unwanted confusions between Roma and Romanians. The process of European integration made it to a certain extent more difficult to openly express anti-Gypsism and to openly reject the Roma, at least on the political level. Nonetheless, it would be short-sighted not to recognize that the pair of philo-Germanism and anti-Gypsism is underlain by Orientalist representations and in effect indicates a conservative and hierarchical vision of Europe. The European identity that Romanian philo-Germanism relates to excludes the Roma as the social Other. Nostalgic representations of a precommunist past are meant to naturalize both previous and contemporary social and ethnic inequalities.

A Bucharest-based national Romanian newspaper presented a documentary film about two ethnically mixed families in Transylvania in an article titled "Bizarre Mixture of Ethnies: Saxons and Gypsies, in Transylvania".[30] The poorly done production was shown in an official institution, the Romanian Cultural Institute in Bucharest.[31] It followed the traces of Saxon-Roma families, seen as an anthropological curiosity. Roma (called Gypsies throughout the entire movie) are presented as having occupied the "empty houses" of the Saxons who left for Germany. The documentary played on the antagonistic representations of the two ethnic groups by stating that Germans and Roma are two "extreme minorities" on their "level of civilization and culture". Germans and Roma being together is bizarre, a sort of weird "cross-breeding", worth being investigated as a curiosity, because within Romanian society the two ethnic groups stand for two different worlds, with two different sets of values, mutually incompatible. An article published in *Adevărul* in November 2007 refers to the situation in a Transylvanian village: "Although they took the place of the Saxons who left to Germany, the Gypsies inherited neither the prosperity nor the German order".[32] If Germans, through their affiliation with German/European culture are seen as a symbol of progress and civilization, Roma are seen as lacking civilization, providing a "catalyst" for the antonymic framing of Romanian national identity discourses (Woodcock, 2007).

Another aspect that makes evident the dichotomy embedded within the representations of Germans and Roma has to do with the physical portrait of Transylvanian Saxons (or Banat Swabians, for all that matters) and of the Roma. On the one hand, the latter are often presented as young, strong, violent, sensual and sexual, gregarious, lively and, last but not least, too numerous. On the other hand,

Germans are often rather symbols of twilight: they are often represented as old, lonely, weak and frail, an extinct species whose last representatives can still be found in Transylvanian or Banat villages, "preparing for Heaven".

Thus, in the Romanian context, Germans seem to be fulfilling the role of the "cultural Other", as opposed to the Roma who are a "social Other". The distinction has been first operationalized in a discussion about the way black Americans are perceived and constructed as a "social Other" in the United States, whereas immigrant groups are perceived and constructed as a "cultural Other". Although different from the in-group, the latter's otherness can be "overcome by learning about the unfamiliar and anchoring it" (Philogène, 2007, 33). Numerous articles in *Formula As* and elsewhere that try to emphasize the Romanian-German compatibility, the character of role model played by the Germans for the Romanian population, the appropriation by Romanians of German habits, show why and how the Germans can be "our Germans". In exchange, the Roma are never "our Roma", just like the poor are never "our poor". The attempt to embrace Germanness and the rejection of the Roma also has an important class dimension: representations of ethnic hierarchies and of social hierarchies are tightly interwoven.

Discourses attempting to go beyond the representation of a conflictual opposition between Roma and Germans in Transylvania and Banat still reproduce similar ethnic hierarchies. German entrepreneurship and guidance can help Roma to escape poverty, as readers of *Adevărul* could find out, for example, from an article I have already referred to in this chapter, about the production of woolen socks in Viscri.[33] The article reported how "under the leadership of a German family" – that is, a German couple who "just like their ancestors, left their native Germany" to move to Transylvania – the local Roma women were able to earn a living by selling in Germany the woolen socks they have been traditionally knitting. Journalist Ruxandra Hurezean (2016) presents, in her recent book titled *Povestea sașilor din Transilvania. Spusă chiar de ei* (The story of Saxons in Transylvania: As told by themselves), how Viscri became a success story despite the fact that many Roma "came" to the village after 1989. The artisans of the transformation of Viscri are one of the last Saxon families in the village, the Prince of Wales and the Mihai Eminescu Trust. The consequence is that "the formerly depopulated villages start to be repopulated again, and the few Saxons show the others how it was and how it could be" (Hurezean, 2016, 80). Under the guidance of Germans and Saxons, as well as of other experts, and with help from the British royal family, the simple inhabitants of the village – some of them Roma – are taught how to have their own businesses and hence how to be free. The ideological horizon of such representations, according to which freedom is connected with having one's own business is salient. In this context, it is also worth referring to how Caroline Fernolend, the *spiritus rector* of the developments taking place in Viscri, spoke about the Roma in the village in an interview granted to *Formula As* in 2002: "After the painful departure of the 240 neighbors, we have tried to build another community, together with the Gypsies and with the Romanians. We have succeeded to a large extent, our Gypsies are thrifty, they have gardens, animals, land".[34]

An article about Viscri published four years later in the same *Formula As* had nonetheless a slightly different tone when referring to the Roma in the village:

> Gypsies in Viscri do not like to be called Gypsies. Only two of them declared to be Gypsies at the last census, although more than half of the village could have easily done the same. Very difficultly, they started following Saxon habits. They hanged in trees rod baskets, where they throw away paper, plastic bottles or plastic bags. Every Saturday, the cart passes to pick up the garbage. *"We pay them 40,000 per cart and they tell us they will carry 7–8. But they never carry more than 5"*, says Caroline smiling. The streets are nonetheless clean. Sometimes, Gypsies forget the Saxon habits and throw the garbage away in the ditch. Caroline has a hint of reproach in her voice: *"They say that it'll go with the water anyway, when it rains"*.[35]

In a chapter about the pastor and writer Eginald Schlattner, Ruxandra Hurezean (2016, 31–59) emphasizes the special relationship that the Lutheran pastor of Roşia has developed with the other inhabitants of the village, Romanians and Roma and in particular his efforts for the schooling of the Roma. At the same time, Hurezean also underlines that the Roma in Schlattner's village are somehow different than the ordinary Roma:

> It [the village] also has many Rroma, recognized as Rroma by the inhabitants, but who declared themselves Romanians at the census. . . . The story of the Gypsies in Roşia is not a common one. They have not come from the chaos of migration, but they are 'household Gypsies', they were the servants of the Saxons. They lived beyond the hill, in a hamlet, where they would go only in the autumn, on Saint Demeter's Day, in order to repair their huts, so that snakes do not enter. After the Saxons left, they came to the village.
>
> (Hurezean, 2016, 45–46)

Although practically acknowledging the existence of a historical relationship of inequality and servitude, Hurezean makes no effort to critically engage with it. She instead suggests that the direct dependence of the Roma of Roşia provided a useful distinction from the other Roma, whose origin in Transylvania is connected with "the chaos of migration". Hierarchies are thus naturalized and essentialized. Economic success and well-being seem to depend on acknowledging and not transgressing them. Acts of transgression are at best possible in carnivalesque contexts, such as the one that Emil Hurezeanu refers to in his preface to the other recent book by Ruxandra Hurezean, dealing with Saxons. Hurezeanu writes about one of the many summer festivals where (the lost) Germanness is performed in Romania, the so-called *Haferlandwoche* (Oats Week), stating how "merry Roma wearing German leather shorts" participate in "a naïve and almost successful attempt to reenchant the past, which cannot avoid the disenchantment of the present" (Hurezeanu, 2017, 9).

7.3. Antagonistic representations of Germans and Hungarians

Alongside the juxtaposition of representations of Germans and Roma in Romania, it is also worth undertaking a similar analytical enterprise and commenting on the German-Hungarian dichotomy within Romanian representations of otherness. It is of a different nature from the constructed German-Roma antagonism, although it is also related to the vision of a potential Romanian-German compatibility, as opposed to a Romanian-Hungarian incompatibility. In an interview published in *Hermannstädter Zeitung* in early 1990, Radu Câmpeanu, the Liberal candidate for presidency in Romania's first post-1989 elections, stated that the ancient Romanian-Hungarian disputes can be solved with wisdom and moderation, and he deplored in the same sentence the disappearance of the German minority from Romania because the Germans always had a civilizational influence on Romanians:

> While the disputes with the Hungarian minority, old as they are, can be solved with wisdom and moderation . . . the ongoing haemorrhage of the German minority is a very sad issue, as the German minority has always been for us an important civilizational factor.[36]

The statement of one of the three candidates for Romanian presidency in the spring of 1990, at the time recently returned to Romania after living in France during the Cold War, openly implied a self-Orientalizing view of Romanianness, informing the representation of the German-Romanian relationship. It also came together with an emphasis on the different character of the Romanian-Hungarian relationship, marked by conflict and disputes. I have already referred to the different values implicitly or explicitly assigned to the German and Hungarian minorities in Romania in comments and statements issued by Romanian politicians in the context of the signing of the Romanian-German Bilateral Treaty.

Against this background, it is appropriate to briefly comment on the Romanian response to and the ensuing Romanian-Hungarian dispute generated by one of the most controversial post-1989 Hungarian legislative issues: the Hungarian Status Law of 2001, or, more accurately, The Act on Hungarians Living in Neighbouring Countries. Juxtaposing and comparing it with the Romanian position on the kin-state politics of the German state, which had an impact on German minorities in Central and Eastern Europe, Romania included, makes evident the differences underlying the representations of Romanian-German and Romanian-Hungarian relationships. By means of this legislative project, the Hungarian government attempted to set up a series of benefits and entitlements for the Hungarians living in the neighboring countries, on the basis of their ethnicity (Aurescu, 2003; Kántor et al., 2004; Waterbury, 2010; Pogonyi, 2017). The most controversial of its provisions involved issuing Hungarian "ethnic identity cards" and granting "labor permits" for ethnic Hungarians living in Hungary's neighboring countries (Waterbury, 2010, 110). The project of the law elicited a great deal of criticism from Romanian authorities. Nonetheless, in its ideological tenets, as well as in its potential impact, the Hungarian Status Law had similarities with the kin-state politics promoted by the German state, which has never made Romanian authorities raise the same type of criticism.

Fundamentally, both Hungary and Germany considered that they have specific duties toward the co-ethnics living outside their borders. In effect, so does Romania in relationship to the ethnic Romanians living outside its borders (Aurescu, 2002). MP Attila Varga (2004), at the time a member of the DAHR, enumerated the main objections of the Romanian part in respect to the Hungarian Status Law: the issue of extraterritoriality, the issue of discrimination, the rejection of the idea of (Hungarian) national unity expressed in the text of the law, the objection to the issue of benefits and entitlements pertaining to educational and cultural support, the criticism of the entitlements granted to non-Hungarian spouses and the contentious issue of the Hungarian certificate, presumably deciding who is and who is not Hungarian. Taking into consideration the heavy symbolic sensibilities often present in Romanian-Hungarian relationships, the political rejection and criticism of this law are not surprising (Kemp, 2006; Waterbury, 2010). Nonetheless, although similarities can be drawn, some of the specific critical points brought forth in this Romanian-Hungarian contentious debate have never been critically addressed in Romania with regard to the German policies toward co-ethnics living outside the borders of Germany – Transylvanian Saxons, Banat Swabians and the other German-speaking groups in Romania included.

The first issue of dispute was that of extraterritoriality – that is, enacting the law from a state on the territory of another state and, in its negative understanding, extending the jurisdiction of a state to the citizens of another state. However, there had always been effects of German legislation, for example of the *Bundesvertriebenengesetz* (federal law on expellees) on Romanian citizens of German ethnicity. At the beginning of the 1990s, during Adrian Năstase's tenure as minister of Foreign Affairs, more than 100,000 Romanian citizens migrated to Germany: they were allowed to do that on the basis of German legislation. Despite nominal pleas to stay in the country, never have post-1989 Romanian officials protested against the extraterritoriality implied by German legislation. At the same time, József Antall's declaration from 1990, according to which he considered himself prime minister of 15 million Hungarians (i.e. also of ethnic Hungarians living outside of Hungary) elicited responses and criticism from Romanian authorities (Toró, 2016, 96). The same can be said about subsequent similar declarations by Hungarian officials. The policies and statements of Helmut Kohl and Hans-Dietrich Genscher, who directly led to the migration of Romanian citizens from Romania to Germany and to their acquisition of German citizenship, have never elicited any type of criticism in Romania.

In Germany, a straightforward change in kin-state legislation took place in 1992, when the *Kriegsfolgenbereinigungsgesetz* (War Consequences Conciliation Act) was drafted and then ratified, substantially modifying the legal and ideological framework regulating the relationship of Germany with ethnic Germans in Central and Eastern Europe (Klekowski von Koppenfels, 2002). Until then, this relationship was fundamentally understood in terms of a Wilhelmian legislative framework based on the so-called jus sanguinis (right of blood) and of a historical-moral debt of the German state toward the Germans on the other side of the Iron Curtain. The migration of the Romanian Germans from Romania to Germany had taken place under the aegis of a legislative framework generously permitting the integration first of *Vertriebenen* (expellees) and then of *Aussiedler* (resettlers). However, as a consequence of the War Consequences Conciliation Act, it became much more difficult for the Germans abroad to obtain German citizenship. In theory, this was possible only if ethnic Germans were discriminated against in the country of residence. Nonetheless, proving the existence of discriminations had become almost impossible once the respective countries (in our case, Romania) were officially considered to be on the path of democratization and Europeanization (Weber et al., 2003, 145–183). After 1993, the new legislative measures in Germany practically put a halt to the migration of Romanian Germans. Nonetheless, German policies and the German-Romanian Bilateral Treaty continued to legally sanction the direct responsibility of Germany for the German ethnics in Romania.

The second issue of dispute was the discrimination due to the establishment of an ethnically based distinction between Romanian citizens, which would then lead to a discrimination against Romanian citizens who are not of Hungarian ethnicity. According to Romanian Constitution, the support for the preservation and development of minority identity cannot lead to the discrimination against other Romanian citizens (a provision also sanctioned in other bilateral treaties, including the Romanian-German Bilateral Treaty). However, the Hungarian attempt was not the only "positive discrimination" attempt that could have been interpreted as leading to discrimination against other Romanian citizens. For example, the *Anwerbestoppausnahmeverordnung* (regulation on the exceptions from recruitment ban) regulated the exceptions from the ban on foreign labor in Germany. Between 1991 and 1994, paragraph 10 of the legal ordinance allowed ethnic Germans from outside Germany in possession of a notification of acceptance (*Aufnahmebescheid*) or who were visiting relatives to be granted a work permit.[37] The notification of acceptance was a document issued to Germans in Central and Eastern European countries and in the former Soviet Union acknowledging their belonging to the German nation. In 1994, the ordinance would be modified, eliminating the possibility of those visiting relatives to get a temporary work permit.[38] The latter provision established a series of bureaucratic hurdles to be overcome by Romanian Germans trying to get a work permit in Germany. However, paragraph 10 indirectly permitted specific Romanian citizens, on the basis of their German ethnicity that was proven through the ownership of a specific document released by German authorities and asserting their German *Volkszugehörigkeit* (ethnic belonging), to be granted a work permit.[39]

Thus, paragraph 10 established a positive discrimination in favor of specific ethnic Germans who were not German citizens, whereas the same paragraph indirectly established a case of positive discrimination on ethnic grounds in Romania: Romanian citizens of German ethnicity, having an *Aufnahmebescheid* (notification of admission), could be granted a work permit on the basis of a German legislative act. The *Aufnahmebescheid* has its similarities with the Hungarian identification card proposed through the Status Law, as it practically established who was "German" (i.e. eligible for German citizenship on the basis of jus sanguinis). During 2001–2002, when the whole Hungarian-Romanian debate on the Status Law was at its height, the *Anwerbestoppausnahmeverordnung* was still in force.

The third issue of dispute for Romanian officials regarded the involvement of Hungary in matters going beyond educational and cultural support. However, Germany's involvement in Romania, on behalf of the German minority, has always gone beyond educational and cultural support, the economic aspect being highly important for the envisaged stabilization of ethnic Germans in Romania. The bilateral Romanian-German Treaty includes a reference to the "reorganization of the social, cultural and economic life" of the German minority in Romania. The main difference stems from the fact that, in one case, the involvement of the kin state in the economic life of the kin minority has been regulated through a bilateral treaty and, in another case, the attempt was to regulate it through an internal kin-state law. Nonetheless, the opposition "in principle" to economic entitlements in the Romanian-Hungarian case is also telling of the existence of slightly different Romanian approaches to the minority issue and, in effect, of a hierarchization of minority groups, Germans faring best and being thus entitled to most benefits, as compared to Hungarians and others.

On a different level, several press articles about Satu Mare Swabians also provide relevant illustrations of the existence of a German-Hungarian dichotomy within Romanian representations of otherness. This particular Romanian-German group rarely reaches the foreground of the public interest, dominated first and foremost by Transylvanian Saxons and, to a lesser extent, by Banat Swabians. There is also not too much academic literature on the topic, although this has slowly begun to change (Roşu, 2015; Dácz, 2017). Satu Mare Swabians often declare Hungarian as their mother tongue, which makes them a peculiar "German" group in Romania. Against this backdrop, particular Romanian-Hungarian tensions and Romanian-Hungarian-German entanglements can be played out in discourses about this group.

Romanian accounts have been representing Satu Mare Swabians as being threatened with assimilation by Hungarians, hence as in need of salvation. The salvation is presented as coming from Romanian authorities and institutions. This is, for example, the tenor underlying a 1991 article in which journalist Silviu Achim called the Satu Mare Swabians "the most isolated and hence the most exposed branch to the hostility of times, amongst our entire population of German extraction".[40] The danger was that of denationalization, more precisely Magyarization, a phenomenon that had started during the Austro-Hungarian dualism, yet continued up to the first decades of the communist regime, Achim wrote. The need was, therefore, to "recover the ethnic identity of the Swabians".[41] An interview granted by Helmut Berner, the president of the Homeland Association of Satu Mare Swabians in Germany, to Silviu Achim, was even more virulent in its criticism of the perceived Magyarization. Berner was extremely critical of "these gentlemen" who continued the Magyarization actions instead of admitting that this type of politics belonged to the nineteenth century. It is not spelled out who the "gentlemen" were, yet readers could easily understand that Berner was referring to Hungarian political and religious elites in Romania and presumably in Hungary as well. The need for saving an ethnic identity under threat was made clearer through references to Europe: "we want that the people in the Satu Mare clime get along well, all preserving their ethnic identity in this small Europe that is Satu Mare county. Our wish is that this small Europe enters big Europe; of course, together with the entire Romania".[42]

The discourse propagated in 1992 by Berner, an ethnopolitical entrepreneur within the Satu Mare Swabian community, tied in perfectly with the discourses usually disseminated by Achim, a nationalistically oriented Romanian journalist, in other instances an apologist of the Antonescu regime and of anti-Hungarianism. In the same year, the already mentioned Silviu Achim was referring to the German migration out of Romania, bewailing it as a "painful loss".[43] The two attitudes fit well together. The Germans are often deemed more valuable than the Hungarians, or, even better, the Germans and their apparently good relationship with Romanians offer a way for discourses emphasizing the Romanian magnanimity and their more tolerant nature compared to Hungarians.

Furthermore, the aforementioned article on Satu Mare Swabians discursively instrumentalized the latter group to make anti-Hungarian claims while also resorting to a "Europeanizing" argument. The forced assimilation (Magyarization) of Satu Mare Swabians was also the topic of an article in the same newspaper, by Val Vâlcu, published in 1995.[44] It is an account about the village Palota (Neu Palota in German, Újpalota in Hungarian) in Bihor County, with a simple message: German-speaking Swabians are being Magyarized. Vâlcu did not come forth with too many comments, but some subtle observations are necessary to understand that the message of the text is a clear critique of Hungarian politicians in Romania. A byline of the article stated "*À propos* forced assimilation", an innuendo referring to the accusations often made by representatives of the Hungarians in Romania regarding the presumed forced assimilation that ethnic Hungarians are victims of. Once again, we find an open instrumentalization of Germans, who become, in the accounts of Romanian journalists, an object of Hungarian ethnic politics in the Satu Mare region. Thus, the historical image of the assimilationist Hungarian elites got reinforced, while the representation of the Satu Mare Swabians as an ethnic group in peril ties in perfectly with the broader representations of the Romanian Germans as a whole, also endangered given their extremely small number.

In 2004, *România liberă* also approached the issue of the Satu Mare Swabians. The author dealt with the question of German versus Hungarian identity of the Swabians in the Satu Mare region and did that in the most salient way, announcing it from the very title: "The Swabians – our Germans or their Hungarians?".[45] The antagonism between Romanians and Hungarians was played on, at stake this time being the Germanness of the Swabians – that is, their "true" ethnic identity. The author offered from the first lines an answer to the question in the title, by stating that they "are Swabians: our Germans".⁴⁶ The Swabians/Germans can therefore be "ours", even if they are Germans, another discursive proof of an imagined Romanian-German compatibility, in contrast to the Hungarians who are never "ours", but always "theirs".

At times, one can discern that Germans enjoy a specific prestige in Romania even from topics that are absent. In 2006, *Formula As* published a series of articles and interviews severely criticizing the restitutions taking place in Transylvania, especially in the city center of Cluj-Napoca, the unofficial capital of the unofficial region.⁴⁷ The authors and the interviewees spoke about a marginalization of Romanians, who "lose" the city centers in Transylvania, the most sensitive case being that of Cluj-Napoca, in a situation reminding them of the pre-1918 discriminations against Romanians in the Habsburg Empire. Nonetheless, a similar process of restitution of buildings to various institutions belonging to minority churches also took place in Sibiu, mostly in favor of the Lutheran Church or the Democratic Forum of Germans. Yet a Transylvanian town center "occupied" by Germans was (at least at the time) not perceived as dangerous and anti-Romanian as one "occupied" by Hungarians. Such a critical stance would also have been largely at odds with the eulogizing interviews with Klaus Iohannis, the then mayor of Sibiu, published in the same *Formula As*. In effect, in the immediate subsequent issue of the magazine, such an interview with Iohannis was published, emphasizing the Europeanness of Sibiu, linking this Europeanness with the upcoming official accession of Romania into the European Union. At the same time, Iohannis distinctly expressed his opposition toward the granting of ethnic autonomy in Romania, an implicit reference to Hungarian claims for autonomy in Szeklerland.⁴⁸

Such implicit or explicit hierarchizations can also be found in academic literature, for example in a book by Adrian Liviu Ivan, historian at the Babeş-Bolyai University in Cluj-Napoca, who teaches a wide number of courses on the European Union. Ivan's book won the Dimitrie Gusti Award of the Romanian Academy. Ivan polemicized with Irina Livezeanu's well-known study (1995) on the nation-building and assimilationist policies of the Romanian state in the interwar period, a compulsory reference for scholars of interwar Romania since it was first published in English in 1995. The book was then also translated into Romanian and published in 1998. Unlike Livezeanu, Ivan fundamentally argued that Greater Romania was a state whose policies were aiming not toward assimilation but instead generously toward integration. One of the main theoretical operative distinctions used in his comparative study of the Hungarian and the German minority between 1919 and 1933 is that between *national minorities* (the presumed case of the former) and *ethnic minorities* (the presumed case of the latter). For Ivan, the distinction is fundamentally based on the relationship of the minorities with their "kin state" (Brubaker, 1996). Hungarians looked toward Budapest and used the help of Hungarian state officialdom in shaping their relationship with Romania, thus being practically in a state of constant conflict with Romanian authorities. At the same time, Hungarian authorities tended to externalize this conflict to the League of Nations, while Germans, in Ivan's vision, allegedly did not nurture politico-national relationships with Germany and hence were much more predisposed to attempt to solve the contested issues with Romanian authorities on an internal level. This (largely artificial) distinction between *ethnic* and *national* minorities undergirds Ivan's entire line of argumentation. He went as far as to state that Transylvanian Saxons did not aspire "towards an integration in the bosom of a German nation, understood in a Herderian or political sense", an attitude that, in his view, is fundamentally different from the Hungarian one (Ivan, 2006, 296).

Ivan's argument contains several flaws. Weimar Germany did not encourage the externalization of the issues related to the German minority in Romania toward the League of Nations, yet this political pragmatism did not mirror the lack of "Germanizing" aspirations of the Transylvanian Saxons. Literature on Transylvanian Saxon identity and on Transylvanian Saxon history emphasizes the existence of a German myth mostly from German unification onward, but with much deeper roots. Furthermore, the eventual success of Hitlerism can be comprehended only if we consider the reputation enjoyed by Germany among Saxons. For ideological reasons, Nazi Germany took its role as a "kin state" for ethnic Germans abroad much more seriously than Weimar Germany. Nonetheless, relationships between Transylvanian Saxons and German institutions, such as Gustav-Adolf-Werk, existed during Weimar Germany as well. Saxons aimed toward a cultural integration in the German nation, very much understood in a Romantic-Herderian sense, hence the colder relationships with the German state and its political and cultural environment between 1919 and 1933. Transylvanian Saxon self-identification discourses and their German-speaking education (the alternative of promoting Saxon-speaking education could have been imagined, at least in theory) emphasize the allegiance to the German *Kulturnation* (cultural nation), which eventually will be doubled by a political allegiance to Germany. The main difference between Saxon and Hungarian attitudes toward cooperation with the Romanian state originates not so much in the former being an *ethnic minority* and the latter being a *national minority* but rather in the absence versus the presence of potential irredentist claims and of a de facto irredentist ideology. Fundamentally due to geographical reasons, Transylvanian Saxons never envisaged anything of the sort, very much unlike Hungarians and Hungarian political representatives in both Hungary and Romania in the interwar period.

Ivan's investigation also strikes through the discrepancy between the number of pages dedicated to the Hungarian minority and the number of pages dedicated to Germans in Transylvania. The book looks more like an analysis of the relationship between the Hungarian minority and the Romanian state during the period 1919–1933, with some appendices related to Transylvanian Saxons. The considerations regarding the latter seem to be an instrument within the much more comprehensive analysis of the Hungarian minority. Thus, in Ivan's interpretation, Saxons become an exemplary minority, because they accept the new state order and the status of a minority in Romania, aiming to improve their condition and to attain their objectives through cooperation with Romanian authorities or through internal ways of attacking the implementation of unwanted measures. Hungarians, on the other hand, by constantly resorting to the League of Nations, also via Budapest, attempt to erode Romanian authority, the ideological pillar of this endeavor being mainly the non-acceptance of the new state order. Indeed, Ivan singled out two distinct minority attitudes toward the relationship with the Romanian state between 1919 and 1933, but he did that by departing from a partially flawed theoretical distinction, which impeded him from fairly investigating the underlying reasons for Transylvanian Saxon attitudes toward the Romanian state. Nonetheless, given the argument I advance in this book, what is most relevant is the idea that Saxons can become a sort of an analytical trump, used to show that Romanian interwar policies were not aiming toward assimilation and that minorities enjoyed internal means to aim to improve their situation. Thus, Saxons become an exemplary minority in Romania's interwar period, being seen in largely positive terms.[49] The real stake seems nonetheless to be that of coming up with an argument critical of Hungarian ethnic politics in interwar Romania.

Notes

1 Pop is not the only historian to come up with considerations of the sort. I have come across other similar ascriptions of the origin of Transylvanian Saxons, such as in works by Neagu Djuvara (2005, 45) and Vasile Pascu (1998, 128) and in a history textbook for the fourth grade (Burlec, Lazăr & Teodorescu, 1998, 33). The simplistic etymological connective thread is false because "Saxon" (lat. *saxones* / germ. *Sachse*) was more a judicial status than a geographical reference (Gündisch, 1998, 30).
2 Emil Hurezeanu, "Transilvania, *mon amour* – despre cetățile fortificate," *Dilema veche* 306, 24 December 2009.
3 Sorana Coroamă Stanca, "Românii-germani," *România liberă*, 3 October 1990.
4 Adrian Bucurescu, "Cine salvează Sighișoara?" *România liberă*, 29 June 1991; Adrian Bucurescu, "Va mai fi salvată Sighișoara?" *România liberă*, 14 May 1992; Ciprian Chirvasiu, Dumitru Manolache, "Cetăți care mor în picioare," *România liberă*, 1 September 1993; Mariana Petcu and Irina Pop, "O cetate fortificată și un castel care nu mai interesează pe nimeni," *România liberă*, 13 December 1996; Carmen Chihaia, "Cetățile-săsești din Transilvania – un patrimoniu-unicat în pericol de pulverizare," *Adevărul*, 14 December 1996.
5 Chirvasiu and Manolache, "Cetăți care mor în picioare".
6 In 2002, under the headline "DRACULAREA" *România liberă* has frequently published critical articles about Dracula Park. See, for example, the issues between 21 February and 8 March.
7 Iulia Blaga, "Sibiul, 'un colț nealterat al Europei'," *România liberă*, 5 May 2000.
8 Horia Țurcanu, "Transilvania – dulce patrie," *Formula As* 519, 10 June 2002.
9 Ioan T. Morar (2006), in his novel *Lindenfeld*, also addressed the phenomenon of the contemporary performance of Germanness by non-Germans, whose underlying reasons are fundamentally of economic nature.
10 Coroamă Stanca, "Românii-germani," *România liberă*, 3 October 1990.
11 Ibid.
12 Ibid.
13 Annemarie and Horst Weber, "Selbstgerecht im Wohlstand," *Hermannstädter Zeitung*, 14 December 1990.
14 Ibid.
15 Ibid.
16 Hertha Böhme, "An die Redaktion der 'Hermannstädter Zeitung'," *Hermannstädter Zeitung*, 14 December 1990.

17 Grete Tischler, "Fünf verlorene Jahre," *Hermannstädter Zeitung*, 11 January 1991.
18 Ibid.
19 Ibid.
20 Andreas Homm, "1990 ist nicht 1945," *Hermannstädter Zeitung*, 11 January 1991.
21 Wolfgang Rehner, "Revoluția a venit prea târziu," interview by Mircea Bunea, *Adevărul*, 23 July 1990.
22 Șelaru, "O localitate săsească"; Dan Tapalagă, "Satul cu blazon," *Formula As*, 9 October 2006.
23 Bogdan Burileanu, "Sibiu. O capitală transnațională a țiganilor?!" *România liberă*, 5 August 1996. For another article about the Gypsy influence in Sibiu, in defiance of laws and authorities, but without reference to the Saxon past, see Mariana Petcu and Flavius Popa, "Sfidarea autorităților," *România liberă*, 2 April 1997.
24 Ion Medoia, "'Mica Vienă', târâtă spre 'Fâșia Gaza'," *România liberă*, 24 October 1997; Ion Medoia, "Timișoara. 'Palatele' țigănești cu 'turnulețe' iau locul construcțiilor în stil vienez," *România liberă*, 10 July 1998; Ion Medoia, "Bulevardul C.D. Loga, îmbâcsit de turnuri și turnulețe orientale," *România liberă*, 10 November 2000.
25 Adrian Bucurescu, "Cetatea Viscri," *România liberă*, 23 November 2000.
26 Adrian Popescu, "Viscri – satul care s-a scos din foame cu 'ora de șosete," *Adevărul*, 5 October 2004.
27 Irina Pop, "Satele săsești vor fi repopulate, dar la primăvară," *România liberă*, 7 December 1996.
28 Sânziana Pop, "Sașii din Ardeal," *Formula As* 388, 15 November 1999.
29 Pop, "Istorie cu ochii în lacrimi."
30 A. E. G., "Combinație bizară de etnii: sași și țigani în Transilvania," *Ziua*, 28 July 2008, http://ziarero.antena3.ro/articol.php?id=1217244520 (accessed 23 September 2018).
31 Geo Scripcariu, *Adela & Agnetha*, www.youtube.com/watch?v=bvOB8KTGhYc (accessed 23 September 2018).
32 Sorin Ghica, "Vătrașii din Sibiu s-au mutat din corturi în casele sașilor," *Adevărul*, 14 November 2007.
33 Popescu, "Viscri". See also Hurezean, 2016, 88–90.
34 Caroline Fernolend, "'Prințul Charles a spus că satul nostru este cel mai frumos din lume și nu înțelege de ce ne trebuie în România Dracula Park'," interview by Ion Longin Popescu, *Formula As* 519, 10 June 2002.
35 Tapalagă, "Satul cu blazon."
36 Radu Câmpeanu, "Rumänien im 4 Jahren ein Sozialstaat?" interview by Annemarie Schuller, *Hermannstädter Zeitung*, 27 April 1990.
37 "Verordnung über Ausnahmeregelungen für die Erteilung einer Arbeitserlaubnis an neueinreisende ausländische Arbeitnehmer (Anwerbestoppausnahme-Verordnung)," http://archiv.jura.uni-saarland.de/BGBl/TEIL1/1990/19903014.1.HTML#GL10 (accessed 20 June 2018).
38 "Zweite Verordnung zur Änderung der Anwerbestoppausnahme-Verordnung," http://archiv.jura.uni-saarland.de/BGBl/TEIL1/1994/19942794.1.HTML (accessed 20 June 2018).
39 The bureaucratic difficulties in this respect were nonetheless critically seen by Romanian Germans and by the representatives of the Forum. See Philippi ([1995] 1996).
40 Silviu Achim, "Întâlnirea șvabilor," *Adevărul*, 11 July 1992.
41 Silviu Achim, "Viitorul șvabilor din România," *Adevărul*, 13 July 1992.
42 Helmut Berner, "Aici naționalitățile se înțeleg bine," interview by Silviu Achim, *Adevărul*, 23 July 1992.
43 Achim, "O etnie de opt ori seculară".
44 Val Vâlcu, "În satul Palota, din Bihor, șvabii vorbesc ungurește," *Adevărul*, 12 August 1995.

45 Mihnea-Petru Pârvu, "Şvabii – nemţii noştri sau ungurii lor?" *România liberă*, 17 August 2004.
46 Ibid.
47 Sânziana Demian, "Despre retrocedările clădirilor vechi din Cluj," *Formula As* 748, 18 December 2006.
48 Klaus Iohannis, "La o Ţară Europeană se cuvine şi o Capitală Europeană," interview by Ion Longin Popescu, *Formula As* 749, 25 December 2006.
49 The representation of Saxons as an almost exemplary minority, blossoming and prospering in the interwar period and nourishing a fundamentally good relationship with Romanian authorities, can also be found in works by other historians (see, for example, Bolovan & Bolovan, 2000; also Ciobanu, 2001).

8 Conclusions

8.1. Romanian philo-Germanism in a broader context

In an article analyzing the effects of twentieth-century forced migrations from Eastern Europe, sociologist Ewa Morawska singled out, within so-called sending societies, several consequences of the phenomenon, related to a number of different societal fields. Some of the effects she mentioned have to do with "self-perceptions and representations of others", as well as with "collective memory and representations of history" (Morawska, 2000, 1053). Surely, only if we stretch the meaning of the term can we categorize the mass departure of Romanian Germans to the Federal Republic of Germany as a case of "forced migration", but the observations Morawska makes do open up a space for analytically addressing some of the implicit and explicit consequences of the phenomenon. At the same time, it also ought to be emphasized that in Romania and elsewhere in (Central and Eastern) Europe the postwar self-perceptions and representations of ethnic otherness, on the one hand, and the postwar interpretations of the recent and less recent past, on the other hand, are also related and communicate with the broader historical context – that is, with identity discourses and with discourses on otherness that have a longer tradition.

Both before and after 1989, the historical experiences of German occupation during the Second World War in particular and of interethnic enmity and conflict in general have played an important role in shaping social and cultural representations of Germanness, as well as of concrete policies in countries such as Poland or Czechoslovakia (and after the dissolution of Czechoslovakia particularly in the Czech Republic). In the 2009 *New York Times* article about Klaus Iohannis, already quoted in the introductory chapter of this book, the author Nicholas Kulish referred to the fact that the former is of German ethnicity as something that "would be a major liability in other countries in Eastern Europe", thus highlighting the peculiarity of the Romanian case.[1] Indeed, negatively laden representations of German alterity in Poland or Czech Republic played a key role in the construction of the respective national identities (LeCaine Agnew, 2003). In post-communist Czech Republic, anti-German prejudice continued to be prevalent, with Germans being represented as the archenemy in history textbooks and even in mass-media discourses (Cordell & Wolff, 2005, 117). In Poland, Germans and

Russians have been historically represented as the "chief external Polish enemies" (Michlic, 2006, 53). The evolutions of the postwar German-Polish relations have been determined by historical legacies and territorial conflicts, but also by the German occupation of Poland during the Second World War, as well as by the immediate consequences of the conflagration, including border changes. Competing memories and narratives about the Second World War played a key role within these evolutions, because they were related to and also left their mark on the representations of otherness. Analyzing the image of the ethnic German in Polish cinema after the Second World War, historian Eugeniusz Cezary Król (2006) reached the conclusion that the quest for a "good ethnic German" is fruitless, thus emphasizing the perception of the German within Polish society as one of the quintessential enemies of Poland and of the Polish people.

Thus, although the post-1989 political context brought forth to a certain extent a much-needed revaluation of Polish-German relationships and even something of a Polish-German rapprochement, the fabric of conflicting and traumatic collective memory did not get easily softened (Cordell & Wolff, 2005). The anti-German rhetoric promoted by the Kaczyński brothers and their Law and Justice Party was able to garner substantial electoral support in the 2000s (Cordell, 2009, 2). At the same time, the process of European integration initially seemed to lead to a normalization in Polish-German relations and to an embrace of discourses emphasizing multicultural cosmopolitanism and the common German-Polish past, at least in various local contexts (Thum, 2011, 393–408). However, looking at the Polish political landscape and particularly at the discourses disseminated by the Law and Justice Party after their new electoral success of 2015, one can easily notice that anti-German positions, sometimes garbed in an anti-EU apparel, continue to play a highly important role.

Poland has also been a prime example illustrating the existence of the so-called anti-Semitism without Jews in the region after the fall of state socialism (Eschenazi & Nissim, 2004, 196–216). Nonetheless, this anti-Semitism without Jews also had an older genealogy: it was in effect preceded by a virulent anti-Semitism with Jews. Joanna Beata Michlic (2006), in her analysis of the image of the Jew in Poland, traced the emergence, the development and the recycling of specific anti-Semitic tropes in Poland, from the nineteenth century onward, thus emphasizing the lengthy chronological span of stereotypes and Polish "anti-Jewish idioms" and of related Polish-Jewish tensions (Michlic, 2006, 8). More specifically, she focused on the representation of the Jew as the "threatening other", showing its importance for modern Polish society and culture and for the process of modern Polish nation building. The last chapter in Michlic's overview is dedicated to the post-1989 period, showing how "the myth of the Jew as the threatening other" (Michlic, 2006, 264) has continued to play an important role in Polish society and culture even after the fall of state socialism.

Nonetheless, as Michlic also suggested, this was only one side of the story. Beginning with the 1980s, the "memory void" surrounding the Jewish community in Poland after the Holocaust started in effect to be filled up. The construction of memory and the relationship between the existence of a "Jewish memory project"

Conclusions 165

and particular Polish identification discourses were analyzed at the time by Iwona Irwin-Zarecka (1989) by means of what she called a "layer-by-layer interpretive approach". The approach implied paying particular attention to the political aspects connected with the phenomenon, since they were directly interwoven with this "Jewish memory project". Thus, Irwin-Zarecka persuasively showed that representations of otherness and perceptions of the past are strongly and almost intrinsically connected with politics, in an excellent illustration of how to interconnect the study of images of alterity and the study of memory. The study of Irwin-Zarecka put under the spotlight the first steps toward the rediscovery of the Jewish material and immaterial heritage in Poland, also emphasizing that this did not entail a disappearance of anti-Semitic tropes and anti-Semitism. The phenomenon investigated by Irwin-Zarecka in its infancy has been subsequently researched in the 1990s, this time emphasizing its almost Pan-European dimension (Gruber, 2002). Its paradoxes have been summed up in the title of Ruth Ellen Gruber's study, *Virtually Jewish*, which underlines the ambivalence embedded within the romanticized and artificial rediscovery of the Jewish past, also taking place in the name of a sanitized European multiculturalism, at odds with both the non-Jewish present as well as with the anti-Semitic manifestations of both past and present.

In the same vein, the Polish case also illustrates how anti-German rhetoric can exist alongside a reinterpretation of the multiethnic past into something of a "marketable multiculturalism" (Chu, 2012b). Such cosmopolitan and sanitized instantiations of an "idealized multiculturalism" (Chu, 2012b, 240) have come together with a recalibration of the importance of German (or Habsburg) past and heritage in Poland, in the name of tolerance and Europeanness (Chu, 2012b; Thum, 2012). Nonetheless, as already suggested, recent political and ideological developments in Poland indicate that this Europeanizing recalibration inclusive of German heritage is far from being fully embraced and accepted, finding itself under attack, particularly in recent years, in the name of Polish ethnic nationalism.

Another case shedding interesting light on the relationship between memory, the production and reproduction of identities and the production and reproduction of otherness in post-1989 Eastern Europe is that of Estonia. At the crux of questions related to memory and ethnic otherness lies a dense web of interconnected interethnic relationships. Germans, Russians and Swedes play an important role in the interpretations of the Estonian past and present. In an anthropological study set in Noarootsi (Swedish: Nuckö) parish, once largely inhabited by members of the Swedish minority, who then left the country in the 1940s, questions related to past and present, perceptions of Estonianness and Swedishness, identity and otherness have been analyzed. Interestingly and at first glance surprisingly, following the demise of the communist regime in Estonia, a revival of Swedish heritage has been noticeable, a "restoration of Swedishness" with a double purpose: "providing an alternative identity after the rupture from the Soviet past (when the remaining Swedes had become almost completely assimilated)" and at the same time "attracting aid and interest from Sweden in order to build an economic future for the area" (Rausing, 2004, 26). Thus, as Sigrid Rausing (2004) persuasively showed, the multilateral relationship between Estonian identity, Swedish heritage and memory within the postcommunist setting is apt to be understood by considering the appeal of Westernness and Europeanness in Estonian society. This appeal also explains the paradoxical appropriation of Swedishness and the assertion of a bereft Swedish past in a forlorn Estonian village.

Moreover, not only the Swedish Other casts light on the relevance of constructing memory for understanding contemporary interests and contemporary Estonian identification discourses. In the same vein, the memory and the contemporary construction of both the Russian and the German Other among Estonians are quintessential. The analysis of the stereotypical images associated with Germany and the Germans in Estonia led to the conclusion that the contemporary positive representations of Germanness in the Baltic country are closely linked to the implicit and explicit comparison and juxtaposition of Germans and Russians, the latter being mainly represented as a threatening Other (Kaljund, 2006, 2012).

Thus, as discourses about Germanness in post-1989 Romania also suggest, in Central and Eastern European countries, representations of Western Others in positive terms and interpretations emphasizing the role of such Western Others in the development of one's own historical identity seem to be directly related to Europeanizing aspirations. Regarding the Estonian relationship to Swedes, Rausing (2004, 5) noted that it was actually a "relationship to a neighbour that also represents an imagined future and the what-might-have-been of the past". Mutatis mutandis, her observation also accounts for the representations of Germanness and of the German neighbors circulating in Romanian society. On the one hand, such representations elicit images of a potential future Western identity of Romania, while on the other hand, they are meant to highlight a past European and Western identity in Romania, yet never fully developed, curtailed by Romanian liminality, by the Orient, by the imposition of state socialism. The quest for internal Western Others, whenever present within Eastern European societies, is mostly a legitimizing quest, whose goal is that of proving the cultural and political belonging of these societies to Europe. It indicates the insidious hegemonic nature of the representations of a West-East divide. The Romanian philo-Germanism without Germans is an exemplification of this quest. Its post-1989 instantiations are comprehensible and make sense if one considers the "return-to-Europe" frenzy typical for countries in the Eastern part of the European continent and for Romania as well, balancing between unwieldiness and proud self-assertion. Furthermore, sanitized representations of a European multicultural past and present also tie in well with these instantiations.

8.2. Liberal entrepreneurship and conservative hierarchies

Romanian philo-Germanism is strongly connected with the production and reproduction of symbolic geographies aiming to discursively insert Romania into what is perceived to be the "civilized" Western/European world. Germans are the others who seem to possess "all that we lack" – centuries-old European culture, work ethic, entrepreneurial spirit – and who are often embraced with "love, ardour, and desire", in what is to a large extent a textbook case of discursive "self-colonization" and "self-Orientalization". Thus, Germans in Romania, whose ancestors largely came to the current regions of Transylvania and Banat as colonists in the twelfth and eighteenth centuries, become a resource for Europeanness, a way of emphasizing Romania's European belonging, which oscillates between being understood as a potentiality and as a reality. According to philo-German discourses, if the European/Western belonging of Romania is real, this is so because of the German influence on Romanian society. If it is only a potentiality, it is because this German influence has not been nurtured and sustained enough. Concerted efforts are needed in this respect, although they might fail due to those who are represented as not being able to put them into practice, as hindering Romania's Europeanization.

Albeit largely hailed by public opinion in Romania and elsewhere as a positive phenomenon, seen as a ray of light among plenty of xenophobia and rejection of otherness, Romanian philo-Germanism is far from being an innocuous and commendatory discourse as it might seem at first glance. Philo-German panegyrics in Romania reinforce a broad range of positive stereotypes and representations, but at the same time, they are more often than not tightly connected with self-deprecating views of the Romanian Self or part and parcel of discourses excluding other Others, such as the Roma or the Hungarians. The implicit and explicit class dimension of the philo-German easternist representations in Romania is also telling of processes of social exclusion, intertwined with exclusion on ethnic grounds, as the case of the Roma suggests. Philo-Germanism and the nostalgia for a German past in Transylvania and Banat act as discursive legitimation mechanisms apt to make acceptable such positions and stances that ought to be regarded critically.

In one of her analyses of post-1989 Romania, anthropologist Katherine Verdery (1996, 97) argued that images of ethnic groups are "important symbols for discussing particular kinds of social dislocation attendant on the exit from socialism". Further on, she commented on the xenophobic sentiment present in Romanian society at the beginning of the 1990s and directed against Jews and Roma:

> Whereas intolerance of Gypsies suggests problems related specifically to the market, anti-Semitism suggests a broader hostility to things of "the West," including democracy and private property, as well as markets; and it embraces themes of concern to a broad array of groups, distressed either at past injustices under socialism or at present dislocations. To say that one dislikes Jews is easier and less revealing than to say one dislikes democracy or international lending institutions. One can make this statement employing Jews as a symbol even if there are few actual Jews around.
>
> (Verdery, 1996, 99)

Verdery's observations on the relationship between past injustices and present dislocations, on the one hand, and representations of ethnic groups, on the other hand, are definitely applicable to the case of Romania after 1989. If anti-Roma feeling at the beginning of the 1990s stood for an uneasy relationship with the market economy and anti-Semitism suggested a general hostility toward things associated with the West, post-1989 Romanian philo-Germanism calls forth the opposite, namely a rather uncritical embrace of particular representations of things Western, a way of entering the select European club through the appropriation of the "German" as a symbol, through making the "German" "ours". At the same time, Verdery's observations also have to be qualified in the sense that contemporary intolerance against Roma and anti-Roma statements are to a large extent about social exclusion. Representations of Roma as a burden on the state's finance, as well as on entrepreneurs and those who produce economic development, not willing to work and living off social welfare, stand for an ideological hostility toward ideas of social justice and social equality. In exchange, philo-Germanism in Romania, the emphasis on German-induced economic know-how and economic development indicate an unabated and not-to-be-questioned support for things such as market economy or economic freedom, which come together with an obliteration and an obscuring of broader social issues.

On the occasion of the beginning of the 2018/2019 school year, the official message of Romania's president Klaus Iohannis touched upon, among other things, the issue of patriotism. In his definition of patriotism, Iohannis included "putting into practice one's entrepreneurial ideas".[2] The emphasis on entrepreneurship, which largely informs Iohannis's political program, is also often embedded within the representations of Germanness circulating in Romania that have constituted the object of analysis of this book. It is one of the key aspects underlying the construction of a potential Romanian-German compatibility in post-1989 Romania. The entrepreneurial spirit is meant to be nurtured and cultivated in Romania. Germans and Romanian Germans are often represented as the ones to be followed in this respect.

However, this apparently future-oriented and entrepreneurship-friendly liberal horizon in which philo-Germanism in Romania is situated comes rather often together with a conservative nostalgia. Romanian philo-German discourses, as well as Romanian German self-representations, endow Germans with both entrepreneurial spirit – thus placing them in the first line of Romania's post-1989 transition to market capitalism – and an ethical, even religious, value. The discursive reconciliation of the two produces conservative and strongly hierarchical representations of how society should look like. The naturalization of particular social and ethnic hierarchies largely informs Romanian philo-Germanism. Representations of a particular Romanian-German compatibility and of a Romanian-German elective affinity are tightly related to the production and reproduction of such hierarchies whose relationship with ideas of social equality is rather tense, to say the least. To a significant extent, the visions of Romania and of Europe that the Romanian philo-Germanism stands for also seem to be informed by a nostalgia for an idealized pre-1945 Romania, for an idealized pre-1945 Europe, largely erasing any questions about the reasons leading to the social, economic and political conflicts that underlay the interwar and the horrors of the Second World War. Beyond the symbolic idea of coming to terms with the past and of repairing past injustices, beyond the discursive recognition of Romanian Germans as the paradigmatic victims of Romanian twentieth-century history, one finds a wistful yearning for the conservative hierarchies of the Europe of yore, a legitimation of social and economic antagonisms from the perspective of a middle class with aristocratic aspirations and desires. Romanian philo-Germanism looks like the expression of the anti-communist liberal-conservative marriage underlying contemporary understandings of European identity that either tend to belittle fascism while scapegoating communism as the root of all evil or tend to put the equal sign between the two. The Europe that Romanian philo-Germanism suggests it wants to embrace is a Europe where social and cultural hierarchies are reinforced rather than critically questioned.

8.3. Anti-Germanism

It would undoubtedly be erroneous to argue that there is no criticism of and no opposition to philo-German discourses in Romania or that xenophobic representations of Germanness discourses play no role in Romania. In effect, the step made by Klaus Iohannis, from a political career in local administration to one at the national level, was bound to also have an impact on the image of the German minority in Romania. Constantly playing the "German" card, implicitly or explicitly suggesting that Iohannis's German ethnicity is a quality in itself, can also have a boomerang effect. Consequently, opposition to or dissatisfaction with the political performance of Iohannis can easily take the form of anti-German positions. Over the past five years, this has been increasingly the case.

In the context of the presidential elections of 2014, Iohannis's main countercandidate, Social Democrat Victor Ponta, attempted to play the nationalistic card in order to garner votes and support. In doing this, he emphasized that Iohannis is not an ethnic Romanian, thus showing that being German in Romania does not imply fully avoiding being the target of discursive xenophobic attacks. Nonetheless, Iohannis, running on behalf of the Liberal Party, did win the presidential elections.

However, the Social Democrats in the meantime won the parliamentary elections of 2016 and are the main party in government. At the time of writing these considerations (October 2018), there is an open conflict between them and Iohannis. This also means that nationalistic, xenophobic and particularly anti-German discourses meant to delegitimize Iohannis (and, by extension, the German minority in Romania in general) are much more visible than some years ago. This practically happens by an appropriation of some previously rather marginal anti-German positions, which were found mainly in the radically nationalist camp, ideologically close to the Romanian extreme right movement whose traditions go back to the interwar period. Paradoxically, this criticism relates to the fascist past of the German minority in Romania. It mainly relies on arguments suggesting that the Democratic Forum of Germans in Sibiu and the Lutheran Church were restituted properties having actually belonged to the German Ethnic Group. Since the latter was officially declared a Nazi organization at the end of the Second World War, the argument goes, it would result that the German Forum and the Lutheran Church are de jure continuators of a former Nazi organization.

The subject was first addressed by journalist Marius Albin Marinescu from Sibiu, who has made a career out of opposing Iohannis at the local level mainly in the pages of his journal, *Justițiarul*. Marinescu's positions tick all the boxes of radical Romanian conservative nationalism: anti-Semitic, anti-Roma, anti-Hungarian, anti-LGBT, Orthodoxist and also anti-German. The rostrum for disseminating his positions is the newspaper *Justițiarul*, a "magazine of attitude against corruptions and abuses".[3] Marinescu's anti-Iohannis and anti-German rants were not taken seriously by too many people while Iohannis was the mayor of Sibiu. Yet in connection with Iohannis's move from local to national politics, some of the topics he addressed were taken up by national publications, with even a TV show on a national channel (B1 TV) amateurishly and inflamingly discussing the connection between the German Ethnic Group, the Nazi organization of the German minority in Romania during the Second World War and the Democratic Forum of Germans in Romania. Following the broadcast, the television channel was fined for the defamatory statements against the German minority in Romania.[4] The topic was also addressed, in rather similar terms, by historian Ioan Scurtu, member of the Romanian Academy, and by journalists such as Ion Cristoiu and Corneliu Nistorescu.[5] Economist Radu Golban is also disseminating a mixture of Eurosceptic and anti-German stances, including criticism of German politics in the European Union and criticism of Romanian German minority politics.[6] Such positions used to be largely niche positions, but over the last two years, they have been slowly making their way to the foreground of public debate. In this context, in their conflict with Klaus Iohannis, Social Democratic politicians also increasingly employ an anti-German rhetoric, without shying away from referring to the German and Romanian German Nazi past.[7] Their handling of such topics is painfully embarrassing, to say the least. At the same time, the issues underlying these anti-German positions are relevant social, political, and economic issues that do require a critical assessment. The Nazi past of the Romanian German institutions during the interwar period and the during the Second World War, or the configuration of power hierarchies and of inequalities in post-1989 Romania as a consequence of the process of property restitution, do need to be critically addressed, in a way that avoids mimetic and self-Orientalizing philo-Germanism, as well as xenophobic anti-Germanism.

At the core of these frictions lies the post-1989 liberal, business-friendly consensus, mixed with cultural conservatism. The Europeanizing desires inscribed within the self-Orientalized Romanian philo-Germanism fit in well within this liberal-conservative marriage, which seems to be more of a love marriage rather than a marriage of convenience. The challenge is to recognize this. The challenge is also that of coming up with a critical discourse addressing the philo-Germanism in Romania, a discourse that does not fall into the easy trap of anti-Germanism. This book has hopefully contributed to this aim.

Notes

1 Nicholas Kulish, "Grim Romanians Brighten Over a German Connection," *New York Times*, 5 December 2009, www.nytimes.com/2009/12/06/world/europe/06romania.html?scp=1&sq=grim%20romanians&st=cse (accessed 12 June 2018).
2 "Alocuţiunea Preşedintelui României, domnul Klaus Iohannis, susţinută în cadrul festivităţii de deschidere a anului şcolar preuniversitar 2018–2019," 10 September 2018, www.presidency.ro/ro/media/discursuri/alocutiunea-presedintelui-romaniei-domnul-klaus-iohannis-sustinuta-in-cadrul-festivitatii-de-deschidere-a-anului-scolar-preuniversitar-2018-2019 (accessed 16 September 2018).
3 It is enough to search for the keywords "Klaus Iohannis" on the following website of the publication to find a plethora of articles criticizing Iohannis in particular and Germany and Germans in general: www.justitiarul.ro/?s=klaus+iohannis&submit=Search (accessed 16 September 2018).
4 Consiliul Naţional al Audiovizualului, "Decizia nr. 316 din 13.06.2017 privind amendarea cu 50.000 lei a S.C. B1 TV CHANNEL S.R.L.," www.cna.ro/IMG/pdf/Dec316-B1TV.pdf (accessed 16 September 2018).
5 Ion Cristoiu, "Grupul Etnic German, moştenit cu imobile cu tot de FDGR a lui Klaus Iohannis, i-a dat mari bătăi de cap şi Mareşalului Antonescu," 25 February 2017, www.cristoiublog.ro/gindul-de-simbata-25-februarie-2017/ (accessed 16 September 2018); Cornel Nistorescu, "Klaus Iohannis, beneficiar de case şi proprietăţi naziste," *Cotidianul.ro*, 15 February 2017, www.cotidianul.ro/klaus-iohannis-beneficiar-de-case-si-proprietati-naziste/ (accessed 16 September 2018); Ioan Scurtu, "Schimbarea la faţă a Grupului Etnic German din România," *Cotidianul.ro*, 15 February 2017, www.cotidianul.ro/schimbarea-la-fata-a-grupului-etnic-german-din-romania/ (accessed 16 September 2018).
6 See http://radugolban.ro (accessed 16 September 2018).
7 Cristian Citre, "Olguţa Vasilescu, aluzie jignitoare la adresa lui Klaus Iohannis şi a poporului german: Ca neamţ, să vorbeşti de gazare, trebuie să ai mult curaj," *G4media.ro*, 24 August 2018, www.g4media.ro/olguta-vasilescu-aluzie-jignitoare-la-adresa-lui-klaus-iohannis-si-a-poporului-german-ca-neamt-sa-vorbesti-de-gazare-trebuie-sa-ai-mult-curaj.html (accessed 16 September 2018); "Liviu Pop: Preşedintele Klaus Iohannis a condus o organizaţie care este un 'continuator' al unui grup nazist," 23 August 2018, www.news.ro/politic-intern/liviu-pop-presedintele-klaus-iohannis-a-condus-o-organizatie-care-este-continuator-al-unui-grup-nazist-1922400523002018082118364193 (accessed 16 September 2018).

Bibliography

Achim, V. (2004). *The Roma in Romanian History*, trans. R. Davies. Budapest: Central European University Press.
Ackrill, U. (2015). *Zeiden, im Januar*. Berlin: Verlag Klaus Wagenbach.
Adamovsky, E. (2005). "Euro-Orientalism and the Making of the Concept of Eastern Europe in France, 1810–1880". *Journal of Modern History* 77(3), 591–628.
———. (2006). *Euro-Orientalism: Liberal Ideology and the Image of Russia in France (c. 1740–1880)*. Oxford: Peter Lang.
Ahonen, P. (2003). *After the Expulsion: West Germany and Eastern Europe 1945–1990*. Oxford: Oxford University Press.
Alionescu, C. C. (2004). "Parliamentary Representation of Minorities in Romania." *Southeast European Politics* 5(1), 60–75.
Almási, G. (2010). "Constructing the Wallach 'Other' in the Late Renaissance." In *Whose Love of Which Country? Composite States, National Histories and Patriotic Discourses in Early Modern East Central Europe*, eds. B. Trencsényi and M. Zászkaliczky. Leiden: Brill, 91–130.
Andreescu, G. (2001). *Ruleta. Români și maghiari, 1990–2000 – jurnal tematic*. Iași: Polirom.
———. (2004). *Națiuni și minorități*. Iași: Polirom.
Andreescu, G., Stan, V. and Weber, R. (1995). "Pact on Stability in Europe: Romania's Interests." *International Studies* 1, 5–11.
Antohi, S. (1999). "Cioran și stigmatul românesc. Mecanisme identitare și definiții radicale ale etnicității." In *Civitas imaginalis. Istorie și utopie în cultura română*, 2nd revised edition, 235–324. Iași: Polirom.
Arfire, R. (2011). "The Moral Regulation of the Second Europe: Transition, Europeanization, and the Romanians." *Critical Sociology* 37(6), 853–870.
Armbruster, A. (1980). *Dacoromano-Saxonica. Cronicari români despre sași. Românii în cronica săsească*. Bucharest: Editura Științifică și Enciclopedică.
———. (1991). *Auf die Spuren der eigenen Identität*. Bucharest: Editura Științifică și Enciclopedică.
Ash, T. G. (1999). *History of the Present: Essays, Sketches and Despatches from Europe in the 1990s*. London: Allen Lane, The Penguin Press.
Aurescu, B. (2002). "Romanian Legislation on Kin-Minorities." In *The Protection of National Minorities by Their Kin-State/La protection des minorités nationales par leur État-parent*, ed. European Commission for Democracy Through Law/Commission européenne pour la démocratie par le droit, 175–193. Strasbourg: Council of Europe Publishing/Éditions du Conseil de l'Europe.

174 Bibliography

———. (2003). "Bilateral Agreements as a Means of Solving Minority Issues: The Case of the Hungarian Status Law." *European Yearbook of Minority Issues* 3, 519–530.

Baier, H., ed. (1994). *Deportarea etnicilor germani din România în Uniunea Sovietică 1945. Culegere de documente de arhivă*. Sibiu: Forumul Democrat al Germanilor din România.

———, ed. (2003). *Departe, în Rusia, la Stalino: amintiri şi documente cu privire la deportarea în Uniunea Sovietică a etnicilor germani din România (1945–1950)*. Reşiţa: InterGraf.

———. (2010). "In der Heimat Europa heimisch. Glanzlichter in der 20-jährigen Geschichte des Demokratischen Forums der Deutschen in Rumänien." *Deutsches Jahrbuch für Rumänien*, 27–30.

Bakić-Hayden, M. (1995). "Nesting Orientalisms: The Case of Former Yugoslavia." *Slavic Review* 54(4), 917–931.

Ballinger, P. (2017). "Whatever Happened to Eastern Europe? Revisiting Europe's Eastern Peripheries." *East European Politics and Societies and Cultures* 31(1), 44–67.

Ban, C. (2013). "From Cocktail to Dependence: Revisiting the Foundations of Dependent Market Economies." *GEGI Working Paper*, 2 December. www.bu.edu/pardeeschool/files/2014/11/Dependent-market-economy-Working-Paper.pdf (accessed 22 September 2018).

Baranowski, S. (2011). *Nazi Empire: German Colonialism and Imperialism from Bismarck to Hitler*. New York: Cambridge University Press.

Barcan, M. and Millitz, A. (1978). *The German Nationality in Romania*, trans. Anda Teodorescu-Bantaş. Bucharest: Meridiane.

Bárdi, N., Gidó, A. and Novák, C. Z., eds. (2014). *Primele forme de autoorganizare a maghiarilor din România: 1989–1990*. Cluj-Napoca: Editura Institutului pentru Studierea Problemelor Minorităţilor Naţionale.

Batt, J. (2002). "Reinventing Banat." *Regional and Federal Studies* 12(2), 178–202.

Bavaj, R. and Steber, M., eds. (2015a). *Germany and 'the West': The History of a Modern Concept*. New York: Berghahn Books.

———. (2015b). "Germany and 'the West': The Vagaries of a Modern Relationship." In Bavaj and Steber. *Germany and the 'West'*, 1–37.

Beer, M. (1998). "Der Zweite Weltkrieg und die Nachkriegszeit." In Gündisch. *Siebenbürgen und die Siebenbürger Sachsen*, 201–250.

———. (2002). "Die Landler. Versuch eines geschichtlichen Überblicks." In *Die Siebenbürgischen Landler. Eine Spurensicherung*, vol. 1, eds. M. Bottesch, F. Grieshofer and W. Schabus, 23–80. Vienna: Böhlau Verlag.

———. (2009). "Rumänien: Regionale Spezifika des Umgangs mit deutschen Minderheiten am Ende des Zweiten Weltkriegs in Südosteuropa." In *Deutschsein als Grenzerfahrung. Minderheitenpolitik in Europa zwischen 1914 und 1950*, eds. M. Beer, D. Beyrau and C. Rauh, 279–303. Essen: Klartext.

Békés, C., Borhi, L., Ruggenthaler, P. and Traşcă, O. (2015). "Introduction." In *Soviet Occupation of Romania, Hungary, and Austria 1944/45–1948/49*, eds. C. Békés, L. Borhi, P. Ruggenthaler and O. Traşcă, 1–28. Budapest: Central European University Press.

Bell, A. (1996). "The Hungarians in Romania Since 1989." *Nationalities Papers* 24(3), 491–507.

Bergel, H. (1976). *Die Siebenbürger Sachsen nach dreißig Jahren Kommunismus. Eine Studie über Menschenrechte am Beispiel einer ethnischen Gruppe hinter dem Eisernen Vorhang*. Innsbruck: Wort und Welt Verlag.

Berger, S. (2010). "Rising Like a Phoenix . . . The Renaissance of National History Writing in Germany and Britain Since the 1980s." In *Nationalizing the Past: Historians as Nation Builders in Modern Europe*, eds. S. Berger and C. Lorenz, 426–451. Basingstoke: Palgrave Macmillan.

———. (2015). "Building the Nation Among Visions of German Empire." In *Nationalizing Empires*, eds. S. Berger and A. Miller, 247–308. Budapest: Central European University Press.

Berner, H. and Radosav, D., eds. (1996). *und keiner weiß warum. Donbaß. Eine deportierte Geschichte*. Ravensburg: Landsmannschaft der Sathmarer Schwaben.

Best, U. (2007). *Transgression as a Rule: German-Polish Cross-Border Cooperation, Border Discourse and EU-Enlargement*. Berlin: LIT Verlag.

Betea, L., Diac, C., Mihai, F-R. and Țiu, I., eds. (2012). *Lungul drum spre nicăieri. Germanii din România deportați în URSS*. Târgoviște: Editura Cetatea de Scaun.

Bideleux, R. (2015). "The 'Orientalization' and 'de-Orientalization' of East Central Europe and the Balkan Peninsula." *Journal of Contemporary Central and Eastern Europe* 23(1), 9–44.

Binder, L. (1988). "Die Evangelische Kirche, 1849–1914." In *Die Siebenbürger Sachsen in den Jahren 1849–1918*, ed. C. Göllner, 227–242. Cologne: Böhlau Verlag.

Binder-Iijima, E., Löwe, H-D. and Volkmer, G., eds. (2010). *Die Hohenzollern in Rumänien 1866–1947. Eine monarchische Herrschaftsordnung im europäischen Kontext*. Cologne: Böhlau Verlag.

Blackbourn, D. (2006). "Das Kaiserreich transnational. Eine Skizze." In *Das Kaiserreich transnational. Deutschland in der Welt 1871–1914*, eds. S. Conrad and J. Osterhammel, 302–324. Göttingen: Vandenhoeck & Ruprecht.

Blaga, L. (2011). *Trilogia culturii*. Bucharest: Humanitas.

Blaut, J. M. (1993). *The Colonizer's Model of the World: Geographical Diffusionism and Eurocentric History*. New York, London: The Guildford Press.

Bodnár, J. (2014). "Shamed by Comparison – Eastern Europe and the 'Rest'." In *EUtROPEs: The Paradox of European Empire*, eds. J. W. Boyer and B. Molden, 256–268. Chicago: University of Chicago.

Böhm, J. (1985). *Das Nationalsozialistische Deutschland und die Deutsche Volksgruppe in Rumänien 1936–1944. Das Verhältnis der Deutschen Volksgruppe zum Dritten Reich und zum rumänischen Staat sowie der interne Widerstreit zwischen den politischen Gruppen*. Frankfurt am Main: Peter Lang.

———. (1993). *Die Deutschen in Rumänien und die Weimarer Republik 1919–1933*. Ippesheim: AGK.

———. (1999). *Die Deutschen in Rumänien und das Dritte Reich 1933–1940*. Frankfurt am Main: Peter Lang.

———. (2003). *Die Gleichschaltung der Deutschen Volksgruppe in Rumänien und das "Dritte Reich"*. Frankfurt am Main: Peter Lang.

———. (2006). *Hitlers Vassallen der Deutschen Volksgruppe in Rumänien vor und nach 1945*. Frankfurt am Main: Peter Lang.

———. (2008). *Nationalsozialistische Indoktrination der Deutschen in Rumänien 1932–1944*. Frankfurt am Main: Peter Lang.

Boia, L. (2001). *Romania: Borderland of Europe*, trans. J. C. Brown. London: Reaktion Books.

———. (2014). *"Germanofilii". Elita intelectuală românească în anii Primului Război Mondial*, 3rd edition. Bucharest: Humanitas.

Bibliography

Boldur-Lățescu, G. (1992). *Genocidul Comunist în România, vol. I: Dimensiunile genocidului*. Bucharest: Albatros.
———. (1998). *Genocidul Comunist în România, vol. III: Destine Strivite*. Bucharest: Albatros.
Bolovan, S. P. and Bolovan, I. (2000). *Germanii din România. Perspective istorice și demografice*. Cluj-Napoca: Centrul de Studii Transilvane.
Botea, B. (2008). "'Valoare colectivă' și discurs performativ asupra interculturalității: o abordare a noilor procese de dezvoltare la Jimbolia." In *Banatul din memorie. Studii de caz*, ed. S. Vultur, 223–246. Timișoara: Marineasa.
Böttcher, B. (2009). *Gefallen für Volk und Heimat. Kriegerdenkmäler deutscher Minderheiten in Ostmitteleuropa während der Zwischenkriegszeit*. Cologne: Böhlau Verlag.
Bottesch, M. (2002). "Identität und Ethnizität der Landler." In *Die Siebenbürgischen Landler. Eine Spurensicherung*, vol. 1, eds. M. Bottesch, F. Grieshofer and W. Schabus, 155–177. Cologne: Böhlau Verlag.
———. (2004). "Gedanken über die Zukunft des deutschsprachigen Schulwesens in Rumänien." In *15 Jahre Demokratisches Forum der Deutschen in Rumänien, ed. Demokratisches Forum der Deutschen in Rumänien*, eds. Einblick and Ausblick, 105–110. Hermannstadt: Honterus Verlag.
———. (2015). "Zur Lage der deutschen Minderheit in Rumänien von 1990 bis 2014." *Deutsches Jahrbuch für Rumänien* 19–35.
Bourdieu, R. (1991). "Identity and Representation: Elements for a Critical Reflection on the Idea of Region." In *Language and Symbolic Power*, trans. G. Raymond and M. Adamson, 220–228. Cambridge: Polity Press.
Boym, S. (2001). *The Future of Nostalgia*. New York: Basic Books.
Bracewell, W. (2009). "Balkan Travel Writing: Points of Departure." In *Balkan Departures: Travel Writing from Southeastern Europe*, eds. W. Bracewell and A. Drace-Francis, 1–24. New York: Berghahn Books.
Brubaker, R. (1992). *Citizenship and Nationhood in France and Germany*. Cambridge, MA: Harvard University Press.
———. (1996). *Nationalism Reframed: Nationhood and the National Question in the New Europe*. Cambridge: Cambridge University Press.
———. (1998). "Migrations of Ethnic Unmixing in the 'New Europe'." *The International Migration Review* 32(4), 1047–1065.
———. (2005). "The 'Diaspora' Diaspora." *Ethnic and Racial Studies* 28(1), 1–19.
———. (2006). *Ethnicity Without Groups*. Cambridge, MA: Harvard University Press.
———. (2013). "Categories of Analysis and Categories of Practice: A Note on the Study of Muslims in European Countries of Immigration." *Ethnic and Racial Studies* 36(1), 1–8.
Brubaker, R., Feischmidt, M., Fox, J. and Grancea, L. (2006). *Nationalist Politics and Everyday Ethnicity in a Transylvanian Town*. Princeton: Princeton University Press.
Budeancă, C. (2016). *Imaginea etnicilor germani la românii din Transilvania după 1918. Studiu de caz: județele Hunedoara, Alba, Sibiu. Cercetare de istorie orală*. Târgoviște: Editura Cetatea de Scaun.
Burgess, A. (1997). *Divided Europe: The New Domination of the East*. London: Pluto Press.
Burlec, L., Lazăr, L. and Teodorescu, B. (1998). *Istoria românilor. Manual pentru clasa a IV-a*. Bucharest: All Educațional.
Burnett, G. and Nocasian, M. (2008). "A Romania of the Imagination: *Formula As*, Virtual Community, and Normative Behavior." *First Monday* 13(11). http://firstmonday.org/htbin/cgiwrap/bin/ojs/index.php/fm/article/view/2257/2040 (accessed 28 July 2017).

Câmpeanu, C. N. (2008). "Material Desires: Cultural Production, Post-Socialist Transformations, and Heritage Tourism in a Transylvanian Town." Doctoral dissertation, University of Texas at Austin.

———. (2012). "Celebrating Crown Day After the 1990s Saxon Migration: Reconfigurations of Ethnicity in a South Transylvanian Village." *Studia Universitatis Babeş-Bolyai Sociologia* 57(2), 101–119.

Case, H. (2009). *Between States: The Transylvanian Question and the European Idea During World War II*. Stanford: Stanford University Press.

Casteel, J. (2016). *Russia in the German Global Imaginary: Imperial Visions and Utopian Desires*. Pittsburgh: University of Pittsburgh Press.

Castellan, G. (1971). "The Germans of Rumania." *Journal of Contemporary History* 6(1), 52–75.

Cento Bull, A. and Hansen, H. L. (2016). "On Agonistic Memory." *Memory Studies* 9(4), 390–404.

Cercel, C. (2009). "Gli Altri Tedeschi." *Equilibri* 13(3), 423–428.

———. (2011). "The Relationship Between Religious and National Identity in the Case of Transylvanian Saxons (1933–1944)." *Nationalities Papers* 39(2), 161–180.

———. (2012). "Transylvanian Saxon Symbolic Geographies." *Civilisations* 60(2), 83–101.

———. (2015). "Philo-Germanism Without Germans in Romania After 1989." *East European Politics and Societies and Cultures* 29(4), 811–830.

———. (2016). "Romanian Germans After the Second World War: Transnational History, Transnational Memory." *Jahrbuch des Bundesinstituts für Kultur und Geschichte der Deutschem im östlichen Europa* 24, 357–379.

———. (2017). "Postwar (West) German-Romanian Relations: Expanding Brubaker's Analytic Triad." *Nationalism and Ethnic Politics* 23(3), 297–317.

Chelcea, L. and Lăţea, P. (2000). *România profundă în comunism. Dileme identitare, istorie locală şi economie secundară în Sântana*. Bucharest: Nemira.

Chirot, D. (1976). *Social Change in a Peripheral Society: The Creation of a Balkan Colony*. New York: Academic Press.

Chu, W. (2012a). *The German Minority in Interwar Poland*. Cambridge: Cambridge University Press.

———. (2012b). "The 'Lodzermensch': From Cultural Contamination to Marketable Multiculturalism." In *Germany, Poland and Postmemorial Relations: In Search of a Livable Past*, eds. K. Kopp and J. Niżyńska, 239–258. New York: Palgrave Macmillan.

Ciobanu, V. (1991). "Wer ist der Autor der Broschüre 'Ce sunt şi ce vor saşii din Ardeal?'" *Zeitschrift für siebenbürgische Landeskunde* 14(1), 37–39.

———. (2001). *Contribuţii la cunoaşterea istoriei saşilor transilvăneni, 1918–1944*. Sibiu: Editura hora.

———. (2013). *Germanii din România în anii 1918–1919*. Sibiu: Editura Honterus.

———. (2016). "Germani." In *Cronologia minorităţilor naţionale din România, vol. I: Albanezi, armeni, bulgari, croaţi, eleni, evrei şi germani*, ed. A. Gidó, second edition, 303–364. Cluj: Editura Institutului pentru Studierea Problemelor Minorităţilor Naţionale.

Cioran, E. M. (1995). *Scrisori către cei de-acasă*, trans. T. Radu. Bucharest: Humanitas.

Cioroianu, A. (2002). "The Impossible Escape: Romanians and the Balkans." In *Balkan as Metaphor. Between Globalization and Fragmentation*, eds. D. I. Bjelić and O. Savić, 209–233. Cambridge, MA: MIT Press.

———. (2007). *Pe umerii lui Marx. O introducere în istoria comunismului românesc*, second edition. Bucharest: Curtea Veche.

Cistelecan, A. (2015). "From Region to Culture, from Culture to Class." *Debatte: Journal of Contemporary Central and Eastern Europe* 23(1), 45–60.
Ciuhandu, G. (2009). "Bis an den Rand physischer Erschöpfung." Interview by A. Săliște and W. Kremm. *Deutsches Jahrbuch für Rumänien* 41–45.
Comisia Națională pentru Statistică (1992). *Recensămîntul populației și locuințelor din 7 ianuarie 1992. Rezultate preliminare*. Bucharest: Comisia Națională pentru Statistică.
Comisia Prezidențială pentru Analiza Dictaturii Comuniste din România. (2006). *Raport Final*. www.wilsoncenter.org/sites/default/files/RAPORT%20FINAL_%20CADCR.pdf (accessed 22 September 2018).
Confino, M. (1994). "Re-Inventing the Enlightenment: Western Images of Eastern Realities in the Eighteenth Century." *Canadian Slavonic Papers* 36(3–4), 505–523.
Connerton, P. (1989). *How Societies Remember*. Cambridge: Cambridge University Press.
Conrad, S. (2010). *Globalisation and the Nation in Imperial Germany*, trans. S. O' Horgan. Cambridge: Cambridge University Press.
Copilaș, E. (2015). *Națiunea socialistă. Politica identității în epoca de aur*. Iași: Polirom.
Cordell, K. (2009). "Memory, Identity and Poland's German Minority." *German Politics and Society* 27(4), 1–23.
Cordell, K. and Wolff, S. (2005). *Germany's Foreign Policy Towards Poland and the Czech Republic: Ostpolitik Revisited*. London: Routledge.
———. (2007). "Germany as a Kin-State: The Development and Implementation of a Norm-Consistent External Minority Policy Towards Central and Eastern Europe." *Nationalities Papers* 35(2), 289–315.
Corsale, A. and Iorio, M. (2014). "Transylvanian Saxon Culture as Heritage: Insights from Viscri, Romania." *Geoforum* 52, 22–31.
Csergő, Z. (2002). "Beyond Ethnic Division: Majority-Minority Debate About the Postcommunist State in Romania and Slovakia." *East European Politics and Societies* 16(1), 1–29.
Custred, G. (1992). "Dual Ethnic Identity of the Transylvanian Saxons." *East European Quarterly* 25(4), 483–491.
Dácz, E. (2017). "Fragen der Ethnizität der Sathmarer Schwaben nach 1989." In *Deutsch in Mittel-, Ost und Südosteuropa. Geschichtliche Grundlagen und aktuelle Einbettung*, eds. H. Philipp and A. Ströbel, 262–284. Regensburg: Verlag Friedrich Pustet.
David-Fox, M. (2010). "Conclusion: Transnational History and the East-West Divide." In *Imagining the West in Eastern Europe and the Soviet Union*, ed. G. Péteri, 258–267. Pittsburgh: University of Pittsburgh Press.
Danneberg, S. (2017). "Das Verhältnis zwischen Sachsen und Rumänen in Siebenbürgen." In *Umbruch mit Schlachtenlärm. Siebenbürgen und der Erste Weltkrieg*, ed. H. Heppner, 113–127. Cologne: Böhlau Verlag.
Dascălu, B. M. (2006). *Germanitatea și literele române*. Bucharest: Ideea Europeană.
Davis, S. (2011). "East-West Discourses in Transylvania: Transitional *Erdély*, German-Western *Siebenbürgen* or Latin-Western *Ardeal*?" In *The East-West Discourse: Symbolic Geography and Its Consequences*, ed. A. Maxwell, 127–153. Bern: Peter Lang.
———. (2016). "Constructing the *Volksgemeinschaft*: Saxon Particularism and the Myth of the German East, 1919–1933." *German Studies Review* 39(1), 41–64.
———. (2017). "Competitive Civilizing Missions: Hungarian Germans, Modernization, and Ethnographic Descriptions of the *Zigeuner* before World War I." *Central European History* 50(1), 6–33.
Demokratisches Forum der Deutschen in Rumänien. ([1990] 1993). "Erklärung des Demokratischen Forums der Deutschen in Rumänien 9. Juli 1990." *Zugänge* 14, 45–49.

―――, ed. (2014). *Die deutsche Minderheit in Rumänien. Geschichte und Gegenwart im vereinten Europa.* Hermannstadt: Honterus Verlag.

De Trégomain, P. (2003). "Le syndrome du peuple élu: les Saxons de Transylvanie et la destruction des confins." *Cultures d'Europe Centrale* 5. www.circe.paris-sorbonne.fr/spip.php?article61&lang=fr (accessed 22 September 2018).

―――. (2006). "Les frontières du dicible. Les Saxons de Transylvanie et la Seconde Guerre mondiale." Doctoral dissertation, Université Paris III, Sorbonne Nouvelle.

―――. (2007). "'Normales'? Les relations germano-roumaines avant et après la chute du Mur." *Allemagne d'aujourd'hui* 182, 81–89.

Detrez, R. (2002). "Colonialism in the Balkans: Historic Realities and Contemporary Perceptions." *Kakanien Revisited*, 15 May. www.kakanien-revisited.at/beitr/theorie/RDetrez1.pdf (accessed 29 June 2018).

Devere, H., Simon, M. and Verbitsky, J. (2011). "A History of the Language of Friendship in International Treaties." *International Politics* 48(1), 46–70.

Direcția Generală de Statistică. (1969). *Recensământul populației și locuințelor din 15 martie 1966, vol. I: Rezultate generale. Partea întâi – populație.* Bucharest: Direcția Centrală de Statistică.

―――. (1980). *Recensământul populației și al locuințelor din 5 ianuarie 1977, vol. I: Populație – structura demografică.* Bucharest: Direcția Centrală de Statistică.

Djuvara, N. (1989). *Le Pays Roumain entre Orient et Occident. Les Principautés danubiennes au début du XIXe siècle.* N.p.: Publications Orientalistes de France.

―――. (2005). *O scurtă istorie a românilor povestită celor tineri,* fifth revised edition. Bucharest: Humanitas.

Dobre, A. M. (2004). "The Europeanisation of the Romanian Minority Rights Policy: Misfit, Change and Controversies." *Studia Politica. Romanian Political Science Review* 4(3), 631–666.

Dobre, F., Banu, F., Banu, L. and Stancu, L., eds. (2011). *Acțiunea "Recuperarea". Securitatea și emigrarea germanilor din România (1962–1989).* Bucharest: Editura Enciclopedică.

Dowling, W. C. (1991). "Germanissimi Germanorum: Romania's Vanishing German Culture." *East European Politics and Societies* 5(2), 341–355.

Drace-Francis, A. (2006). *The Making of Modern Romanian Culture: Literacy and the Development of National Identity.* London: Tauris Academic Studies.

―――. (2013). *The Traditions of Invention: Romanian Ethnic and Social Stereotypes in Historical Context.* Leiden: Brill.

Dragoman, D. (2005). "La recomposition du champ politique régional en Roumanie. Le succès du Forum Allemand à Sibiu/Hermannstadt." *Studia Politica* 5(1), 181–201.

―――. (2013). "The Success of the German Democratic Forum in Sibiu: Non-Ethnic Voting, Political Neutrality and Economic Performance." *Transitions* 53(1–2), 95–117.

Dragoman, D. and Zamfira, A. (2008). "L'influence des stéréotypes sur les performances électorales des partis des minorités ethniques en Roumanie. Allemands et hongrois en perspective comparée." *Transitions* 48(1), 135–161.

Dupcsik, C. (1999). "Postcolonial Studies and the Inventing of Eastern Europe." *East Central Europe/L'Europe du Centre-Est. Eine wissenschaftliche Zeitschrift* 26(1), 1–14.

―――. (2001). "The West, the East, and the Border-Lining." *Newsletter Social Science in Eastern Europe,* special edition 31–39. www.gesis.org/fileadmin/upload/dienstleistung/fachinformationen/newsletterssee/dokumente/archiv/nl2001s.pdf (accessed 24 April 2017).

180 Bibliography

Durst, M. (1993). "Initiativgruppe Auswanderer, gegründet am 15. Januar 1990 in Großscheuern." *Zugänge* 14, 43–45.

Ehrmann, K. A. (2003). "Zehn Kerzen auf der Geburtstagstorte." *Deutsches Jahrbuch für Rumänien* 32–37.

Eiwen, D. (1988). "Das Bild Deutschlands und des Deutschen in der rumänischen Literatur." Doctoral dissertation, University of Cologne.

———. (1998). "Das Bild der Siebenbürger Deutschen in rumänischen Schrifttum. Momentaufnahmen aus seiner Entstehung und Entwicklung." In *Das Bild des Anderen in Siebenbürgen*, eds. K. Gündisch, W. Höpken and M. Markel, 263–284. Cologne: Böhlau Verlag.

Eliade, P. (1898). *De l'influence française sur l'esprit public en Roumanie. Les origines. Étude sur l'état de la société roumaine à l'époque des règnes phanariotes*. Paris: Ernest Leroux.

Ernu, V., Rogozanu, C., Șiulea, C. and Țichindeleanu, O., eds. (2008). *Iluzia anticomunismului. Lecturi critice ale raportului Tismăneanu*. Chișinău: Cartier.

Eschenazi, G. and Nissim, G. (2004). *Ebrei invisibili. I sopravvisuti dell'Europa Orientale dal communismo a oggi*. Milano: Oscar Mondadori.

Evans, R. J. W. (2006). "Transylvanian Saxons." In *Austria, Hungary and the Habsburgs: Essays on Central Europe c. 1683–1867*, 209–227. Oxford: Oxford University Press.

Feichtinger, J., Prutsch, U. and Csáky, M., eds. (2003). *Habsburg Postcolonial. Machtstrukturen und kollektives Gedächtnis*. Innsbruck: StudienVerlag.

Fischer, E. (1911). *Die Kulturarbeit des Deutschtums in Rumänien. Ein Versuch zur Grundlegung ihrer Geschichte*. Hermannstadt: W. Krafft.

Fleck, G. and Rughiniș, C., eds. (2008). *Come Closer: Inclusion and Exclusion of Roma in Present-Day Romanian Society*. Bucharest: Human Dynamics.

Fleming, K. E. (2000). "*Orientalism*, the Balkans, and Balkan Historiography." *American Historical Review* 105(4), 1218–1233.

Florian, C., Preda, D. and Trașcă, O., eds. (2009). *România – Republica Federală Germania, vol. I: Începutul relațiilor diplomatice 1966–1967*. Bucharest: Editura Enciclopedică.

Forstenheizler, J. (2004). "Identität und Identitätssuche der Sathmarschwaben." In *Einblick & Ausblick. 15 Jahre Demokratisches Forum der Deutschen in Rumänien*, ed. Demokratisches Forum der Deutschen in Rumänien, 87–97. Sibiu: Honterus Verlag.

Foucault, M. (1980). "The Confession of the Flesh." In *Power/Knowledge: Selected Interviews and Other Writings 1972–1977*, ed. C. Gordon, trans. C. Gordon, L. Marshall, J. Mapham and K. Soper, 194–228. New York: Pantheon Books.

Franzinetti, G. (2008). "The Idea and the Reality of Eastern Europe in the Eighteenth-Century." *History of European Ideas* 34(4), 361–368.

Frotscher, M. (2015). "A Lost Homeland, a Reinvented Homeland. Diaspora and the 'Culture of Memory' in the Colony of Danube Swabians of Entre Rios." Trans. S. Stroud. *German History* 33(3), 439–461.

Gabanyi, A. U. (1991) "Bleiben, gehen, wiederkehren? Zur Lage der deutschen Minderheit in Rumänien." *Südosteuropa. Zeitschrift für Gegenwartsforschung* 40, 493–517.

———. (2016). "Cuvânt înainte." In Hurezean. *Povestea sașilor* 9–13.

Gallagher, J. J. and Tucker, P. N. (2000). "Aussiedler Migration and Its Impact on Brașov's Ethnic German Population and Its Built Environment." *Geojournal* 50(2–3), 305–309.

Gallagher, T. (1995). *Romania After Ceaușescu: The Politics of Intolerance*. Edinburgh: Edinburgh University Press.

Ganț, O. (2013). "Das Reservoir für den Arbeitsmarkt ist in unseren Schulen." *Deutsches Jahrbuch für Rumänien* 23–24.

Gassert, P. (2015). "No Place for 'the West': National Socialism and the 'Defence of Europe'." In Bavaj and Steber. *Germany and the 'West'* 216–229.
Gavreliuc, A. (2003). *Mentalitate și societate. Cartografii ale imaginarului identitar în Banatul contemporan*. Timișoara: Editura Universității de Vest.
Georgescu, T. (2016). *The Eugenic Fortress: The Transylvanian Saxon Experiment in Interwar Romania*. Budapest: Central European University Press.
Gheorghiu, L. (2015). *Comunitatea dispărută. Germanii din România între anii 1945 și 1967*. Bucharest: Tritonic.
Girtler, R. (1992). *Verbannt und vergessen. Eine untergehende deutschsprachige Kultur in Rumänien*. Linz: Veritas.
———, ed. (1997). *Die Letzten der Verbannten: Der Untergang der altösterreichischen Landler in Siebenbürgen/Rumänien*. Vienna: Böhlau Verlag.
———, ed. (2007). *Das letzte Lied vor Hermannstadt: Das Verklingen einer deutschen Bauernkultur in Rumänien*. Cologne: Böhlau Verlag.
Giurescu, C. C. (1941). *Die europäische Rolle des rumänischen Volkes*. Bucharest: Dacia.
Giurescu, D. C. (1990). *The Razing of Romania's Past*. London: World Monuments Fund.
Golescu, D. ([1826] 1990). "Însemnare a călătoriii mele Constandin Radovici din Golești făcută în anul 1824, 1825, 1826." In *Scrieri*, ed. Mircea Anghelescu, 1–116. Bucharest: Minerva.
Golopenția, A. and Georgescu, D. C. (1948). *Populația Republicii Populare Române la 25 ianuarie 1948. Rezultatele provizorii ale recensământului. Extras din 'Probleme economice', nr. 2. Martie 1948*. Bucharest: Institutul Central de Statistică.
Göllner, C., ed. (1979). *Geschichte der Deutschen auf dem Gebiete Rumäniens*. Bucharest: Kriterion Verlag.
Gräf, R. (2018). "Germanii din Banat sau istoria între două emigrări. Cercul care s-a închis." In *Germanii din Banat prin povestirile lor*, ed. S. Vultur, 13–32. Iași: Polirom.
Grama, E. (2010). "Searching for Heritage, Building Politics: Architecture, Archaeology, and Imageries of Social Order in Romania (1947–2007)." Doctoral dissertation, University of Michigan.
Grancea, M. and Ciobanu, A. (2002). "Criza identitară românească. Discurs istoriografic și stereotipuri etnoculturale." In *Identitate și alteritate: Studii de imagologie III*, eds. N. Bocșan, S. Mitu and T. Nicoară, 363–378. Cluj-Napoca: Presa Universitară Clujeană.
Gross, S. G. (2015). *Export Empire: German Soft Power in Southeastern Europe*. Cambridge: Cambridge University Press.
Gruber, R. E. (2002). *Virtually Jewish: Reinventing Jewish Culture in Europe*. Berkeley, Los Angeles, London: University of California Press.
Gündisch, K. (1998). *Siebenbürgen und die Siebenbürger Sachsen*. Munich: Langen Müller.
Hahn, E. and Hahn, H. H. (2008). "The 'Germans and the East': Back to Normality – But What Is Normal?" In *The Germans and the East*, eds. C. Ingrao and F. A. J. Szabo, 421–438. West Lafayette: Purdue University Press.
Haynes, R. (2000). *Romanian Policy Towards Germany, 1936–40*. Houndmills: Palgrave Macmillan.
Hamlin, D. (2010). "'Wo sind wir?' Orientalism, Gender and War in the German Encounter with Romania." *German History* 28(4), 424–452.
———. (2017a). "Disease, Microbiology, and the Construction of a Colonial Space: Romania and the Central Powers in the First World War." *War and Society* 36(1), 31–43.
———. (2017b). *Germany's Empire in the East: Germans and Romania in an Era of Globalization and Total War*. Cambridge: Cambridge University Press.

182 Bibliography

Hammond, A. (2004). "Introduction." In *The Balkans and the West: Constructing the European Other, 1945–2003*, ed. A. Hammond, xi–xxiii. Aldershot: Ashgate.

Hartl, H. (1985). *Die Deutschen in Rumänien: 1918–1940, 1945–1985. Zur Geschichte ihres Niedergangs als Volksgruppe.*

Hasdeu, I. (2008). "Imagining the Gypsy Woman." Trans. M. Scott. *Third Text* 22(3), 347–357.

Hausleitner, M. (2001). *Die Rumänisierung der Bukowina: die Durchsetzung des nationalstaatlichen Anspruchs Grossrumäniens*. Munich: Oldenbourg Wissenschaftsverlag.

———. (2005). *Deutsche und Juden in Bessarabien 1814–1941. Zur Minderheitenpolitik Russlands und Großrumäniens*. München: IKGS Verlag.

———. (2014). *Die Donauschwaben 1868–1948. Ihre Rolle im rumänischen und serbischen Banat*. Stuttgart: Franz Steiner Verlag.

Heitmann, K. (1985). *Das Rumänenbild im deutschen Sprachraum, 1775–1918. Eine imagologische Studie*. Cologne: Böhlau Verlag.

———. (1998). "Die Rumänen Siebenbürgens aus deutscher Sicht im 19. Jahrhundert. Das Porträt der Ethnie von Rudolf Bergner (1884)." In *Das Bild des Anderen in Siebenbürgen*, eds. K. Gündisch, W. Höpken and M. Markel, 33–56. Cologne: Böhlau Verlag.

Hienz, H. A. (1998). "Fischer, Dr. med. Emil." In *Schriftsteller-Lexikon der Siebenbürger Deutschen: D-G*, ed. H. A. Hienz, 70–79. Cologne: Böhlau Verlag.

Higounet, C. (1989). *Les Allemands en Europe centrale et orientale au Moyen Age*. Paris: Aubier.

Hîncu, D. (1998). *'Noi' și germanii 'noștri' 1800–1914. Un studiu imagologic urmat de Tablouri dintr-o lume care a fost*. Bucharest: Editura Univers.

Hitchins, K. (1994). *Rumania: 1866–1947*. Oxford: Clarendon Press.

———. (1996). *The Romanians: 1774–1866*. Oxford: Clarendon Press.

———. (1999). *A Nation Discovered: Romanian Intellectuals in Transylvania and the Idea of Nation 1700/1848*. Bucharest: Editura Enciclopedică.

Hrenciuc, D. (2013). *Între destin și istorie. Germanii în Bucovina (1918–2012)*. Cluj-Napoca: Argonaut.

Hughes, A. (2011). "Germanicity Without Germans and Beyond: Post-Saxon Rural Transylvania." Paper presented at the conference "The Flight and Expulsion of Germans in Contemporary German Culture", Nottingham Trent University, 21 October.

Hughes, T., Hughes, A. and Koranyi, J. (2010). "Transylvanian Villages: Conservationism, but at What Price?" *Open Democracy*, 26 August. www.opendemocracy.net/james-korany-tom-hughes-alina-hughes/conservation-at-what-price (accessed 29 July 2017).

Hurezean, R. (2016). *Povestea sașilor din Transilvania. Spusă chiar de ei*. Cluj-Napoca: Editura Școala Ardeleană.

———. (2017). *Criț. Istoria, poveștile și viața unui sat de sași*. Bucharest: Curtea Veche.

Hurezeanu, E. (2017). "Trecutul este o altă țară." In Hurezean. *Criț*, 7–11.

Hüsch, H-G., Baier, H. and Meinhardt, E., eds. (2013). *Kauf von Freiheit*. Hermannstadt: Honterus Verlag.

Hüsch, H-G., Leber, P-D. and Baier, H., eds. (2016). *Wege in die Freiheit. Deutschrumänische Dokumente zur Familienzusammenführung und Aussiedlung 1969–1989*. Aachen: Landsmannschaft der Banater Schwaben e.V.

Iancu, B. (2007). "Sibiu CCE 2007. Moduri de întrebuințare." *Secolul 21* 1–6, 75–83.

Ibryamova, N. (2013). "European Union Political Conditionality and Minority Rights: Compliance in Bulgaria and Romania." *The International Journal of Human Rights* 17(3), 350–367.

Idel, M. (2009). "Foreword." In Oișteanu. *Inventing the Jew* ix–x.

Bibliography 183

Iliescu, I. (1995). *Momente de istorie. I: Documente, interviuri, comentarii: decembrie 1989-iunie 1990*. Bucharest: Editura Enciclopedică.

Ingrao, C. (2008). "The Early Modern Period." In *The Germans and the East*, eds. C. Ingrao and F. A. J. Szabo, 59–63. West Lafayette: Purdue University Press.

Institutul Național de Statistică. (2003). "Populația după etnie." www.insse.ro/cms/files/rpl2002rezgen1/14.pdf (accessed 29 June 2018).

———. (2011). "Recensământul populației și al locuințelor 2011. Rezultate definitive. Tabelul 7 (stânga). Populația stabilă pe sexe, după etnie – categorii de localități, macroregiuni, regiuni de dezvoltare și județe." www.rpl2011.djsct.ro/inceputj.php?cod=9&codj=0 (accessed 29 June 2018).

International Commission on the Holocaust in Romania. (2004). *Final Report*. Iași: Polirom.

Ioanid, R. (2005). *The Ransom of the Jews: The Story of the Extraordinary Secret Bargain between Romania and Israel*. Chicago: Ivan R. Dee.

Iohannis, K. (2010). "Im Amt des Bürgermeisters." In *Zwanzig Jahre Demokratisches Forum der Deutschen Hermannstadt*, ed. Demokratisches Forum der Deutschen in Hermannstadt, 17–21. Hermannstadt: Honterus Verlag.

———. (2014). *Pas cu pas*. Bucharest: Curtea Veche.

———. (2015). *Primul pas*. Bucharest: Curtea Veche.

Iorga, N. (1919). "Prefață." In *Ce sînt și ce vor sașii din Ardeal: Expunere din izvor competent*, 3–8. București: Tipografia Cultura Neamului Românesc.

———. (1977). *Pagini alese din însemnările de călătorie prin Ardeal și Banat*, 2 vols., ed. L. Cursaru. Bucharest: Minerva.

Irgang, W. (2012). "Mittelalterlicher Landesausbau/Ostsiedlung." *Online-Lexikon zur Kultur und Geschichte der Deutschen im östlichen Europa*. https://ome-lexikon.uni-oldenburg.de/begriffe/mittelalterlicher-landesausbau-ostsiedlung/ (accessed 29 June 2018).

Irwin-Zarecka, I. (1989). *Neutralizing Memory: The Jew in Contemporary Poland*. New Brunswick, Oxford: Transaction Publishers.

Ivan, A. L. (2006). *Stat, majoritate și minoritate națională în România (1919–1933). Cazul maghiarilor și germanilor din Transilvania*. Cluj-Napoca: Eikon.

Ivanov, L. (2004). *Imaginea rusului și a Rusiei în literatura română 1840–1948*. Chișinău: Cartier.

Jachomowski, D. (1984). *Die Umsiedlung der Bessarabien-, Bukowina- und Dobrudschadeutschen. Von der Volksgruppe in Rumänien zur "Siedlungsbrücke" an der Reichsgrenze*. Munich: R. Oldenbourg Verlag.

Jacobsen, H. A. and Tomala, M., eds. (1992). *Bonn-Warschau 1945–1991. Die deutschpolnischen Beziehungen 1945–1991*. Cologne: Verlag Wissenschaft und Politik.

Janowski, M., Iordachi, C. and Trencsényi, B. (2005). "Why Bother About Historical Regions? Debates About Central Europe in Hungary, Poland and Romania." *East-Central Europe* 32(1–2), 5–58.

Judson, P. (2005). "When Is a Diaspora Not a Diaspora? Rethinking Nation-Centered Narratives About Germans in Habsburg East Central Europe." In *The Heimat Abroad: The Boundaries of Germanness*, eds. K. O'Donnell, R. Bridenthal and N. Reagin, 219–247. Ann Arbor: The University of Michigan Press.

Kaindl, R. F. (1911). *Geschichte der Deutschen in den Karpathenländern, vol. III: Geschichte der Deutschen in Galizien, Ungarn, der Bukowina und Rumänien seit etwa 1770 bis zur Gegenwart*. Gotha: Friedrich Andreas Perthes.

Kaljund, K. (2006). "Zur Rolle des stereotypisierenden Deutschenbildes der Esten in Geschichte und Gegenwart." Doctoral dissertation, Ludwig Maximilians University Munich.

184 Bibliography

———. (2012). "East-West Dichotomies in the Construction of Estonian National Identity." *Central and Eastern European Review* 6, 1–31.

Kántor, Z., Majtényi, B., Ieda, O., Vizi, B. and Haléasz, I., eds., 2004. *The Hungarian Status Law: Nation Building and/or Minority Protection*. Sapporo: Slavic Research Center, Hokkaido University. http://src-h.slav.hokudai.ac.jp/coe21/publish/no4_ses/contents.html (accessed 18 August 2017).

Karl, J. C. (2006). "Die Minderheitenorganisation Demokratisches Forum der Deutschen in Rumänien (DFDR)/ Forumul Democrat al Germanilor din România (F.D.G.R.) seit 1989: Politisches Subjekt oder Objekt." *Trans. Internet-Zeitschrift für Kulturwissenschaften* 16 (May). www.inst.at/trans/16Nr/14_6/karl16.htm (accessed 22 September 2018).

———. (2011). "Ethnic Minorities Between Political Participation and Cultural Representation in Post-Communist Romania with a Special Focus on the Democratic Forum of the Germans in Romania (DFDR/F.D.G.R.)." Doctoral dissertation, University of Bucharest.

Karnoouh, C. (2008). *L'invention du peuple: Chroniques de Roumanie et d'Europe orientale*. Paris: Éditions L'Harmattan.

Kellogg, F. (1995). *The Road to Romanian Independence*. West Lafayette: Purdue University Press.

Kemp, W. (2006). "Kin-States Protecting National Minorities: Positive Trend or Dangerous Precedent?" In *European Integration and the Nationalities Question*, eds. J. McGarry and M. Keating, 103–123. London: Routledge.

Kift, D. (2010). "Neither Here Nor There? Memorialization of the Expulsion of Ethnic Germans." In *Memorialization in Germany since 1945*, eds. B. Niven and C. Paver, 78–87. Basingstoke: Palgrave Macmillan.

Kiossev, A. (1999). "Notes on Self-Colonising Cultures." In *Art and Culture in Post-Communist Europe*, eds. Bojana Pejić and David Elliott, 114–117. Stockholm: Moderna Museet, Modern Museum.

Kiss, T. and Székely, I. G. (2016). "Shifting Linkages in Ethnic Mobilization: The Case of RMDSZ and the Hungarians in Transylvania." *Nationalities Papers* 44(4), 591–610.

Klein, H. (2010). "Zwanzig Jahre deutsches Forum Hermannstadt." In *Zwanzig Jahre Demokratisches Forum der Deutschen in Hermannstadt*, ed. Demokratisches Forum der Deutschen in Hermannstadt, 9–15 Sibiu: Honterus Verlag.

Klekowski von Koppenfels, A. (2002). "The Decline of Privilege: The Legal Background to the Migration of Ethnic Germans." In *Coming Home to Germany? The Integration of Ethnic Germans from Central and Eastern Europe in the Federal Republic*, eds. D. Rock and S. Wolff, 102–118. New York: Berghahn Books.

Klimaszewski, C., Bader, G. E., Nyce, J. M. and Beasley, B. E. (2010). "Who Wins? Who Loses? Representation and 'Restoration' of the Past in a Rural Romanian Community." *Library Review* 59(2), 92–106.

König, W. (1979). "Haben die Siebenbürger Sachsen und die Banater Schwaben 1918/19 bedingungslos dem Anschluß an Rumänien zugestimmt?" *Zeitschrift für siebenbürgische Landeskunde* 2, 101–110.

Kontje, T. (2004). *German Orientalisms*. Ann Arbor: The University of Michigan Press.

Kopp, K. (2012). *Germany's Wild East: Constructing Poland as Colonial Space*. Ann Arbor: The University of Michigan Press.

Koranyi, J. (2008). "Between East and West: Romanian German Identities Since 1945." Doctoral dissertation, University of Exeter.

———. (2011). "Reinventing the Banat: Cosmopolitanism as a German Cultural Export." *German Politics and Society* 29(3), 97–112.

———. (2014). "Voyages of Socialist Discovery: German-German Exchanges Between the GDR and Romania." *The Slavonic and East European Review* 92(3), 479–506.
Koranyi, J. and Wittlinger, R. (2011). "From Diaspora to Diaspora: The Case of Transylvanian Saxons in Romania and Germany." *Nationalism and Ethnic Politics* 17(1), 96–115.
Kremm, W. (2002). "Mehr als nur Kabelbäume." *Deutsches Jahrbuch für Rumänien* 128–130.
———. (2009). "Vom Stammtisch zum Wirtschaftsclub." *Deutsches Jahrbuch für Rumänien* 51–54.
Król, E. C. (2006). "Das Bild des ethnischen Deutschen im polnischen Film." Trans. into German by B. Karwen. In *Die "Volksdeutschen" in Polen, Frankreich, Ungarn und der Tschechoslowakei. Mythos und Realität*, eds. J. Kochanowski and M. Sach, 367–389. Osnabrück: Fibre Verlag.
Kührer-Wielach, F. (2014). *Siebenbürgen ohne Siebenbürger? Zentralstaatliche Integration und politischer Regionalismus nach dem Ersten Weltkrieg*. Munich: De Gruyter Oldenbourg.
Kuus, M. (2004). "Europe's Eastern Expansion and the Reinscription of Otherness in East-Central Europe." *Progress in Human Geography* 28(4), 472–489.
Lăcătuş, A. (2009). "Tradiţie, autonomie şi realizare de sine în *Die Stadt im Osten* de Adolf Meschendörfer." In *Modernitatea conservatoare: aspecte ale culturii Europei Centrale*, 73–79. Braşov: Editura Universităţii "Transilvania".
Lascu, S. (2006). "Integrarea germanilor dobrogeni în societatea românească modernă (1878–1916) – între tradiţii proprii şi realităţi ponto-dunărene." In *Germanii dobrogeni. Istorie şi civilizaţie*, ed. V. Ciorbea, 51–84. Constanţa: Muntenia.
Leber, P-D. (2016). "Zur Aussiedlungsgeschichte der Deutschen aus Rumänien. Familienzusammenführung, Flucht, Auswanderung." In *Wege in die Freiheit. Deutsch-rumänische Dokumente zur Familienzusammenführung und Aussiedlung 1969–1989*, eds. H-G. Hüsch, P-D. Leber and H. Baier, 9–17. Aachen: Landsmannschaft der Banater Schwaben e.V.
LeCaine Agnew, H. (2003). "Czechs, Germans, Bohemians? Images of Self and Other in Bohemia to 1848." In *Creating the Other: Ethnic Conflict and Nationalism in Habsburg Central Europe*, ed. N. M. Wingfield, 56–77. New York: Berghahn Books.
Lemberg, H. (1985). "Zur Entstehung des Osteuropabegriffs im 19. Jahrhundert. Vom 'Norden' zum 'Osten' Europas." *Jahrbücher für Geschichte Osteuropas* 33, 48–91.
Lendvai, P. (1971). *Anti-Semitism Without Jews: Communist Eastern Europe*. New York: Doubleday.
Lengyel, Z. K. (2001). "Politisches System und Minderheiten in Rumänien 1918–1989. Abriß über die inneren Integrationsprobleme des zentralistischen Einheitsstaates am Beispiel der Deutschen und der Magyaren." *Zeitschrift für siebenbürgische Landeskunde* 24(2), 1–23.
Leu, V. (1996). "Imaginea 'neamţului' în însemnările de pe cărţile vechi româneşti din Banat." In Zub. *Identitate şi alteritate* 240–246.
———. (2018). "Imaginea germanului la românii din Banat." In Vultur. *Germanii din Banat* 35–58.
Levy, D. (2002). "Integrating Ethnic Germans in West Germany: The Early Postwar Period." In *Coming Home to Germany? The Integration of Ethnic Germans from Central and Eastern Europe in the Federal Republic*, eds. D. Rock and S. Wolff, 19–37. New York, Oxford: Berghahn Books.
Lewis, M. W. and Wigen, K. E. (1997). *The Myth of Continents: A Critique of Metageography*. Berkeley: University of California Press.

Bibliography

Liiceanu, A. (2005). "Alteritate etnică și imaginar colectiv." In *Barometrul relațiilor etnice 1994–2002. O perspectivă asupra climatului interetnic din România*, eds. G. Bădescu, M. Kivu and M. Robotin, 55–64. Cluj-Napoca: Centrul de Resurse pentru Diversitate Etnoculturală.

Liulevicius, V. G. (2009). *The German Myth of the East: 1800 to the Present*. Oxford: Oxford University Press.

Livezeanu, I. (1995). *Cultural Politics in Greater Romania: Regionalism, Nation Building and Ethnic Struggle, 1918–1930*. Ithaca: Cornell University Press.

Llanque, M. (2015). "The First World War and the Invention of 'Western Democracy'." In Bavaj and Steber. *Germany and the 'West'* 69–80.

Lower, W. (2005). *Nazi Empire-Building and the Holocaust in Ukraine*. Chapel Hill: University of North Carolina Press.

Lumans, V. O. (1993). *Himmler's Auxiliaries: The Volksdeutsche Mittelstelle and the German National Minorities of Europe, 1933–1945*. Chapel Hill: The University of North Carolina Press.

Lupșiasca, K. L. (1993). "Was kann das Forum?" *Zugänge* 14, 70–73.

———. (2013). "Zeittafel zur Ansiedlung im Banater Bergland." In *Die Banater Berglanddeutschen. Ein Handbuch*, eds. W. G. König, K. L. Lupșiasca and E. J. Țigla, 29–39. Reșița: Banatul Montan.

Maeder, P. (2011). *Forging a New Heimat: Expellees in Post-War Germany and Canada*. Göttingen: V&R Press.

Manuilă, S. (1938). *Recensământul general al populației României din 29 decemvrie 1930, vol. II: Neam, limbă maternă, religie*. București: Editura Institutului Central de Statistică.

Manz, S. (2014). *Constructing a German Diaspora: The 'Greater German Empire', 1871–1914*. New York: Routledge.

Marchand, S. (2009). *German Orientalism in the Age of Empire: Religion, Race, and Scholarship*. New York: Cambridge University Press.

Marian, L. (1920). *Coloniștii nemți din Basarabia. Considerații istorice, politice și etnografice*. Bucharest: Tipografia "Providența".

Măries, S. (1996). "Das Fremdenbild im rumänischen Raum in der Mitte des XIX. Jahrhunderts." In *Identitate și alteritate în spațiul cultural românesc*, ed. A. Zub, 207–227. Iași: Ed. Universității Alexandru Ioan Cuza.

Marineasa, V. and Vighi, D., eds. (1994). *Rusalii '51: fragmente din deportarea în Bărăgan*. Timișoara: Marineasa.

———, ed. (1996). *Deportarea în Bărăgan: destine, documente, reportaje*. Timișoara: Mirton.

Marte, K. P. (2003). " Gespräch mit Klaus-Peter Marte, Konsul der Bundesrepublik Deutschland in Temeswar." *Jahrbuch des Demokratischen Forums der Deutschen in Temeswar* 29–30.

Martin, B. G. (2016). *The Nazi-Fascist New Order for European Culture*. Cambridge, MA: Harvard University Press.

Martin, H. (2002). "Zehn Jahre 'BVIK Banatia'." *Deutsches Jahrbuch für Rumänien* 29–34.

———. (2011). "Jugendförderung durch Stiftungsarbeit." In *Einblick & Ausblick. 15 Jahre Demokratisches Forum der Deutschen in Rumänien*, ed. Demokratisches Forum der Deutschen in Rumänien, 111–117. Hermannstadt: Honterus Verlag.

Maxwell, A. (2011) "Introduction. Bridges and Bulwarks: A Historiographic Overview of East-West Discourses." In *The East-West Discourse: Symbolic Geography and Its Consequences*, ed. Alexander Maxwell, 1–32. Bern: Peter Lang.

Mazower, M. (2009). *Hitler's Empire: How the Nazis Ruled Europe*. London: Penguin Books.
McArthur, M. (1981). "The Politics of Identity: Transylvanian Saxons in Socialist Romania." Doctoral dissertation, University of Massachussets.
Melegh, A. (2006). *On the East-West Slope: Globalization, Nationalism, Racism and Discourses on Central and Eastern Europe*. Budapest: Central European University Press.
Meschendörfer, A. (1931). *Die Stadt im Osten*. Hermannstadt: Verlag Krafft & Drotleff.
Meyer, H. C. (1955). *Mitteleuropa in German Thought and Action 1815–1945*. The Hague: Martinus Nijhoff.
Michalon, B. (2003). "Migration des Saxons de Roumanie en Allemagne. Mythe, interdepéndance et alterité dans le retour." Doctoral dissertation, Université de Poitiers.
Michlic, J. B. (2006). *Poland's Threatening Other: The Image of the Jew from 1880 to the Present*. Lincoln: University of Nebraska Press.
Mihăilescu, V. (2014). "De ce urâm țiganii. Eseu despre partea blestemată, manele și manelism." In *Condiția romă și schimbarea discursului*, eds. V. Mihăilescu and P. Matei, 189–223. Iași: Polirom.
———. (2017). "Despre exceptionalism și ipostazele sale românești." In *De ce este România astfel? Avatarurile excepționalismului românesc*, ed. V. Mihăilescu, 43–71. Iași: Polirom.
Mihăilescu, V., Coman, G. and Pozsony, F., eds. (2002). *Vecini și vecinătăți în Transilvania*. Bucharest: Paideia.
Milata, P. (2009). *Zwischen Hitler, Stalin und Antonescu. Rumäniendeutsche in der Waffen-SS*, second revised edition. Cologne: Böhlau Verlag.
Miloiu, S., Dragomir, E. and Ștefănescu, A. (2007). "Projects for a United Europe During World War II? The Axis, Romanian and Finnish Perceptions." In *Europe as Viewed from the Margins: An East-Central European Perspective from World War I to the Cold War*, eds. I. Stanciu, S. Miloiu and I. Oncescu, 95–145. Târgoviște: Editura Cetatea de Scaun.
Minkiewicz, L. (2004). *Einblick & Ausblick. 15 Jahre Demokratisches Forum der Deutschen in Rumänien*, ed. Demokratisches Forum der Deutschen in Rumänien, 127–130. Hermannstadt: Honterus Verlag.
———. (2005). "Von Jassy bis Tulcea." *Deutsches Jahrbuch für Rumänien* 47–49.
Mironescu, V. (1911). *Privire retrospectivă. Asupra trecutului nostru paralel cu cel al vecinilor; răspuns la "Kulturarbeit des Deutschtums in Rumänien" de Dr. Emil Fischer*. Iași: Institutul de Arte Grafice N. V. Ștefaniu & Co.
Mishkova, D. (2008). "Symbolic Geographies and Visions of Identity: A Balkan Perspective." *European Journal of Social Theory* 11(2), 237–256.
Miskolczy, A. (1999). "Das Bild vom Anderen in Siebenbürgen." In *Das Bild vom Anderen: Identitäten, Mentalitäten, Mythen und Stereotypen in multiethnischen europäischen Regionen*, eds. V. Heuberger, A. Suppan and E. Vyslonzil, 169–175. Frankfurt am Main: Peter Lang.
Mitu, M. and Mitu, S. (2014). *Ungurii despre români. Nașterea unei imagini etnice*. Iași: Polirom.
Mitu, S. (2001). *National Identity of Romanians in Transylvania*, trans. S. Corneanu. Budapest: Central European University Press.
———. (2006). *Transilvania mea. Istorii, mentalități, identități*. Iași: Polirom.
———. (2007). *Europa Centrală, Răsăritul, Balcanii: geografii simbolice comparate*. Cluj: International Book Access.
Mitu, S. (2016). *Identități moderne în Transilvania*. Cluj-Napoca: Argonaut.

188 Bibliography

Möckel, A. (1994). "Kleinsächsisch oder Alldeutsch? Zum Selbstverständis der Siebenbürger Sachsen von 1867 bis 1933." In *Siebenbürgen zwischen den beiden Weltkriegen*, ed. W. König, 129–141. Cologne: Böhlau Verlag.

Möckel, G. (1977). "Fatum oder Datum? Gedanken zum Schicksalsweg der Siebenbürger Sachsen." In *Siebenbürgisch-sächsische Geschichte in ihrem neunten Jahrhundert*, ed. G. Möckel, 61–72. Munich: Im Eigenverlag des Hilfskomitees der Siebenbürger Sachsen.

Morar, I. T. (2006). *Lindenfeld*. Iași: Polirom.

Morar, V. (2011). "Stări și destine colective. Despre sași, morală și tăcere." In *Morala elementară. Stări, praguri, virtuți*, 289–308. Bucharest: Paideia.

Morawska, E. (2000). "Intended and Unintended Consequences of Forced Migrations: A Neglected Aspect of East Europe's Twentieth Century History." *International Migration Review* 34(4), 1049–1087.

Motzan, P. and Sienerth, S., eds. (1993). *Worte als Gefahr und Gefährdung: fünf deutsche Schriftsteller vor Gericht (15. September 1959 – Kronstadt); Zusammenhänge und Hintergründe. Selbstzeugnisse und Dokumente*. Munich: Südostdeutsches Kulturwerk.

Müller, C. (2004). "Zwölf Jahre Hilfe zur Selbsthilfe." *Deutsches Jahrbuch für Rumänien* 39–40.

———. (2005). "Wer einen besseren Lohn wittert, ist weg." *Deutsches Jahrbuch für Rumänien* 153–155.

Müller-Langenthal, F. (1922). *Die Siebenbürger Sachsen und ihr Land*, fourth revised edition. Stuttgart: Heimat und Welt-Verlag Dieck & Co.

Murgescu, B. (2010). *România și Europa. Acumularea decalajelor economice (1500–2010)*. Iași: Polirom.

Nachum, I. and Schaefer, S. (2018). "The Semantics of Political Integration: Public Debates about the Term 'Expellees' in Post-War Western Germany." *Contemporary European History* 27(1), 42–58.

Nägler, T. (1992). *Die Ansiedlung der Siebenbürger Sachsen*, second edition. Bucharest: Kriterion.

Năstase, A. (2007). *România după Malta. 875 de zile la Externe, vol. IV: 1 martie-30 aprilie 1991*. Bucharest: Fundația Europeană Titulescu.

Naumescu, V. (2018). "Introducere. O sută de ani de periferie. România, în căutarea garanțiilor." In *România, marile puteri și ordinea europeană*, ed. V. Naumescu, 17–31. Iași: Polirom.

Nelson, R. L., ed. (2009). *Germans, Poland, and Colonial Expansion to the East: 1850 Through the Present*. New York: Palgrave Macmillan.

Neubauer, J., Cornis-Pope, M., Kibedi-Varga, S. and Harsanyi, N. (2006), "Transylvania's Literary Cultures: Rivalry and Interaction." In *History of the Literary Cultures of East-Central Europe: Junctures and Disjunctures in the 19th and 20th Centuries*, vol. II, eds. M. Cornis-Pope and J. Neubauer, 245–282. Amsterdam, Philadelphia: John Benjamins Publishing Company.

Neugeboren, E. (1919). *Ce sînt și ce vor sașii din Ardeal: Expunere din izvor competent*. București: Tipografia Cultura Neamului Românesc.

Neumann, I. B. (1998). *Uses of the Other: "The East" in European Identity Formation*. Minneapolis: University of Minnesota Press.

Niven, B., ed. (2006). *Germans as Victims: Remembering the Past in Contemporary Germany*. Basingstoke: Palgrave Macmillan.

Nobles, M. (2008). *The Politics of Official Apologies*. Cambridge: Cambridge University Press.

Novák, C. Z. (2013). "Relațiile româno-maghiare și schimbarea de regim din 1989." *Anuarul Institutului de Cercetări Socio-Umane "Gheorghe Șincai"* 16, 43–63.

Oanca, A. (2010). "Governing the European Capital of Culture and Urban Regimes in Sibiu." MA Thesis, Central European University.

Oișteanu, A. (2009). *Inventing the Jew: Antisemitic Stereotypes in Romanian and Other Central East-European Cultures*, trans. M. Adăscăliței. Lincoln: University of Nebraska Press.

Okey, R. (1992). "Central Europe/Eastern Europe: Behind the Definitions." *Past & Present* 137(1), 102–133.

Paikert, G. C. (1967). *The Danube Swabians: German Populations in Hungary, Rumania and Yugoslavia and Hitler's Impact on Their Patterns*. The Hague: Martinus Nijhoff.

Pál-Antal, S. (2009). "Die Szekler unter den Völkern Siebenbürgens." In *Die Szekler in Siebenbürgen: von der privilegierten Sondergemeinschaft zur ethnischen Gruppe*, eds. H. Roth, P. Niedermaier and G. Olasz, 1–10. Cologne: Böhlau Verlag.

Panagiotidis, J. (2015). "What Is the German's Fatherland? The GDR and the Resettlement of Ethnic Germans from Socialist Countries (1949–1989)." *East European Politics and Societies and Cultures* 29(1), 120–146.

Pascu, V. (1998). *Istoria antică și medievală a românilor*. Bucharest: Clio.

Pavel, D. and Huiu, I. (2003). *"Nu putem reuși decît împreună". O istorie analitică a Convenției Democratice, 1989–2000*. Iași: Polirom.

Petrescu, D. (2008). "Conflicting Perceptions of (Western) Europe: The Case of Communist Romania, 1958–1989." In *Europa im Ostblock. Vorstellungen und Diskurse (1945–1991)/Europe in the Eastern Bloc. Imaginations and Discourses (1945–1991)*, eds. J. M. Faraldo, P. Gulińska-Jurgiel and C. Domnitz, 199–220. Cologne: Böhlau Verlag.

Petri, H. (1956). *Geschichte der deutschen Siedlungen in der Dobrudscha: hundert Jahre deutschen Lebens am Schwarzen Meer*. Munich: Verlag des Südostdeutschen Kulturwerks.

"Philo-Germanism without Germans in Romania after 1989", in *East European Politics and Societies and Cultures* 29:4 (2015), pp. 811–830, and "Transylvanian Saxon Symbolic Geographies", in *Civilisations* 60:2 (2012), pp. 83–101.

Philogène, G. (2007). "Social Representations of Alterity in the United States." In *Social Representations and Identity: Content, Process, and Power*, eds. G. Moloney and I. Walker, 31–42. New York: Palgrave Macmillan.

Pietz, W. (1988). "The 'Post-Colonialism' of Cold War Discourse." *Social Text* 19–20, 55–75.

Philippi, P. (1993). "Was sollte das Forum sein und tun?" *Zugänge* 14, 13–19.

———. (1994). "Nation und Nationalgefühl der Siebenbürger Sachsen." In *Die Siebenbürger Sachsen in der Geschichte und Gegenwart*, ed. H. Rothe, 69–86. Cologne: Böhlau Verlag.

———. ([1995] 1996). "Brief an Bundespräsident Roman Herzog (mit Anlagen)." *Zugänge* 19–20, 149–159.

———. (2002). "Ziele der Forumsgründung 1989. Eine Retrospektive." *Deutsches Jahrbuch für Rumänien*, 19–28.

———. ([1993] 2006). "Blick zurück in Betroffenheit. Vor 50 Jahren: Rumäniendeutsche in die Waffen-SS." In *Kirche und Politik. Siebenbürgische Anamnesen und Diagnosen aus fünf Jahrzehnten. Teil II: zwischen 1992 und 2005*, 41–43. Hermannstadt: Hora Verlag.

———. ([1995] 1996). "Die deutsche Minderheit in Rumänien. Referat beim FUEV-Kongreß in St. Moritz (25. Mai 1995)." *Zugänge* 19–20, 8–11.

Bibliography

———. ([1995] 2006). "Zum 50. Jahrestag der Deportation in die Sowjetunion (12. Januar 1995)." In *Kirche und Politik. Siebenbürgische Anamnesen und Diagnosen aus fünf Jahrzehnten. Teil II: zwischen 1992 und 2005*, 97–104. Hermannstadt: Hora Verlag.

———. ([1996] 2006). "Verstrickung, Schuld und Opfer." In *Kirche und Politik. Siebenbürgische Anamnesen und Diagnosen aus fünf Jahrzehnten. Teil II: zwischen 1992 und 2005*, 150–151. Hermannstadt: Hora Verlag.

———. ([1997] 2006). "Zur NATO-Mitgliedschaft Rumäniens." *In Kirche und Politik. Siebenbürgische Anamnesen und Diagnosen aus fünf Jahrzehnten. Teil II: zwischen 1992 und 2005*, 188–190. Hermannstadt: Hora Verlag.

———. ([2001] 2006). "Die Zukunft der Siebenbürger Sachsen nach zehn Jahren im freien Rumänien." In *Kirche und Politik. Siebenbürgische Anamnesen und Diagnosen aus fünf Jahrzehnten. Teil II: zwischen 1992 und 2005*, 266–292. Hermannstadt: Hora Verlag.

———. ([2005] 2006). "Deportationsgedenken heute – und auch übermorgen? Referat bei der zentralen Gedenkveranstaltung am 22. Januar 2005 in Reschitza." In *Kirche und Politik. Siebenbürgische Anamnesen und Diagnosen aus fünf Jahrzehnten. Teil II: zwischen 1992 und 2005*, 393–400. Hermannstadt: Hora Verlag.

———. (2010). "Subjekt sein und mitbestimmen: Zwanzig Jahre Demokratisches Forum der Deutschen in Rumänien." *Deutsches Jahrbuch für Rumänien* 23–26.

Phinnemore, D. (2010). "And We'd Like to Thank . . . Romania's Integration in the European Union." *Journal of European Integration* 32(3), 291–308.

Pintilescu, C. (2008). *Procesul Biserica Neagră 1958*. Braşov: Aldus; Heidelberg: Arbeitskreis für Siebenbürgische Landeskunde.

Poenaru, F. (2017). *Locuri comune. Clasă, anticomunism, stânga*. Cluj-Napoca: Tact.

Pogonyi, S. (2017). *Extra-Territorial Ethnic Politics, Discourses and Identities in Hungary*. New York: Palgrave Macmillan.

Polaschegg, A. (2005). *Der andere Orientalismus. Regeln deutsch-morgenländischer Imagination im 19. Jahrhundert*. Berlin, New York: Walter de Gruyter.

Pop, I-A. (1998). *Naţiunea română medievală: solidarităţi etnice româneşti în secolele XIII-XVI*. Bucharest: Editura Enciclopedică.

———. (2016). *Transilvania: starea noastră de veghe*. Cluj-Napoca: Editura Şcoala Ardeleană.

———. (2018). "Făurirea României în secolele al XIX-lea şi XX – câteva repere istorice." In *România, marile puteri şi ordinea europeană*, ed. V. Naumescu, 35–48. Iaşi: Polirom.

Pop Reteganul, I. (1900). *Pilde şi sfaturi pentru popor*. Gherla: Edit. proprietatea şi tiparul Tipografiei "Aurora" A. Todoran.

Popovici, V. and Pop, O. (2016). "From Over Here, in the Periphery: A Decolonial Method for Romanian Cultural and Political Discourses." Trans. by R. Pârvu. *LeftEast*. www.criticatac.ro/lefteast/from-over-here-in-the-periphery-a-decolonial-method-for-romania/ (accessed 23 August 2017).

Porr, P-J. (1993). "Was alles unter der Schirmherrschaft des Forums geschieht." *Zugänge* 14, 88–90.

———. (2015a). "Ein Erfolg: 25 Jahre Deutsches Forum." Interview by H. Baier. *Deutsches Jahrbuch für Rumänien* 36–40.

———. (2015b). "Liebe Leserinnen und Leser." *Deutsches Jahrbuch für Rumänien* 15.

———. (2017). "Statt mit Abblend- oder Standlicht mit Fernlicht denken." Interview by H. Baier. *Deutsches Jahrbuch für Rumänien* 19–23.

Preda, C. (2013). "Partide, voturi şi mandate la alegerile din România (1990–2012)." *Studia Politica: Romanian Political Science Review* 13(1), 27–110.

Protsyk, O. and Matichescu, L. M. (2010). "Electoral Rules and Minority Representation in Romania." *Communist and Post-Communist Studies* 43(1), 31–41.

Ram, Melanie H. (2003). "Democratization Through European Integration: The Case of Minority Rights in the Czech Republic and Romania." *Studies in Comparative International Development* 38(2), 28–56.

———. (2009). "Romania: From Laggard to Leader?" In *Minority Rights in Central and Eastern Europe*, ed. B. Rechel, 180–194. London: Routledge.

Rațiu, I. (2001). *Istoria unei candidaturi deturnate. Note zilnice. Ianuarie-Decembrie 1992*. Bucharest: Regent House Printing & Publishing.

Rausing, S. (2004). *History, Memory, and Identity in Post-Soviet Estonia: The End of a Collective Farm*. Oxford: Oxford University Press.

Rădvan, L. (2011). "Coloniștii germani, fondarea orașelor din Țările Române și metamorfozele istoriografiei românești din secolul al XX-lea." *Historia Urbana* XIX, 119–140.

Rehner, H. (1993). *Wir waren Sklaven: Tagebuch eines nach Rußland Verschleppten*. Bucharest: Concordia.

Rieser, H-H. (2001). *Das rumänische Banat – eine multikulturelle Region im Umbruch. Geographische Transformationsforschungen am Beispiel der jüngeren Kulturlandschaftsentwicklung in Südwestrumänien*. Stuttgart: Jan Thorbecke Verlag.

Rigo, E. (2005). "Citizenship at Europe's Borders: Some Reflections on the Post-Colonial Condition in the Context of EU Enlargement." *Citizenship Studies* 9(1), 3–22.

Roșu, R. (2015). "Zur Identität der Sathmarer Schwaben." *Zeitschrift für Balkanologie* 51(2), 236–253.

Roth, C. (2013). "La Nation entre les lignes. Médias invisibles, discours implicites et invention de tradition chez les Saxons de Transylvanie." Doctoral dissertation, Université Pantheon-Assas.

Roth, H. (1994). *Politische Strukturen und Strömungen bei den Siebenbürger Sachsen 1919–1933*. Cologne: Böhlau Verlag.

———. (1995). "Zum Wandel der politischen Strukturen bei den Siebenbürger Sachsen." In *Minderheit und Nationalstaat. Siebenbürgen seit dem ersten Weltkrieg*, ed. H. Roth, 99–113. Cologne: Böhlau Verlag.

———. (1998). "Autostereotype als Identifikationsmuster. Zum Selbstbild der Siebenbürger Sachsen." In *Das Bild des Anderen in Siebenbürgen*, eds. K. Gündisch, W. Höpken and M. Markel, 178–191. Cologne: Böhlau Verlag.

———. (2003). *Kleine Geschichte Siebenbürgens*. Cologne: Böhlau Verlag.

———. (2007). *Hermannstadt. Kleine Geschichte einer Stadt in Siebenbürgen*, second edition. Cologne: Böhlau Verlag.

Ruthner, C. (2003). "K.u.k. Kolonialismus als Befund, Befindlichkeit und Metapher: Versuch einer weiteren Klärung." In Feichtinger, Prutsch and Csáky. *Habsburg Postcolonial*, 111–128.

Said, E. W. ([1978] 2003) *Orientalism*. London: Penguin Books.

Salat, L. (2008). "Regimul minorităților naționale din România și contextul internațional al acestuia." In *Politici de integrare a minorităților naționale din România. Aspecte legale și instituționale într-o perspectivă comparată*, ed. L. Salat, 9–29. Cluj-Napoca: Fundația CRDE.

Salat, L. and Novák, C. Z. (2015). "Ethnicity, Nationalism, and the Minority Regime." In *Post-Communist Romania at Twenty-Five: Linking Past, Present and Future*, eds. L. Stan and D. Vancea, 63–85. Lanham: Lexington Books.

Sampson, S. (1984). *National Integration Through Socialist Planning: An Anthropological Study of a Romanian New Town*. Boulder: East European Monographs.

Șandru, D. (2009). *Reforma agrară din 1945 și țărănimea germană din România*. Bucharest: Institutul Național pentru Studiul Totalitarismului.

Sasse, G. (2006). "National Minorities and EU Enlargement: External or Domestic Incentives for Accommodation?" In *European Integration and the Nationalities Question*, eds. J. McGarry, M. Keating, 64–84. London: Routledge.

Schaser, A. (1989). *Josephinische Reformen und sozialer Wandel in Siebenbürgen: Die Bedeutung des Konzivilitätsreskriptes für Hermannstadt*. Stuttgart: Franz Steiner Verlag.

Schlattner, E. (1998). *Der geköpfte Hahn*. Wien: Zsolnay Verlag.

Schlesak, D. (2011). *The Druggist of Auschwitz: A Documentary Novel*, trans. J. Hargreaves. New York: Farrar, Straus & Giroux.

Schlögel, K. (2002). "Die Mitte liegt ostwärts. Die Deutschen, der verlorene Osten und Mitteleuropa." In *Die Mitte liegt ostwärts. Europa im Übergang*, 14–64. Munich: Carl Hanser Verlag.

Schmidt, U. (2011). *Bessarabia: German Colonists on the Black Sea*, trans. James T. Gessele. Fargo: NDSU Libraries.

Schüller, S. O. (2009). *Für Glaube, Führer, Volk, Vater- oder Mutterland? Die Kämpfe um die deutsche Jugend im rumänischen Banat (1918–1944)*. Berlin: LIT Verlag.

Schultheiss, G. (1898). *Der Kampf um das Deutschtum: Deutschtum und Magyarisierung*. Munich: Verlag von J. F. Lehmann.

Schuster, H. W. (2009). "Grundzüge der Entwicklung der Landsmannschaft der Siebenbürger Sachsen in Deutschland." In *60 Jahre Verband der Siebenbürger Sachsen in Deutschland. Grundzüge seiner Geschichte*, ed. H. W. Schuster, 9–69. Munich: Landsmannschaft der Siebenbürger Sachsen in Deutschland.

Schwarz, E. (1957). *Die Herkunft der Siebenbürger und Zipser Sachsen. Siebenbürger und Zipser Sachsen, Ostmitteldeutsche, Rheinländer im Spiegel der Mundarten*. Munich: Verlag des Südostdeutschen Kulturwerks.

Schwicker, J. H. (1881). *Die Deutschen in Ungarn und Siebenbürgen*. Vienna: Verlag von Karl Prochaska.

Scridon, I. and Ilovan, O-R. (2015). "The Zipsers' Ethnic Identity in Vişeu de Sus/Oberwischau, Romania, in the Context of Inter-Ethnic Relationships." *Mitteilungen der Österreichischen Geographischen Gesellschaft* 157, 151–168.

Sebaux, G. (2015). *(Post)Colonisation – (Post)Migration. Ces Allemands entre Allemagne et Roumanie*. Paris: Éditions Le Manuscrit.

Senz, I. (1994). *Die Donauschwaben*. Munich: Langen Müller.

Severin, A. and Andreescu, G. (2000). *Locurile unde se construieşte Europa*. Iaşi: Polirom.

Shafir, M. (1991). "Antisemitism Without Jews in Romania." *Report on Eastern Europe* 28 June, 20–32.

———. (2000). "The Political Party as National Holding Company: The Hungarian Democratic Federation of Romania." In *The Politics of National Minority Participation in Post-Communist Europe: State-Building, Democracy, and Ethnic Mobilization*, ed. J. P. Stein, 101–128. Armonk: M.E. Sharpe.

———. (2018). "The Nature of Postcommunist Antisemitism in East Central Europe: Ideology's Backdoor Return." *Journal of Contemporary Antisemitism* 1(2), 33–61.

Sienerth, S. (1994). "Adolf Meschendörfer." *Neue Deutsche Biographie* 17. www.deutsche-biographie.de/pnd118831569.html#ndbcontent (accessed 22 September 2018).

Slavici, I. [1930] (1994). "Lumea prin care am trecut." In *Amintiri. Lumea prin care am trecut*, ed. C. Mohanu, 179–296. Bucharest: Minerva.

Smith, B. G. (2016). "Ethnonationalism as a Source of Stability in the Party Systems of Bulgaria and Romania: Minority Parties, Nationalism, and EU Membership." *Nationalism and Ethnic Politics* 22(4), 433–455.

Bibliography 193

Smith, D. J. (2002). "Framing the National Question in Central and Eastern Europe: A Quadratic Nexus?" *Ethnopolitics* 2(1), 3–16.

Spiridon, M. (2004). *Les dilemmes de l'identité aux confins de l'Europe: le cas roumain.* Paris: L'Harmattan.

Stache, C. and Theilemann, W. G. (2012). "Evangelisch in Alt-Rumänien. Zu Themenrelevanz, Forschungsstand und Konzeption." In *Evangelisch in Altrumänien. Forschungen und Quellen zur Geschichte der deutschsprachigen evangelischen Kirchengemeinden im rumänischen Regat*, eds. C. Stache and W. G. Theilemann, 17–40. Sibiu: Schiller Verlag.

Stan, V. (1995). "Nationalism and European Security: Romania's Euro-Atlantic Integration." *International Studies* 1, 27–48.

Stanciu, L. (2010). *Iluminism Central European: Școala Ardeleană.* Cluj-Napoca: Editura Mega.

Steiner, S. (2007). *Reisen ohne Wiederkehr. Die Deportation von Protestanten aus Kärnten 1734–1736.* Vienna: R. Oldenbourg.

———. (2014). *Rückkehr unerwünscht. Deportationen in der Habsburgermonarchie der Frühen Neuzeit und ihr europäischer Kontext.* Cologne: Böhlau Verlag.

Sterbling, A. (1997). "Historische und aktuelle Aspekte der 'Bodenfrage' und der Agrarkrise in Siebenbürgen." In *Kontinuität und Wandel in Rumänien und Südosteuropa. Historisch-soziologische Analysen.* Munich: Südostdeutsches Kulturwerk.

Stickler, M. (2004). *"Ostdeutsch heißt Gesamtdeutsch." Organisation, Selbstverständnis und heimatpolitische Zielsetzungen der deutschen Vertriebenenverbände 1949–1972.* Düsseldorf: Droste Verlag.

Stroe, M. (2007). "În vitrina europeană." *Secolul 21* 1–6, 84–96.

———. (2011a). "Heterorepresentations of Saxonness and Their Political Meanings in Transylvania." In *European, National and Regional Identity: Proceedings of the International Conference "European, National and Regional Identity", Organized in Oradea, 24–26 March 2011, in the Frame of Research Project HURO/0801/180*, eds. B. Balogh, S. Bălțătescu, K. Bernath and É. Biró-Kaszás, 195–209. Oradea: Ed. Universității din Oradea.

———. (2011b). "Sibiu European Capital of Culture 2007: Saxonness as a Romanian Cultural Brand." In *Every Day's a Festival! Diversity on Show*, eds. S. Küchler, L. Kürti and H. Elkadi, 83–112. Wantage: Sean Kingston Publishing.

———. (2017). *Gustul locului. Producția de peisaje culturale agro-alimentare în sudul Transilvaniei.* Bucharest: Tritonic.

Swanson, J. C. (2017). *Tangible Belonging: Negotiating Germanness in Twentieth-Century Hungary.* Pittsburgh: University of Pittsburgh Press.

Szegedi, E. (2006). *Tradiție și inovație în istoriografia săsească între baroc și iluminism.* Cluj-Napoca: Casa Cărții de Știință.

Szelényi, B. A. (2007). "From Minority to Übermensch: The Social Roots of Ethnic Conflict in the German Diaspora of Hungary, Romania and Slovakia." *Past and Present* 196, 215–251.

Takle, M. (2011). "(Spät)Aussiedler: From Germans to Immigrants." *Nationalism and Ethnic Politics* 17(2), 161–181.

Teutsch, F. (1916). *Die Siebenbürger Sachsen in Vergangenheit und Gegenwart.* Leipzig: Verlag von K. F. Koehler.

———. (1924). *Die Siebenbürger Sachsen in Vergangenheit und Gegenwart*, 2nd augmented edition. Hermannstadt: W. Krafft Verlag.

Todorova, M. ([1997] 2009). *Imagining the Balkans*, second edition. New York: Oxford University Press.

Bibliography

Torrey, G. E. (1992). "Romania in the First World War: The Years of Engagement, 1916–1918." *The International History Review* 14(3), 462–479.

Thiel, S. (2006). "Geglückter Tapetenwechsel für Banater Ingenieurin." *Deutsches Jahrbuch für Rumänien* 96–99.

———. (2008). "Querdenken, Initiativfreude, Mut: Schwäbin schaffte frühzeitig EU-Standard." *Deutsches Jahrbuch für Rumänien* 58–60.

Thum, G., ed. (2006a). *Mythische Landschaften. Das Bild vom "deutschen Osten" und die Zäsuren des 20. Jahrhunderts.* Göttingen: Vandenhoeck & Ruprecht, 181–211.

———. (2006b). "Mythische Landschaften. Das Bild vom 'deutschen Osten' und die Zäsuren des 20. Jahrhunderts." In Thum. *Mythische Landschaften*.

———. (2011). *Uprooted: How Breslau Became Wrocław During the Century of Expulsions*, trans. T. Lampert and A. Brown. Princeton: Princeton University Press.

———. (2012). "'We Are Prussia Today': Polish-German Variations on a Vanished State." In *Germany, Poland and Postmemorial Relations: In Search of a Livable Past*, eds. K. Kopp and J. Niżyńska, 259–279. New York: Palgrave Macmillan.

Tismăneanu, V. (1998). *Fantasies of Salvation: Democracy, Nationalism, and Myth in Post-Communist Europe*. Princeton: Princeton University Press.

———. (2003). *Stalinism for All Seasons: A Political History of Romanian Communism*. Berkeley: University of California Press.

Topor, C. L. (2012). "Der 'Inländische' Feind – das Schicksal der Deutschen in Altrumänien zwischen nationaler Identität und Rhetorik des Krieges (1914–1916)." *Forschungen zur Volks- und Landeskunde* 55, 145–154.

Toró, T. (2016). "Hungarian Minority Politics in Post-Socialist Romania: Interests, Strategies and Discourses." *Acta Universitatis Sapientiae, European and Regional Studies* 10, 79–106.

Totok, W. (1988). *Die Zwänge der Erinnerung. Aufzeichnungen aus Rumänien*. Hamburg: Junius Verlag.

Török, B. Z. (2016). *Exploring Transylvania: Geographies of Knowledge and Entangled Histories in a Multiethnic Province, 1790–1918*. Leiden: Brill.

Traşcă, O. (2013). *Relaţiile politice şi militare româno-germane: septembrie 1940 – august 1944*. Cluj-Napoca: Argonaut.

Tudor, C. V. (1996). *Jurnal de vacanţă*. Bucharest: Ed. Fundaţiei România Mare.

Turliuc, M. N. (2004). *Imaginar, identitate şi reprezentări sociale. Imaginea elementului alogen în mentalul colectiv românesc*. Iaşi: Ed. Universităţii Al. Ioan Cuza.

Ţichindeleanu, O. (2009). "The Modernity of Post-Communism." In *Genealogies of Post-Communism*, eds. A. T. Sîrbu and A. Polgár, 117–138. Cluj-Napoca: Idea Design & Print.

Uhl, H. (2003). "Zwischen 'Habsburgischem Mythos' und (Post-)Kolonialismus. Zentraleuropa als Paradigma für Identitätskonstruktionen in der (Post-)Moderne." In Feichtinger, Prutsch and Csáky. *Habsburg Postcolonial* 45–54.

Ulrich, E. (2005). *Din cartea vieţii mele: am fost deportat în U.R.S.S.* Petroşani: Editura Fundaţiei Culturale "Ion D. Sîrbu".

Varga, A. (2004). "Legislative Aspects and Political Excuses: Hungarian-Romanian Disagreements on the 'Act on Hungarians Living in Neighbouring Countries'." Translated by Bob Dent. In Kántor et al. *The Hungarian Status Law*, 461–474. http://src-h.slav.hokudai.ac.jp/coe21/publish/no4_ses/chapter19.pdf (accessed 23 September 2018).

Vasiliu, F. and Dragoman, D. (2008). "Politici culturale şi afirmarea identităţii. Luxemburg şi Marea Regiune – Sibiu. Capitale Culturale Europene în 2007." *Sociologie Românească* 6(2), 30–39.

Verdery, K. (1983). *Transylvanian Villagers: Three Centuries of Political, Economic, and Ethnic Change*. Berkeley: University of California Press.

———. (1985). "The Unmaking of an Ethnic Collectivity: Transylvania's Germans." *American Ethnologist* 12(1), 62–83.

———. (1991). *National Ideology Under Socialism: Identity and Cultural Politics in Ceauşescu's Romania*. Berkeley: University of California Press.

———. (1996). "Nationalism and National Sentiment in Postsocialist Romania." In *What Was Socialism, and What Comes Next?* 83–103. Princeton: Princeton University Press.

———. (2003). *The Vanishing Hectare: Property and Value in Postsocialist Transylvania*. Ithaca: Cornell University Press.

Volovici, L. (1991). *Nationalist Ideology and Antisemitism: The Case of Romanian Intellectuals in the 1930s*, trans. C. Kormos. Oxford: Pergamon Press.

Vultur, S. (1997). *Istorie trăită – istorie povestită: deportarea în Bărăgan 1951–1956*. Timişoara: Amarcord.

———. (2012). *Francezi în Banat, bănăţeni în Franţa*. Timişoara: Marineasa.

Wagner, R. (2000). "Ethnic Germans in Romania." In *German Minorities in Europe: Ethnic Identity and Cultural Belonging*, ed. S. Wolff, 135–142. New York: Berghahn Books.

Waterbury, M. A. (2010). *Between State and Nation: Diaspora Politics and Kin-State Nationalism in Hungary*. New York: Palgrave Macmillan.

Weber, A. (2010). *Rumäniendeutsche? Diskurse zur Gruppenidentität einer Minderheit (1944–1971)*. Cologne: Böhlau Verlag.

Weber, G., Nassehi, A., Weber-Schlenther, R., Sill, O., Kneer, G., Nollmann, G. and Saake, I. (2003). *Emigration der Siebenbürger Sachsen. Studien zu Ost-West-Wanderungen im 20. Jahrhundert*. Wiesbaden: Westdeutscher Verlag.

Weber, G., Weber-Schlenther, R., Nassehi, A., Sill, O. and Kneer, G. (1995). *Die Deportation von Siebenbürger Sachsen in die Sowjetunion*, vol. 3. Cologne: Böhlau Verlag.

Weber, H. (1991). "Die Rumäniendeutschen – gestern, heute und vielleicht morgen." In *Nachdenken über die Zukunft. Aufsätze und Dokumente über die Rumäniendeutschen*, ed. H. Weber. Sibiu: Im Selbstverlag des Demokratischen Forums der Deutschen in Rumänien.

———. (1993a). "Minderheitenverständnis, Minderheitenrechte und Minderheitenschutz in Rumänien." *Zugänge* 14, 5–13.

———. (1993b). "Das DFDR – Was es ist und was es will." *Zugänge* 14, 60–67.

Wedekind, M. (2004). "Der siebenbürgische Karpatenverein (1880–1944). Ein Beitrag zur Sozialgeschichte Siebenbürgens." *Amnis. Revue de civilisation contemporaine Europe/ Ameriques* 1. http://amnis.revues.org/1088 (accessed 22 September 2018).

Welisch, S. A. (1986). "The Bukovina-Germans During the Habsburg Period: Settlement, Ethnic Interaction, Contributions." *Immigrants & Minorities* 5(1), 73–106.

Weniger, L. (1994). *Schatten am Don. Als Zwangsdeportierte aus Siebenbürgen in Kohlebergwerken in Russland, 1945–1946*. Dortmund: Forschungsstelle Osmitteleuropa.

Wermke, H. (2013). "Vom Unternehmerstammtisch zum Wirtschaftsklub." *Deutsches Jahrbuch für Rumänien* 33–38.

Wien, U. A. (2002). *Friedrich Müller-Langenthal. Leben und Dienst in der evangelischen Kirche in Rumänien im 20. Jahrhundert*. Sibiu: Monumenta Verlag.

Winkler, H. A. (2006/2007). *Germany: The Long Road West*, vol. 2, trans. A. J. Sager. Oxford: Oxford University Press.

Wittstock, W. (2004). "Mitreden und mitentscheiden. Schwierigkeiten der parlamentarischen Vertretung eines Minderheitenverbandes." In *Einblick & Ausblick. 15 Jahre Demokratisches Forum der Deutschen in Rumänien*, ed. Demokratisches Forum der Deutschen in Rumänien, 31–39. Hermannstadt: Honterus Verlag.

Wokoeck, U. (2009). *German Orientalism: The Study of the Middle East and Islam from 1800 to 1945*. London: Routledge.

Wolff, L. (1994). *Inventing Eastern Europe: The Map of Civilization on the Mind of the Enlightenment*. Stanford: Stanford University Press.

Wolff, S. (2006). "The Impact of Post-Communist Regime Change and European Integration on Ethnic Minorities: The 'Special' Case of Ethnic Germans in Eastern Europe." In *European Integration and the Nationalities Question*, eds. J. McGarry and M. Keating, 139–168. London: Routledge.

Woodcock, S. (2005). " 'The Țigan is not a Man': The Țigan Other as a Catalyst for Romanian Ethnonational Identity." Doctoral dissertation, University of Sydney.

——. (2007). "Romania and Europe: Roma, Rroma and Țigani as Sites for the Contestation of Ethno-National Identities." *Patterns of Prejudice* 41(5), 493–515.

Wright, J. (1998). "The Protection of Minority Rights in Europe: From Conference to Implementation." *International Journal of Human Rights* 2(1), 1–31.

Zach, K. (1998). "Religiöse Toleranz und Stereotypenbildung in einer multikulturellen Region. Volkskirchen in Siebenbürgen." In *Das Bild des Anderen in Siebenbürgen*, eds. Konrad Gündisch, Wolfgang Höpken and Michael Markel, 109–154. Cologne: Böhlau Verlag.

Zăloagă, M. (2004). "Imaginea Celuilalt în Chronica românilor. Viziunea șincaiană asupra populațiilor germanice din Transilvania." *Libraria. Studii și cercetări de bibliologie. Anuar* 3, 209–218.

——. (2015). *Romii în cultura săsească în secolele al XVIII-lea și al XIX-lea*. Cluj-Napoca: Editura Institutului pentru Studierea Problemelor Minorităților Naționale.

Zillich, H. (1937). *Zwischen Grenzen und Zeiten*. Munich: Albert Langen-Georg Müller.

——. (1950). *Der Schicksalsweg der Siebenbürger Sachsen*. Munich: Verband der Siebenbürger Sachsen in Deutschland.

Zub, A., ed. (1996). *Identitate și alteritate în spațiul cultural românesc*. Iași: Ed. Universității Alexandru Ioan Cuza.

Index

anti-communism 59, 62, 63, 104, 105, 111, 113, 117, 169
anti-Germanism 31, 35n3, 43, 46, 64, 84, 102, 103, 105, 163–165, 169–170
anti-Semitism 5, 45, 61, 67, 72, 164–165, 167–168, 170
Aurel Vlaicu 19, 25

Balkanism 9–11, 61, 64, 90; *see also* Orientalism
Banat Swabians 30; deportation to Bărăgan 30, 105, 106; identity discourses 25; settlement in Banat 23, 135; *see also* Romanian Germans; Romanian-Swabian relationships/reciprocal representations; Saxon-Swabian relationships/reciprocal representations
Băsescu, T. 2, 88, 110, 113
Berglanddeutsche: settlement in Banat 24
Bessarabia Germans: in the interwar period 27; relocation to the Reich 29; settlement in Bessarabia 25; *see also* Marian, L.
Blaga, L. 59–61
Brașov 40, 52–55, 63, 97–98, 104, 118, 136, 137, 140; Black Church 54, 137; "Junii Brașovului" 54–55
Bukovina Germans: relocation to the Reich 29; settlement in Bukovina 24

Caramitru, I. 109, 148
Carol I 2, 4, 35, 41, 42, 46
Carp, R. 2–3
Carpathian Mountains 20, 52–53, 55, 57, 124, 127
Cărtărescu, M. 2–4
Central European identity 10, 14–15, 17, 107, 127

Charles, Prince of Wales 139, 148
Chebeleu, T. 82
Ciuhandu, G. 94, 148

Declaration of Alba Iulia 27, 55, 70–71
Democratic Alliance of Hungarians in Romania 72–73, 75, 154
Democratic Forum of Germans in Romania 1, 2, 76–79, 84–93, 95–99, 102–105, 108, 119, 138, 145, 158, 161n39, 169–170
Deutsches Jahrbuch für Rumänien 90–99
Dobruja Germans: relocation to the Reich 29; settlement in Dobruja 25

Eastern Europe, invention of 7–9; *see also* Orientalism
easternisms 9, 94, 167; *see also* Orientalism
economic development 84–87, 91–96; *see also* German entrepreneurship
educational system: German-language educational system in Romania 96–97; vocational educational system 97–99
Estonia 165–166
Europe, return to 10–12, 72, 73, 76, 129–130, 166
Europeanization *see* European Union, integration in
European Union, integration in 9, 11, 68, 73–76, 86, 89, 106, 108, 164; *see also* Europe, return to

Fernolend, C. 125, 128, 151
Final Report of the Presidential Commission for the Analysis of the Communist Dictatorship in Romania 110, 113

Index

Formula As 1–2, 88–89, 120–125, 126–129, 139, 148–149, 151–152, 158
Francophilia 42–43, 46

Genscher, H.-D. 70, 78, 81, 154
Georgescu, R. *see Trading Germans*
German colonialism/imperialism in Eastern Europe 13–16, 20, 26, 41–44, 47
German diaspora 24, 43
German entrepreneurship 86–87, 91–94, 98–99, 147
German expertise 88–90; *see also* German entrepreneurship
German myth of the East 14, 15, 47; *see also* German colonialism/imperialism in Eastern Europe
Germans abroad *see* German diaspora
German views of Romanians 41, 44, 48; *see also* German colonialism/imperialism in Eastern Europe; German myth of the East
Germany (Federal Republic of) as a kin state 28–29, 33, 70, 80–84, 108, 153–156
Golescu, D. 40–41

Habsburg Empire 16–17, 22–24, 26, 34
Helsinki Accords 70
hierarchizations 9–11, 17n2, 39, 43, 46, 56, 68, 82, 106, 126–127, 136, 141–142, 146, 149–152, 156, 166–168
Horn, G. 70
Hungary as a kin state 70, 83, 153–156
Hurezean, R. 98, 111–112, 114, 148, 151, 152
Hurezeanu, E. 112, 133n41, 136, 152
Hüsch, H.-G. 115–116

in-betweenness *see* liminality
intimate colonization *see* self-colonization
Iohannis, K. 1–5, 6n3, 6n5, 88–90, 101n24, 101n26, 103, 121, 122–124, 130n2, 133n38, 133n41, 133n44, 158, 163, 168, 169–170, 171nn2–3, 171n5, 171n7
Iorga, N. 56–58, 59
Ivan, A. L. 158–160

Jacobi, P. 111

Kinkel, K. 106–109, 113, 131n15

Landler: settlement in Transylvania 22
lastness 123, 125, 127–128
liminality 9–11, 41–42, 43–44, 56, 58, 68, 135, 144, 166
Lutheran Church in Transylvania 21, 23, 48, 139, 141, 158, 169–170; *see also* Müller-Langenthal, F.; Teutsch, F.
Luxembourg 20, 126, 139, 140–141

Magyarization 23, 24, 39, 50–51, 156–157
Marian, L. 58–59
Meschendörfer, A. 52–55
minority politics in post-1989 Romania 70–76
Mitteleuropa *see* Central European identity
Müller, H. 111
Müller-Langenthal, F. 31, 50–51, 54

Năstase, A. 81–82, 154
National Liberal Party 2, 88–89, 153, 169
National Salvation Front 70–71, 76
NATO, integration in 11, 73, 76, 105–109
Neugeboren, E. 56–57
Noarootsi 165
nostalgia 121, 125–128, 142, 149, 167, 168

Orientalism 7–17; Euro-Orientalism 7–8, 37; German Orientalism 13–16, 43; nesting Orientalisms 10, 17, 107, 127; self-Orientalization 12–13, 39, 40–41, 45–46; *see also* Balkanism; Eastern Europe, invention of; easternisms; self-colonization

Philippi, P. 79, 103, 105, 131n10
Poland 15, 63, 100n13, 107, 163–165
Ponta, V. 88
Pop Reteganul, I. 44–45
property restitution 77, 85, 101n21, 102, 118, 158, 169–170

Rațiu, I. 117
Reșița 111, 131n10
Roma-German antagonism 142–152
Romania: during communism 33, 65–66; during the First World War 26, 46–47; during the interwar period 27; during the Second World War 61–62; in the nineteenth century 42–43
Romanian German representations of Roma 39, 145–147

Romanian Germans 121; categorizations of 18–20; deportation to the Soviet Union 30, 62, 102–106, 110–113, 146; during communism 30–31, 33, 62–66; during the interwar period 27–29, 158–160; during the Second World War 29, 61–62; enrollment in Waffen-SS 29, 111–113, 131n10; heritage 125, 136–142; identity discourses of 62–64; migration to (West) Germany 1, 30, 31–32, 33, 63–66, 77, 119–120; (potential) return migration to Romania 118–119, 124–125, 129–130
Romanian-German Treaty for Friendly Cooperation and Partnership in Europe 79–84
Romanian-Hungarian relationships/reciprocal representations 39, 65–66, 68, 72, 82, 158–160
Romanian identity discourses 36–38, 39–41, 43, 44, 58, 60–61, 65–66, 107–108, 135–136
Romanian migration to Western Europe 77, 143–144
Romanian representations of Jews 45, 67, 167; *see also* anti-Semitism
Romanian representations of Roma 68–69, 72, 167–168; *see also* Roma-German antagonism
Romanians as a demographic danger for Germans 50, 51
Romanian-Saxon relationships/reciprocal representations 26, 37–39, 44–45, 47–58, 59–61, 63–64
Romanian-Swabian relationships/reciprocal representations 45–46, 61

Sălcudeanu, P. 117–119, 132n27, 132n29
Satu Mare 92–93
Satu Mare Swabians 27, 30, 110, 124, 156–157; settlement in northwestern Romania 23–24; *see also* Romanian Germans
Saxon-Swabian relationships/reciprocal representations 25, 50, 78

Schlattner, E. 121–122, 128, 152
Şcoala Ardeleană *see* Transylvanian School
self-colonization 12–13, 39, 40–42, 58, 89, 167; *see also* Orientalism
Severin, A. 106–109, 113, 131n11
Sibiu 1–5, 77, 78, 82, 88–89, 117, 122–123, 125–126, 133n41, 133n55, 136, 140, 147, 158, 169–170; Sibiu as European Capital of Culture 89, 123, 138, 140–141
Sighişoara 126, 137, 138–140, 149
Slavici, I. 45
Social Democratic Party 72, 73, 88, 90, 169–170

technocracy *see* German expertise
Teutsch, F. 48–50, 51, 54
Timişoara 77, 82, 94–96, 98, 117, 147, 148
Trading Germans 115
Transylvanian Saxons: identity discourses 21–22, 23, 25, 38, 47–57, 63–64, 159; in Northern Transylvania 30, 31; Saxon representations of Roma 39; settlement in Transylvania 15, 20–21, 58, 127; *see also* German myth of the East; Romanian Germans; Romanian-Saxon relationships/reciprocal representations; Saxon-Swabian relationships/reciprocal representations
Transylvanian School 37–39, 67
Tudor, C. V. 137–138

Unification of Greater Romania 26–27; *see also* Declaration of Alba Iulia

Văcărescu, I. 40
Văcăroiu, N. 104–106, 109
Viscri 125, 128–129, 140, 141, 147, 148, 151–152

West-East relationships 4, 7–13, 39

Zillich, H. 52–54, 55, 63
Zipser: settlement in Maramureş 24

Printed in the United States
by Baker & Taylor Publisher Services